Alexander von Pock

Strategic Management in Islamic Finance

WIRTSCHAFTSWISSENSCHAFT

Alexander von Pock

Strategic Management in Islamic Finance

Deutscher Universitäts-Verlag

Bibliografische Information Der Deutschen Nationalbibliothek
Die Deutsche Nationalbibliothek verzeichnet diese Publikation in der Deutschen Nationalbibliografie; detaillierte bibliografische Daten sind im Internet über <http://dnb.d-nb.de> abrufbar.

Dissertation Ruhr-Universität Bochum, 2006

1. Auflage August 2007

Lektorat: Frauke Schindler / Anita Wilke

Der Deutsche Universitäts-Verlag ist ein Unternehmen von Springer Science+Business Media.
www.duv.de

Umschlaggestaltung: Regine Zimmer, Dipl.-Designerin, Frankfurt/Main
Gedruckt auf säurefreiem und chlorfrei gebleichtem Papier
Printed in Germany

ISBN 978-3-8350-0723-9

Acknowledgements

This dissertation would not have been possible without the help and support of many people and institutions.

First and foremost, I would like to thank Prof. Dr. Volker Nienhaus, my doctorate supervisor. I am very grateful for his high level of interest and the many hints he provided throughout the study. Furthermore, I would like to thank Prof. Dr. Stephan Paul for his fast and positive review and Prof. Dr. Mario Rese for his willingness to act as a member of the examination board.

I am deeply indebted to all Islamic banks that participated in the empirical part of this study. I would like to thank all the professionals for their input and the time they spent on answering the questionnaires.

This dissertation was generously supported by my employer, the management consulting firm A.T. Kearney. I am grateful for the financial sponsorship as well as the assistance the firm provided during my doctorate leave of absence.

Finally, I would like to thank my family and friends for their continued help and support.

Alexander von Pock

Content

List of Exhibits

1 Introduction

In the last decades, Islamic finance has evolved to become one of the most dynamic and fastest developing business areas in the global financial industry. Although still a niche market, the segment is experiencing ever increasing competition and, especially in recent years, has left its home turf with Islamic financial products being offered in major markets outside the Muslim world, such as the United States and Great Britain. While academic research has extensively covered the basics and a selection of special issues regarding Islamic finance and Islamic economics, the determinants of strategic management in Islamic finance have not drawn the same degree of attention in the literature. As will be presented in the following paragraphs, this study intends to make a contribution to this significant research area.

1.1 Research Problem

> "The foremost belief around which all the Islamic concepts revolve is that the whole universe is created and controlled by One, the only One God. He has created man (...) to fulfill certain objectives through obeying His commands. These commands (...) cover a substantial area of almost every aspect of our life."[1]

It is therefore little surprising that Muslims have to abide by the precepts of Islam even in their financial dealings. The first serious attempts to cater to Muslim banking clients – who wanted to reconcile Islamic principles and their financial requirements – dates back to the 1970s, when the first modern, non-governmental Islamic banks were created. Largely unnoticed by the general public in the West[2], Western financial institutions also began to enter the Islamic financial market in the 1990s. Citibank was the first Western bank to open up an Islamic bank in Bahrain in 1996. Today, Western banks as diverse as the Swiss private bank Pictet & Cie., large universal banks as Deutsche Bank or BNP Paribas, or investment banks such as Goldman Sachs offer Islamic financial products. UBS is for the time being the last Western financial institution that founded its own Islamic bank: Noriba. These Western banks are in competition with purely Islamic banks such as the Saudi Arabian Al Rajhi Banking & Investment Corp. or the Kuwait Finance House, two of the largest Islamic banks originating in the Muslim world.

The ever-increasing importance of Islamic finance is also mirrored by the introduction of Islamic stock market indices. The two key indices are the Dow Jones Islamic Market Index and the FTSE Global Islamic Index, providing a benchmark for the selection of Islamically appropriate companies. Since a number of years, the Islamic finance industry is also striving to develop common accounting, auditing, governance,

---

[1] Usmani (2002), p. xiii.

[2] „West" is meant to comprise Europe, the Americas, Australia and New Zealand, as the term is frequently used.

ethics, and Sharia standards for Islamic financial institutions. These are developed by institutions such as the Accounting and Auditing Organization for Islamic Financial Institutions (AAOIFI) or the Islamic Financial Services Board (IFSB).

However, the Islamic finance industry can still be considered as an emerging market. Moreover, the market seems to be quite inhomogeneous at first glance. It is characterized by a number of different firms with strongly varying market presence and penetration: from globally acting banks such as HSBC Amanah Finance, which draw on the global network and resources of its parent company – the HSBC group – to local, independent banks such as Dubai Islamic Bank; from Islamic finance-specific universal banks catering to corporate and private clients to free riders that selectively offer Islamic financial services as exotic products. Consequently, market players obviously distinguish themselves in terms of their resource endowments and the strategies they employ to position themselves on the market. At the same time, conventional wisdom suggests that Islamic banks most probably differ in their performance. The strategic management determinants of such performance differences are the focal point of this research.

From a broader perspective, the research problem also touches upon general issues of strategic management. There are two different perspectives in strategic management regarding the sources of sustainable competitive advantage. On the one hand, success factors are derived from market requirements. Industry effects, i.e. the relative attractiveness of the industry compared to other industries, largely drive company performance. On the other hand, success factors are derived from the company's endowment with distinctive resources and core competencies. Firm-specific effects are viewed as the major driver of company performance. So far, empirical research has reported contradictory findings and remains inconclusive: the question of the relative impact of industry and firm-specific effects is still open. However, both concepts are more and more regarded as complementary in the literature.

1.2 Research Objective and Approach

The main objective of this research is to identify key success factors of superior firm performance in Islamic finance. This is done on the basis of a holistic conceptual framework, taking into account current practices in Islamic finance, strategic management theories, and previous empirical research from the fields of strategic management and economics. The study examines external factors (global environment and industry forces), internal factors (core competencies), and company strategies as potential explanatory factors of performance differences of Islamic financial institutions.

The theoretically derived hypotheses about explanatory factors of company performance in Islamic finance are empirically tested in a survey of 77 Islamic financial institutions operating across the GCC area and Malaysia. The necessary data was collected using a standardized questionnaire. Out of the 77 Islamic financial institutions contacted, 36 or 47% participated in the study, leading to a highly satisfactory response rate. What is more, the participants represent approx. 80% of the estimated total on-balance sheet Islamic banking assets in the GCC area, and approx. 70% of the estimated total on-balance sheet Islamic banking assets in Malaysia. As both markets are highly concentrated, this also means that the major players are included in the study.

The empirical data analysis follows a two-step approach. First, the reliability and validity of the measurement model is tested. The conceptual model mentioned above consists of the assumed relationships between theoretical constructs. These theoretical constructs or latent variables are abstract, non-observable entities, which cannot be measured directly, but have to be represented by one or more indicators. The operationalisation of these constructs largely draws on factor analysis as statistical tool.

Second, the hypothesized relationships between the constructs are analyzed. For this matter, several statistical tests are applied. The impact of the various factors on the different company performance variables is analyzed using correlation and regression analysis. The investigation of differences of the factors or the performance indicators across various groups or clusters – such as hypothesized strategic groups – are performed using the t-test and ANOVA.

1.3 Research Structure

The present research is organized as follows. The introductory chapter 1 gives an overview of the research problem, the research objective and approach, and the research structure.

Chapter 2 sets the analytical framework of the study. It begins in chapter 2.1 with a depiction of the major theories of strategic management, starting with an exposition of state-of-the-art strategic management approaches – the market-based view of strategic management, the resource-based view of strategic management, and New Institutional Economics approaches. Next, strategic management propositions on banking are derived on the basis of an analysis of the various steps of the strategic management process. For this matter, corporate vision, mission and objectives, external factors, internal factors, company strategies, and strategy implementation are scrutinized.

In chapter 2.2, Islamic finance is presented both in terms of its theoretical basis and its actual manifestations and practices. First, the fundamentals of Islamic finance are depicted, including the sources, methods, and schools of law, followed by an exposition of a set of principles in an attempt to help the reader understand the underpinnings of Islamic finance. Next, there is a detailed description of Islamic financial instruments, where these products are organized according to their economic and financial characteristics into debt-like instruments, equity-like instruments, derivative-like instruments, hybrid instruments and other transactions and services. Finally, the Islamic finance market is illustrated. A market overview presents market size, regional scope, and major market types in Islamic finance. Subsequently, the institutional framework – including the regulatory and supervisory environment, as well as the framework for liquidity management and secondary markets – is depicted. Two regions – namely the GCC area and Malaysia – are then looked at in greater detail – with for example a description of major players, marketed products and the specific regulatory environment – as these regions can be considered to be the most important ones for profit-oriented, free-market Islamic financial institutions.

In chapter 2.3, an empirical literature review is presented. It starts with a review of general studies that analyze the importance of the various factors brought forward in strategic management theories, followed by a depiction of Islamic finance studies, which so far adopted economic rather than strategic management approaches.

Drawing on the previous expositions of Islamic finance, strategic management theories, and empirical research on factors influencing company performance, chapter 2.4 develops a conceptual model – composed of three different partial models – and hypotheses about strategic management in Islamic finance. It starts with an overview of the three models, depicting its various building blocks. Next, detailed hypotheses regarding the building blocks of the models and their interrelation are presented. Finally, a summary complements the exposition.

Chapter 3 contains the empirical validation of the conceptual model and its propositions. It begins with the exposition of the research methodology in chapter 3.1. First, the data collection and sampling process is presented, including a depiction of the data collection tool, and the data generation method. In particular, some descriptive statistics are offered in order to further characterize the firms included in the sample, and to shed some light on a few areas of discussion in the Islamic finance literature, which are not part of the conceptual model of this study. Next, the data analysis methodology and tools are described. The major part of chapter 3.1, however, documents the operationalisation of the theoretical constructs developed previously in the analytical framework. In detail, the operationalisation of the external factors, internal factors, company strategies, and company performance is presented.

Chapter 3.2 presents the findings of the empirical test of all three models with their corresponding hypotheses. The exposition starts with the analysis of the impact of external factors on performance. Next, the impact of internal factors on performance is scrutinized. Then, the impact of company strategies on performance is examined. Finally, the chapter is wrapped up with a summary of the empirical results.

Chapter 4 serves as a summary appraisal of the main arguments and major results of both the analytical framework and the empirical study. It is organized in three sections. Chapter 4.1 presents an analytical and empirical summary. Next, implications of the study for Islamic financial institutions are described in chapter 4.2. Finally, in chapter 4.3, research limitations and suggestions for future research are discussed.

2 Analytical Framework

This chapter lays the analytical foundations for the subsequent empirical analysis of strategic management and competitive strategy in Islamic finance. It is organized in four sections. First, the main theories of strategic management are described with an emphasis on the possible influencing factors of company behavior and the repertory of competitive strategies. Second, Islamic finance is presented both in terms of its theoretical basis and its actual manifestation and practices. Third, an empirical literature review presents previous studies of the determining factors of firm performance. Finally, drawing on the previous sections, a conceptual model is developed that is used as a framework to generate detailed hypotheses for the empirical study.

2.1 Theories of Strategic Management

Strategic management is a relatively new notion in business and economics research, which came into existence at about the same time as modern, non-governmental Islamic banking: the mid 1970s.[3] Theories of strategic management have evolved along several lines, the commonality of all approaches being that they define best practices for steering and managing a company. The current section focuses on the major concepts of strategic management, which view management as the process of corporate planning and governance.[4] It starts with the depiction of various strategic management approaches. After that, strategic management propositions on banking will be detailed.

2.1.1 Strategic Management Approaches

There is no generally accepted definition of "strategy" and "strategic management" in business and economics research.[5] Following Welge and Al-Laham, we define strategy as a fundamental, long-term-oriented behavior (combination of actions) of the firm and its relevant parts vis-à-vis its environment in order to realize its long-term objectives.[6] Inter alia, it covers the scope and domain of the firm's activities, its distinctive competences, and its competitive advantage. Strategic management shall

---

[3] Cf. Welge and Al-Laham (1999), p. 8 and Bea and Haas (2001), p. 6. However, the term "strategy" was introduced into managerial economics by Ansoff and other followers of the "Harvard approach" in the 1960s already. Cf. Eschenbach (1993), p. V and Welge and Al-Laham (1999), p. 12.

[4] In this respect, the predominant Anglo-Saxon strategic management approaches are followed. Evolutionary approaches – such as the approach of Kirsch (1996) – are discarded.

[5] For an overview of different strategy and strategic management definitions cf. Hammer (1988), p. 53, Kreikebaum (1989), p. 25-26, Hax and Majluf (1991), p. 2-5, Dichtl and Issing (1993), p. 2021, Eschenbach (1993), p. V and Welge and Al-Laham (1999), p. 12 et sqq.

[6] Welge and Al-Laham (1999), p. 19.

be defined as the process of formulating and implementing company strategies.[7] The strategic management approaches brought forward in the literature are manifold.[8] In the following, three approaches will be detailed: the market-based view, the resource-based view and new institutional economics. The first two are generally considered as state-of-the-art approaches of strategic management.[9] The last is gaining increased relevance in the strategic management literature.[10]

2.1.1.1 The Market-based View of Strategic Management

Basis of the market-based view of strategic management is the classical industrial organization (I-O) "structure-conduct-performance paradigm" of Mason and Bain.[11] According to this paradigm, the industry structure or competitive environment influences the conduct or strategic choice of a company, which in turn affects the performance or economic success of that company. The primary constitutive elements of the industry structure are the number and size of market players including suppliers and customers, the extent of product differentiation, demand elasticity and barriers to market entry. Conduct is defined as the strategic choices of the individual companies, essentially regarding price, promotion, product features and quality, research and development or production capacity. Performance relates to the companies' economic success and is often equated with return, technical efficiency or innovation capabilities (e.g. rate of new product introductions).[12]

Porter, who is regarded as the exponent of new industrial organization and as a pioneer of strategic management, has further developed the classical structure-conduct-performance approach. He observed that the classical paradigm had major drawbacks regarding its usefulness for strategic management research[13]: First, classical I-O focuses on the allocation efficiency of the whole industry rather than the profitability of individual firms. Second, firms are modeled as single-product companies operating in a single industry rather than diversified companies with multiple business units operating in various sectors. Third, classical I-O takes the industry structure as given and does not acknowledge any repercussions of the companies' strategic decisions on the industry structure. Last, classical I-O views the companies as single, rational units that maximize profits and not as entities with multiple decision makers and corresponding political processes as well as differentiated goal systems. Starting from these observations, new industrial organization enhanced the structure-conduct-performance paradigm by adopting a

---

[7] Ibid. Despite the missing universally accepted definitions of these terms, usage of the terms in the literature is very similar to our definitions. Cf. Hinterhuber (1992), p. 7 et sqq., Delley (2001), p. 16 et sqq.

[8] For good overviews of these approaches cf. Knyphausen-Aufseß (1995), Bea and Göbel (1999).

[9] Börner (2000b), p. 50. This appraisal is also reflected in the number of articles using market-based view and/or resource-based view in the Strategic Management Journal, the research area's paramount publication channel.

[10] Welge and Al-Laham (1999), p. 43.

[11] Cf. Mason (1939) and Bain (1968).

[12] Cf. Welge and Al-Laham (1999), p. 36-37 and Bea and Haas (2001), p. 24-25.

[13] Porter (1981), p. 611 et sqq.

more dynamic approach and incorporating the impact of performance on strategy as well as the impact of strategy on the industry structure. According to this improved paradigm, companies adapt or revise their strategies subject to their performance. Furthermore, the industry structure can be altered by the conduct or strategic decisions of a company: for example, innovation or product differentiation can create barriers to entry; vertical integration, co-operations or alliances can change the degree of concentration and competition in an industry.[14] With his "five-forces" model, Porter was the first to develop a comprehensive concept of an industry's competitive structure.[15] The five forces, which determine the attractiveness of an industry, are the bargaining power of the suppliers, the bargaining power of the customers, the threat of entry of new market players, the threat of substitutes and the intensity of competition within the industry. Porter holds that the industry attractiveness is inversely correlated with the intensity of these five forces.

The market-based view of strategic management adopts an outside-in perspective of the company: success factors are derived from market requirements; success potentials are sought in product-market combinations. Following Porter, competitive strategies can be divided into two basic forms: cost leadership strategy and differentiation strategy. Both will be detailed in the subsequent section on strategic management propositions on banking.

2.1.1.2 The Resource-based View of Strategic Management

As an alternative to the market-based view of strategic management, the resource-based view developed a "resource-conduct-performance paradigm" to explain the causal logic of companies' rent generation. According to this paradigm, a company's distinctive resource endowment influences the conduct or strategic choice of that company, which in turn affects its performance or economic success. Following Barney, firm resources are defined as "(...) all assets, capabilities, organizational processes, firm attributes, information, knowledge, etc. controlled by a firm that enable the firm to conceive of and implement strategies that improve its efficiency and effectiveness".[16] A variant of the resource-based view – the knowledge-based view – even considers knowledge as *the* crucial resource in modern, dynamic economies.[17] Although there is no generally accepted typology of resources in the literature, resources are often divided into tangible and intangible resources.[18] The former covers physical and financial assets such as IT hardware, production facilities or equity base. The latter is further classified into personal resources – covering skills and capabilities – and impersonal resources – covering intangible assets and organizational routines and processes.

---

[14] Cf. Tirole (1995), p. 169-203 and p. 305-360.

[15] Porter (1980).

[16] Barney (1991), p. 101.

[17] Cf. Nonaka and Takeuchi (1995) and Grant (1996).

[18] Cf. Knaese (1996), p. 17, Börner (2000b), p. 77, Delley (2001), p. 28-29. Barney classifies resources into physical capital resources, human capital resources and organizational resources.

The foundations of the resource-based view have been formulated in a seminal work by Penrose: she held that the heterogeneity of resources determines the uniqueness of companies.[19] Consequently, a company's resources are not all regarded as fungible goods tradable at perfect factor markets – some are specific to the company. At least for a certain time these resources cannot be acquired or imitated by the company's competitors because of information, transfer and replication barriers and the lack of the possibility to substitute them.[20] Information barriers arise for example from causal ambiguities between company-specific resources and the resulting competitive advantages or the social complexity of resource combinations. Imperfect factor markets, patents or the path dependency of the resource built-up are exemplary causes of transfer and replication barriers. Competitive advantages are derived from distinctive resources of a company, which are not only specific to that firm but also offer superior customer value.[21]

Hamel and Prahalad, who introduced the notion of "core competencies", further developed the initial resource-based view of strategic management.[22] They observe that "(…) the real sources of [competitive] advantage are to be found in management's ability to consolidate corporate-wide technologies and production skills into competencies that empower individual businesses to adapt quickly to changing opportunities"[23]. Although the concept of core competencies was quickly adopted in the strategic management literature, there is no single, universally accepted definition of the term. According to Hamel and Prahalad, a core competence has to satisfy three criteria: "First, a core competence provides potential access to a wide variety of markets. (…) Second, a core competence should make a significant contribution to the perceived customer benefits of the end product. (…) Finally, a core competence should be difficult for competitors to imitate."[24] In relation to resources, core competencies can be viewed as distinctive resource bundles. As such, they are intangible, since they result from the integration and unique combination of resources.[25] Core competencies are effective in three areas: market-access core competencies refer to market development activities and cover capabilities in sales, distribution and marketing. Integrity-related core competencies pertain to the co-ordination of the various departments or business units. Functionality-related core competencies refer to product design and the consequent customer value of a company's offering.[26] Competitive advantages arise from an efficient and effective

---

[19] Penrose (1959), p. 75. Penrose's idea has been further developed by Rumelt (1984), Wernerfelt (1984) and Barney (1991) who laid the groundwork for the later conception of core competencies, which will be detailed later in this section.

[20] For a good overview and discussion of the reasons for resource specificity cf. Barney (1991), p. 105-112 and Knaese (1996), p. 18-24. Rumelt (1984) talks of "isolating mechanisms", Wernerfelt (1984) of "resource position barriers".

[21] Cf. Börner (2000b), p. 65-75.

[22] Hamel and Prahalad (1994).

[23] Ibid., p. 80.

[24] Ibid., p. 83 et sqq.

[25] Börner (2000b), p. 80.

[26] Hamel (1994), p. 16.

bundling of resources and a continuous renovation and further development of the resulting core competencies.[27]

The capability of a company to continuously acquire and develop its core competencies is usually regarded as a meta competence. Among these meta competencies are learning and innovation capabilities, communication capabilities, relationship management capabilities and management systems.[28] In the literature, the capability of innovation and organizational learning is often viewed as the most important meta competence, as it is a *conditio sine qua non* of the built-up of competencies.[29] As a consequence, it is stipulated that a firm's organization and culture should be configured in a way favoring this meta competence.

The resource-based view of strategic management adopts an inside-out perspective of the company: success factors are derived from the company's endowment with distinctive resources and core competencies. Although it is sometimes seen as a counterdraft to the market-based view, both concepts are often regarded as complementary. In relation to the SWOT[30] analysis, a traditional strategic planning tool, the resource-based view is often equated with the analysis of internal strengths and weaknesses of the firm, the market-based view with the analysis of external opportunities and threats.[31]

2.1.1.3 New Institutional Economics Approaches

As new institutional economics actually is not part of the realm of strategic management, it does not attempt to explain the economic success of a company but rather deals with problems of economic co-ordination. The three main approaches of new institutional economics – property rights theory, transaction cost theory and principal agent theory – are however of some relevance for strategic management research, as will be highlighted in the following exposition.[32] All three approaches are based on the same assumptions about human behavior[33]: First, individual utility maximization: people are individually pursuing clearly defined goals – specified as utility functions, which are maximized. These utility functions are constant over time, so that changes in behavior cannot be attributed to changes in people's preferences. Second, bounded rationality: both knowledge and information processing capabilities of people are limited. As a consequence, problems cannot be comprehensively structured and solved. People decide and act on simplifications and approximations of

---

[27] Börner (2000b), p. 82, Delley (2001), p. 36.

[28] For a detailed review of these meta competencies cf. Knaese (1996), p. 29-35.

[29] Cf. Börner (2000b), p. 87-88, Delley (2001), p. 35.

[30] SWOT = Strenghts, Weaknesses, Opportunities, Threats

[31] Cf. Wernerfelt (1984), p. 171, Barney (1991), p. 99-101, Knaese (1996), p. 8-13, Börner (2000b), p. 118 et sqq. In particular, Börner formulates an integrated model of both the market-based and the resource-based view.

[32] For an overview of various uses of new institutional economics approaches in strategic management cf. Milgrom and Roberts (1992), Scott (1995), Picot et. al. (1997), Kieser (1999). For a good overview of new institutional economics cf. Williamson (2000).

[33] Cf. Cezanne and Mayer (1998), p. 1345 et sqq. and Welge and Al-Laham (1999), p. 43-44.

the original problem. Finally, opportunistic behavior: people maximize their own utility, regardless of any possible damage to others caused by their actions.

Property rights theory. At the heart of this theory are the content and structure of property rights and their effect on the allocation and uses of resources.[34] Property rights are divided into four forms: First, the rights concerning the use of a good (*usus*). Second, the rights regarding the formal and substantial modification of a good (*abusus*). Third, the rights concerning the appropriation of the gains and losses resulting from the use of a good (*usus fructus*). Finally, the rights to relinquish or sell a good. Attenuations, transaction costs and externalities are important, partly interlinked factors influencing property rights. Attenuations refer to restrictions of the property rights, i.e. a situation where not all four forms of property rights can be executed – for example when the owner of a house has conveyed the right of use to a tenant. Transaction costs may also lead to attenuations, which in turn may lead to positive or negative externalities. Property rights theory is primarily concerned with allocation efficiency and social welfare considerations – its relevance for strategic management research is limited. However, one of its building blocks – the transaction costs – have direct implications for strategic management.

Transaction cost theory. Transaction cost theory deals with the costs of information, communication, negotiation, processing, control and adjustment in connection with an economic exchange – such as the transferal of property rights.[35] It holds that transaction costs are essential for explaining the governance structure of economic transactions or co-ordination, i.e. " (…) the institutional framework within which the integrity of a transaction is decided. Markets and hierarchies are two of the main alternatives."[36] Determinants of potential transaction costs are human factors – both bounded rationality and opportunistic behavior mentioned above – and environmental factors – uncertainty/complexity, idiosyncrasy and frequency of the transaction. Transaction cost theory infers the selection of the optimal governance structure for a specific transaction from these factors. In strategic management research, it is for example used for the determination of vertical integration and co-operation strategies.[37]

Principal agent theory. As the name implies, this theory relates to the relationship of principals and agents and optimal contracts to steer and control this relationship.[38] Information asymmetries between, and diverging target systems as well as opportunistic behavior of both principal and agent lead to agency costs and the need to design incentive, control and information systems that assure largely compliant

---

[34] For a good overview of the theory cf. Cezanne and Mayer (1998), p. 1346-1348. For a more detailed exposition cf. Furubotn and Richter (1991 and 1996).

[35] For an overview cf. Cezanne and Mayer (1998), p. 1348-1350. For a more detailed exposition cf. Coase (1937), Williamson (1975), Rindfleisch and Heide (1997).

[36] Williamson (1979), p. 235.

[37] Cf. Welge and Al-Laham (1999), p. 45-47.

[38] For an overview cf. Cezanne and Mayer (1998), p. 1350-1352. For a more detailed exposition cf. Jensen and Meckling (1976), Grossman and Hart (1983), Arrow (1985), Pratt and Zeckhauser (1985).

behavior of the agent. In the basic principal agent model, the principal cannot observe the actions of his agent (hidden action). Moreover, the principal does not know ex ante whether the agent is capable of performing his contractual obligation (hidden information/hidden characteristics), nor does he know his true intentions (hidden intentions). Finally, the outcome of the agent's task does not only depend on his performance but also on external factors, with the principal not being able to identify the contribution of the former or the latter ex post (moral hazard). The resulting problems are resolved by the principal agent theory in several ways. The principal's uncertainty about the agent's qualifications can be remedied through signaling and self-selection. An agent can for example signal his qualifications by means of guarantees; he can perform self-selection by accepting variable rather than fixed remuneration. The principal's uncertainty about the agent's actions can for example be remedied through performance-related compensation. Accordingly, the theory's relevance for the design of managerial incentive and control systems seems obvious.[39] In a broader perspective, principal agent theory can be of use for strategic management research in all matters of co-ordination, such as management-shareholder relations, joint ventures, or strategic alliances. In industrial organization, major building blocks of the theory – such as asymmetric information - are also used to explain product differentiation and advertising.[40]

2.1.2 Strategic Management Propositions on Banking

It is widely acknowledged in the strategic management field of research that a scientific standard, which truly merits to be designated as "theory", has not been reached yet.[41] On the one hand, the general principles brought forward in the literature often lack a high degree of determination, i.e. they cannot be used as a basis for concrete practical action. On the other hand, empirically relevant observations that relate to actual business practice often refer to individual, isolated cases, i.e. they cannot be used to generate universal conclusions. Research on strategic management therefore often times focuses on typological assertions, which are situated in the middle between singular and general assertions, and are viewed as "theories of minor reach"[42]. In this section, such typological propositions on strategic bank management – which are important for the subsequent formulation of a conceptual model relating to strategic management in Islamic finance – will be depicted. This will be done along the lines of the strategic management process, which can be divided into five steps: First, the formulation of the corporate vision, mission and objectives; second, the assessment of external factors; third, the assessment of internal factors; fourth, the formulation of company strategies; finally, implementation and controlling of these

[39] For an example cf. Hüttemann (1993).

[40] Cf. Tirole (1995), p. 289-294.

[41] Cf. Bea and Haas (2001), p. 3-36. A sound review of the situation is given by Knyphausen-Aufseß (1995).

[42] Cf. Bea and Haas (2001), p. 23.

strategies.[43] In the following exposition, these factors will be analyzed in order to derive strategic management propositions on banking.

2.1.2.1 Bank Performance: The Importance of Corporate Vision, Mission and Objectives

The formulation of the corporate vision, mission and objectives (VMO) is the starting point of the strategic management process. It is based on the development of a vision, which is normally not the outcome of a formalized procedure.[44] Despite a plethora of terms in the literature – e.g. corporate philosophy, corporate policy, charter – there is a common thread in the definitions brought forward: corporate vision and mission set the basic principles of a company, which are stipulated in some sort of mission statement, and define the scope of the company's activities.[45] While corporate vision and mission are rather vague and abstract, they are specified and detailed by the corporate objectives. In addition to the determination of the company's business goals, corporate vision, mission and objectives also have to take into account the company's stakeholders. According to Post et. al., they have to consider social challenges, global economic change, government and public policy, ecological and natural resource concerns, and ethical expectations and public values.[46]

Corporate vision, mission and objectives have to fulfill a number of functions. Among these functions are the decision function, the control function, the legitimization function, the co-ordination function, the motivation function, and the information function.[47] The decision function relates to the importance of VMO as reference criteria for the assessment and selection of competitive strategies. VMO perform a control function by enabling target/actual comparisons, and they may serve as legitimization, for example in the form of social or ecological goals of the company. As a consequence, when analyzing strategic management actions in order to identify best practices, this can only be done when relating them to the degree to which they satisfy the individual bank's VMO. The co-ordination function concerns their relevance for the orientation of the whole company towards common goals – as for example reflected in the concept of management by objectives. The importance of VMO for the motivation of employees is mirrored in the motivation function. Finally, the information function relates to the use of VMO as a source of information, both internally and externally. These three functions point to the importance of a bank's

---

[43] In the literature, strategic management is often modeled in a similar way. Cf. Hinterhuber (1992), Thompson and Strickland III (1998), Welge and Al-Laham (1999), Bea and Haas (2001), Achenbach et. al. (2003). In fact, a lot of the literature on strategic management does not produce individual theoretical propositions that eventually can be tested but concentrates on the development of heuristic methods as a basis for strategic management decisions. This is illustrated in the expositions of strategic management cited above.

[44] Cf. Hinterhuber (1992), p. 41 et sqq., Bea and Haas (2001), p. 67.

[45] Hinterhuber (1992), p. 57.

[46] Post et. al. (1996). For a short discussion of these factors cf. Welge and Al-Laham (1999), p. 101-104.

[47] Bea and Haas (2001), p. 72-73. Cf. also Welge and Al-Laham (1999), p. 109-110.

ability to make all its parts act in its interest. VMO is seen as a tool to do just that – as will become apparent later, companies can develop core competencies in this respect.

There is a multitude of potential corporate objectives of a company, targeting inter alia market service, market position, profitability, corporate financing, power and prestige, employee-related goals, or social goals.[48] Financial objectives and objectives regarding market service as well as market position are by far the most widely used corporate objectives in practice.[49] These include profit, return (on assets, on investments, on equity, on sales), customer satisfaction, market share, product/ service quality and shareholder value. Therefore, it seems fair to take criteria like these as indicators for bank performance.

2.1.2.2 The Impact of External Factors on Bank Performance

External factors relate to opportunities and threats in classical strategic planning terms and their analysis largely draws on approaches of the market-based view of strategic management. In the following, key concepts of external factors will be presented, and propositions on the impact of a bank's global environment, industry structure, and industry dynamic will be detailed.

Global environment. A bank's global environment consists of its macro-economic, socio-cultural, technological, and political/legal environment.[50] All these factors directly and indirectly influence the company's room for maneuver and – being effective for a great number of companies operating in the same industry – can create metatrends. The macro-economic environment includes for example economic growth, the level of disposable household income, the interest level, or the unemployment rate. The socio-cultural environment relates to values and attitudes of the population, lifestyle, demographic development, and the like. It is of particular importance for the determination of customer preferences and requirements. The technological environment is inter alia determined by the level and productivity of research and development, the technological innovation rate, and the pace of technological change. The importance of the technological environment for the banking industry is highlighted by recent revolutionary technological developments, such as the development of the Internet. Finally, the political/legal environment relates for example to the political system, political ideologies, political stability, or the legal system of a country. All parts of a bank's global environment strongly relate to the geographical scope of the bank's activities. Therefore, banks operating in the same geographical area – more precisely in the same country or countries – should be impacted in the same way by the global environment. Consequently, one would

---

[48] Cf. Welge and Al-Laham (1999), p. 111 et sqq.

[49] Al-Laham (1997), p. 104.

[50] Cf. Welge and Al-Laham (1999), p. 185-192, Achenbach et. al. (2003), p. 327-330. Achenbach et. al. also list the natural environment. However, the examples they provide – companies are increasingly being held responsible for environmental damage they create and the increasing demand for ecological products – in our view rather belong to the political/legal and the socio-cultural environment, respectively.

expect in this case that there is no correlation between bank performance and the global environment.[51]

Industry structure. Porter's five forces are the major industry structure concept. Together, the five forces – new market entrants, the bargaining power of suppliers, the bargaining power of customers, substitutes and the rivalry among established competitors – determine the attractiveness or profitability potential of an industry.[52] Market attractiveness is inversely correlated with the strength of these forces; in fact if only a single force is strong enough, an industry can be relatively unattractive. Porter also holds that the performance of a company is essentially industry-driven. Accordingly, companies have to master these forces and – ideally – to change them in their favor.[53]

New market entrants increase the capacity within an industry and consequently exercise pressure on market prices and industry profits. The probability of new players entering a market depends on two factors: the anticipated reaction of established market players and existing barriers to entry. It will be low if new entrants expect hard retaliatory measures, in particular in the form of price competition. This can be the case if previous new entrants already suffered retaliation, if the established market players dispose of substantial means of retaliation (such as excess liquidity or excess production capacity), if they possess idiosyncratic, highly illiquid assets or if the industry is characterized by slow growth and limited ability to absorb more competitors.[54] As for the banking industry, a general statement on expected retaliatory measures cannot be made – this clearly depends on the situation in individual markets – e.g. geographical markets. Barriers to entry are created by economies of scale, brand identity, capital requirements, switching costs, access to distribution, government policy and absolute cost advantages. Economies of scale will lead to a cost disadvantage of new market entrants. Brand identity refers to the existence of well-established brands and consequent customer loyalty due to former promotional effort, product differentiation, superior service or first-mover advantage. Porter regards brand identity as the most important barrier to entry in investment banking.[55] A big amount of capital required for the start-up of a business (e.g. acquisition of production facilities, substantial advertising or research and development expenses) can be another barrier to entry, as capital providers may be reluctant to make it available or may demand a risk premium. In general, a relatively low amount of capital is required for opening up a bank. Switching costs incurred by customers when purchasing the product of the new market entrant may deter them from defecting from the established

[51] As a consequence, many empirical studies on the determinants of company performance focus on a single country, holding the global environment – more or less – constant.

[52] Cf. for the following exposition Porter (1983), p. 25-61 and Porter (1986), p. 22-30. For exemplary reviews of Porter's concept cf. Welge and Al-Laham (1999), p. 193-201, Bea and Haas (2001), p. 95-99, Achenbach et. al. (2003), p. 330-338. In this section, product is used as a term including products and services.

[53] Porter (1986), p. 22.

[54] Porter (1983), p. 37-38.

[55] Ibid., p. 32.

competitors – for example in the case of IT software. Again, these can be expected to be relatively low in the banking industry. Access to distribution channels by the existing market players may also serve as a barrier to entry, as new entrants may need to accept lower margins to get access to hard-fought channels or may even be forced to create their own. In the banking industry, this is especially true for banks targeting the mass and affluent customer segments, as these typically need to be served by branch offices. Government policy, e.g. in the form of subsidies to established market players, can also create barriers to entry. As before, this clearly depends on the situation in individual markets. Finally, absolute cost advantages – for example through better know-how, patents or experience-curve effects – can make market entry of new players cumbersome. Although there can be advantages through better know-how or experience-curve effects in the banking industry, these effects can be assumed to be relatively small; moreover, financial products cannot be protected by patents.

Action parameters of suppliers are pricing, quality and quantity of their products.[56] Suppliers have a high bargaining power if they have a lot of leeway in setting higher prices, lowering their quality or curtailing supply. Factors determining the bargaining power are supplier concentration, presence of substitute inputs, importance of volume to supplier, importance of inputs to buyer, differentiation or switching costs of inputs, and threat of forward integration of supplier. Suppliers will have a high bargaining power if their industry is highly concentrated and more so than their customers; in case of missing substitutes for their products; if the industry they sell to is unimportant in terms of sales volume; if the product they supply is of substantial importance to their customers (e.g. if the flow of the production process depends on this input); if their customers would incur high switching costs in case of product or supplier changes; or if the supplier can pose a credible threat of forward integration. Major suppliers in the banking industry are IT suppliers and people – as suppliers of human resources. Both are important inputs for banks.

Action parameters as well as factors determining the bargaining power of customers largely mirror those of suppliers – and will consequently not be presented again. One additional factor is buyer information, i.e. his knowledge about market prices and the cost structure of his suppliers. The better he is informed, the larger will be his bargaining power. It can be expected that large companies and high net worth individuals have a higher bargaining power than average customers, as it can be assumed that they are better informed, and as their share of business with the bank will be higher.

Substitutes are those products that (can) perform the same function as the original product but do not belong to the same industry.[57] Substitutes account for an upper

---

[56] Porter observes, that workers/human resources very often are suppliers with substantial bargaining power. Cf. Porter (1983), p. 55.

[57] The definition of substitute illustrates a problem of Porter's industry definition. Porter defines industry as a group of companies whose products are close substitutes. One could argue that substitutes performing the same function as the original product will be close substitutes and

price limit in an industry. Special attention should be given to substitutes whose price-performance trade-off improves over time, especially in high-margin industries. As an example for the banking industry, products such as life insurance can be regarded as substitutes for savings products.

Rivalry among established competitors appears in the form of price competition, promotion battles, new product introductions, and the like. It is determined by various structural factors, such as the number of competitors, market growth, production capacity, switching costs, diversity of rivals, or exit barriers. The rivalry within the industry is more intense in case of a large number of competitors or if competitors are very similar in size and resource endowment; if market growth is slow; in case of excess capacity; if switching costs of customers are low; if competitors are very heterogeneous and do not agree on the same market rules; or in case of high exit barriers, e.g. high exit costs such as social plans.

The industry structure can be further refined by identifying strategic groups of companies. Strategic groups are companies that are homogeneous along several strategic dimensions. Porter lists the degree of specialization, brand identity, push or pull strategy, selection of sales channels, product quality, technological edge, vertical integration, cost position, service policy, price policy, power, relation to parent company, and relation to government as major strategic dimensions.[58] He holds that the five forces influence different strategic groups of the same industry to varying degrees. Moreover, similarly to the global environment, most parts of a bank's industry structure strongly relate to the geographical scope of the bank's activities. Therefore, banks operating in the same geographical area – more precisely in the same country or countries – should be impacted in the same way by the industry structure, provided that they belong to the same strategic group. Consequently, one would expect in this case that there is no correlation between bank performance and the industry structure.[59]

Industry dynamic. Porter's five forces analysis of the industry structure is a rather static approach. It yields insights about current characteristics of the competitive forces and is therefore particularly useful for stable, mature industries.[60] Yet most industries undergo constant change, as product life cycles have shortened, barriers to entry have been lowered by factors such as deregulation, technological change has picked up the pace, and competition has intensified. In this context, Porter points out that the strategic behavior of companies can influence structural change of an

---

consequently be part of the industry competition and *not* an external force. It might be more stringent to talk of potential substitutes as one of the five forces, i.e. products that are not already used for the same functions but only have the potential to be used as substitutes.

[58] Porter (1983), p. 174-176. In the literature, one can find also other definitions of strategic groups, such as a definition from a resource-based viewpoint. This will be presented below.

[59] As a matter of course, it is also possible to find identical industry structures or global environments in different geographic areas. In this case again, no correlation between performance and industry structure as well as global environment would be expected.

[60] Cf. Welge and Al-Laham (1999), p. 201. See also Börner (2000b), p. 136-143, who uses this assessment as a basis for his development of an integrated strategic management model.

industry, either as a reaction to strategic moves of its competitors or acting as a first mover. Examples for such (re)actions are the design of license agreements, lobbying, or development of substitute products.

2.1.2.3 The Impact of Internal Factors on Bank Performance

Internal factors relate to strengths and weaknesses of the company in classical strategic planning terms and their analysis largely draws on approaches of the resource-based view of strategic management. In the following, the key concept behind internal factors will be detailed, and propositions on their impact will be presented.

Internal factors are generally equated with core competencies, i.e. distinctive resource bundles.[61] These constitute "hypothetical constructs"[62], which are – due to their intangible character – hard to identify. What is more, core competencies are in essence unique to a single firm; therefore, the identification of core competencies for a whole industry seems – at first glance – absurd. However, firm resource and core competencies endowments can be the basis for the definition of strategic groups: In this case, a strategic group is defined as a group of firms that compete within an industry by deploying similar configurations of strategic resource bundles.[63] Moreover, even though assertions on the exact form of core competencies of banks in general must remain on a rather abstract and generic level, it is possible to define and detail areas of core competencies. As was presented above, core competencies are effective in three areas: market-access core competencies, functionality-related core competencies, and integrity-related core competencies. These three areas will be typified in what follows.[64] As should be apparent from what has been said before about the nature of core competencies, the following does not claim to be exhaustive but tries to identify the most important components of these three areas.

Market-access core competencies. These competencies relate to sales channels, customer contact, and customer counseling as well as acceptance. The sales channels define the access of the bank to its market(s). They are composed of the branch office network – including, where applicable, the ATM network – and direct banking facilities, such as Internet banking or call centers. The resulting entire distribution system can be part of a core competence, if it yields a superior utility to the customer. The customer contact competence is made up of image and brand, the bank's customer orientation through the mix of its human resources and its business processes, and the bank's customer structure. Competencies in customer counseling and acceptance, finally, are those that relate to the interaction of the bank with its customers. They are composed of the professional and social skills of the customer

---

[61] See above chapter 2.2.1.2

[62] Rasche (1994), p. 411.

[63] Cf. McGee and Thomas (1986), Amit and Schoemaker (1993). A derivation of strategic groups based on firm resources could be more useful than the strategic groups based on firm product market strategies, because in general, altering a firm's resource base requires a considerably longer time than changing its market strategies. Cf. Dierickx and Cool (1989).

consultants, of application software, and again of the bank's business processes. If a bank disposes of these competencies, it can take up or detect services required by its customers as well as economically select customers better than others.

Functionality-related core competencies. Among these competencies are the transaction processing competencies, the infrastructure competencies, and the transformation competencies. Transaction processing competencies combine personal as well as technical (mostly IT-related) capabilities of the bank. In other words, these competencies draw heavily on expertise and bank telematics. For example, a bank might be in a position to submit a binding offer faster than its competitors. Another example could be an exceptionally efficient management of customer data, leading to superior account management or marketing activities. The infrastructure competencies relate to supply, and procurement functions. These are mostly involved in the provision of input resources – in particular human resources and IT. Finally, the transformation competencies refer to the bank's treasury and trading capabilities. As an example, a core competence could consist in an extraordinary understanding of financial markets, i.e. the way a bank finds and administers information on financial market developments, leading to superior actions in the financial markets. In this regard, the financial standing of a bank – notably its rating – might be of particular importance.

Integrity-related core competencies. These core competencies relate to the co-ordination of the various departments or business units of a company. Consequently, they mainly affect central management – in particular top management – and comprehensive competencies spanning the entire range of competencies presented before. The former refers to the dispositive actions of the bank's management, the system of rules formulated by management, and the information and control system used by management. It affects in particular the capability of the bank to implement strategic decisions. The latter refers to the interaction and the complexity of the various core competencies detailed above. As an example, the extraordinary understanding of financial markets, which was mentioned as a functionality-related core competence, can be viewed as a comprehensive, integrity-related core competence in the case of investment banks.

The actual occurrence of these core competencies in a bank is determined by the development of the individual firm since its inception. Although the considerations made above about core competencies of banks can be further refined if a specific segment of that industry is selected – such as Islamic finance – predictions of their configuration will remain tentative. However, following the resource-based view, it can be expected that core competencies have an impact on bank performance: stronger competencies should result in superior performance.

[64] The exposition below largely draws on Börner (2000b), p. 230-253.

2.1.2.4 The Impact of Company Strategies on Bank Performance

In the strategic management process, company strategies are developed on the basis of an assessment of both external and internal factors.[65] They are often classified into corporate strategies, business strategies and functional strategies:[66]

> "Corporate strategy defines the scope of the firm's operations and how the management allocates or deploys its resources to make the whole firm a vital, competitive enterprise. Corporate strategy is concerned more with the question of where to compete than with how to compete in a particular business – the latter is the province of business strategy."[67]

Business strategies are detailed at the department level in the form of functional strategies.[68] While in practice, as mentioned above, both external and internal factors are taken into account to develop company strategies, both the market-based view and the resource-based view make an exclusive claim on the development of company strategies. However, the causal relationship between an actual set of external or internal factors, respectively, and the right choice of a company strategy, remains unclear in the strategic management literature – regardless of whether it is based on the market-based view, the resource-based view or whether it expounds heuristics of the strategic management process.

As the present study is focusing on Islamic banking, i.e. a well-defined segment within the greater realm of the banking industry, corporate strategies – the question of where to compete – will not be analyzed here, even though Islamic banking can be further sub-segmented, e.g. into corporate and private banking. Instead, this section will focus on business strategies. As defined above, business strategies are concerned with the question of how to compete in a particular business.[69] In the literature, business strategies are generally presented following Porter's generic strategies category scheme.[70] In his view, competitive strategy is the selection of offensive or defensive measures in order to establish a firm and secure industry position. He distinguishes cost leadership strategy, differentiation strategy and segmentation strategy.

---

[65] The analysis of external and internal factors is usually refined by projecting their possible future development. For this matter, a variety of tools is presented in the literature, such as quantitative forecasting techniques, scenario analysis, or the concept of weak signals. Cf. Welge and Al-Laham (1999), p. 287-302, Bea and Haas (2001), p. 264-300. Part of these tools – in particular scenario planning – are also used for the selection of company strategies.

[66] Obviously, there are many ways how to classify company strategies. Bea and Haas, for instance, list seven different classifications for strategies, but then follow the above-mentioned classification in their own presentation, as is often done in the literature. Cf. Welge and Al-Laham (1999), p. 322-431, Bea and Haas (2001), p. 161-181, Achenbach et. al. (2003), p. 358-390.

[67] Hatten and Hatten (1988), p. 235. In the literature, there are also growth and divestment strategies that are often viewed as an independent strategy type or subsumed under corporate strategies (cf. Welge and Al-Laham (1999), p. 432-483; Bea and Haas (2001), p. 166-176).

[68] For a good overview cf. Welge and Al-Laham (1999), p. 400-431.

[69] For a good overview of business strategies cf. Welge and Al-Laham (1999), p. 375-399 and p. 432-483.

[70] Porter (1983), p. 62 et sqq.

Cost leadership strategy emphasizes efficiency. By producing high volumes of standardized products, the firm hopes to take advantage of economies of scale and experience curve effects. The product is often a basic no-frills product that is produced at a relatively low cost and made available to a very large customer base. Maintaining this strategy requires a continuous search for cost reductions in all aspects of the business. In the banking industry, such a strategy is pursued by discount brokers or direct banking specialists, leveraging a high standardization of products and a largely IT-based transaction processing. The cost leadership strategy also implies that there is a single company, which *is* the cost leader, and not many companies fighting for that position.[71] Therefore, in empirical research analyzing many companies, no correlation or even a negative correlation between cost leadership strategies and performance is expected: if market players are rational entities, there will be only one or an evanescent few companies following that strategy.

A differentiation strategy is pursued if a company offers a unique product in terms of quality and service, whose features provide superior customer value. These features can for example relate to the product's technical configuration, its design, brand image, or sales channel. Because customers see the product as unrivaled and unequaled, the price elasticity of demand tends to be reduced and customers tend to be more brand loyal. Differentiation strategies are often viewed as highly relevant for the banking industry, much more so than cost leadership.[72] Consequently, a positive correlation between the use of differentiation strategies and bank performance is expected.

In the segmentation strategy – also called focus strategy or niche strategy – the firm concentrates on a select few target markets with the intention to better meet the needs of that target market by focusing the marketing efforts and tailoring the marketing mix. The firm typically looks to gain a competitive advantage through effectiveness rather than efficiency. This strategy type is most suitable for relatively small firms. Both cost leadership and differentiation strategy can be combined with the segmentation strategy. The question of what correlation to expect between the use of niche strategies and financial performance depends on the characteristics of the industry. If the industry is made up of a large number of firms with one or a few players dominating the market, a positive correlation is expected, as most firms will be serving a lucrative niche market. If this is not the case, no correlation is expected.

2.1.2.5 The Impact of Strategy Implementation on Bank Performance

The effectiveness of strategies can only be ensured by efficient implementation and controlling. The strategy formulation and implementation process on the one hand and controlling on the other hand are intertwined and interdependent, as planning without control is futile, and control without planning impossible.[73] As a consequence,

[71] Porter (1986), p. 34.

[72] Börner (2000b), p. 387.

[73] Wild (1974)

controlling of the strategic targets, strategic assumptions, strategy implementation and strategy success needs to be conceived as an ongoing task along the strategic management process.[74] Strategy implementation is mainly concerned with business planning, and communication and incentive system. In the following, we limit ourselves to the presentation of these two areas, as controlling is less relevant for our purposes.[75]

Business planning. Strategies and strategic plans need to be transformed into operational plans, detailing individual operational measures. In order to do that, a business plan needs to be developed, which is usually composed of the planning of the corporate strategy and business strategy, and further refined in sales plans, investment plans and innovation plans. The business plan defines the budget that sets the framework for the company's monetary goals. The strategic plan needs to be detailed and specific enough to act as direction setting, yet high-level enough to allow for the indispensable flexibility that is required at the operational level. The operational plans should take the targets of the strategic plan into account and detail them in production plans, procurement plans, resource plans (both personnel and equipment), distribution plans, and administration plans. Both should be interlinked in such a way, that operational measures are logically deducted from strategic directives.

Communication and incentive system. In order for a strategy to become effective, it must have a direct impact on the behavior of the company's employees. Therefore, employees must be made aware of the company's strategy (communication) and their actions must be linked to the company's strategic targets (incentive system). In the literature, the balanced scorecard by Kaplan and Norton is regarded as an eminent tool for effective strategy implementation, in particular with regard to the translation of rather abstract strategies into concrete target figures (communication) and the usage of these figures for management-by-objectives (incentive system).[76] The balanced scorecard transfers in a deductive way a company's strategy into four perspectives, with a balance between internal and external measures, objective and subjective measures, and performance results and the drivers of future results. It considers financial, customer, business process, and learning measures.[77] When used at different hierarchical levels, a system of interlinked balanced scorecards can be developed, detailing the most relevant target figures for the respective level(s).

---

[74] For good expositions of the strategic controlling process cf. Bea and Haas (2001), p. 211-236, Achenbach et. al. (2003), p. 420-425.

[75] For good expositions of the strategic implementation process cf. Hinterhuber (1992), Welge and Al-Laham (1999), p. 523-617, Bea and Haas (2001), p. 188-200, Achenbach et. al. (2003), p. 405-419.

[76] Cf. Welge and Al-Laham (1999), p. 554-561; Bea and Haas (2001), p. 190-193; Achenbach et. al. (2003), p. 415-419. For the original presentation of the concept cf. Kaplan and Norton (1996).

[77] Financial measures are for example operating income, return on capital employed, or economic value added. Among customer measures are customer satisfaction, customer retention, or market share in target segments. Business process measures are e.g. unit costs, throughput, or failure rates. Learning measures include employee productivity, employee satisfaction, employee retention, or product innovation rate. Cf. Kaplan and Norton (1996).

The importance of these two areas for bank performance has become apparent in the exposition above on integrity-related core competencies already. In order to ensure the effective implementation of company strategies, a bank needs to dispose of the relevant capabilities to do so. Consequently, one can regard these two areas as competencies and subsume them under the heading of integrity-related core competencies. Hence, in accordance with what has been expounded above, it can be expected that the implementation capabilities have an impact on bank performance: stronger implementation capabilities should result in superior performance.

2.2 Islamic Finance in Theory and Practice

Although not a new phenomenon, Islamic finance is still a largely untapped area for the majority of academics, finance practitioners and the general public in the West. While Western academic interest has been spurred in the early 1980s already[78], it has been and still is confined to a selected few and the ever-increasing popularity of the topic in Islamic countries is widely ignored in the Western world, where it has remained a subject-matter of experts. Therefore, the current section introduces theory and practice of Islamic finance. It starts with the exposition of the fundamentals of Islamic finance, followed by a detailed description of Islamic financial instruments. After that, Islamic finance markets are depicted – including a presentation of their institutional framework – with special emphasis on the markets in the GCC countries and Malaysia.

2.2.1 The Fundamentals of Islamic Finance

> "One of the more striking facts about the rise of Islamic banking and finance is that it represents an assertion of religious law in the area of commercial life, where secularism rules almost unquestioned throughout the rest of the world."[79]

In fact, the importance and the sheer existence of Islamic finance can only be understood with respect to Islam's claim of sovereignty over all spheres of life. While in the Christian world, in the wake of the enlightenment, faith has for the majority of people become restricted to the realm of spirituality, Islam is seen by the believer as an all-encompassing way of life, and Islamic law as the criterion for right action in all circumstances. What is more, there are explicit rulings regarding areas such as property rights, gain, risk-taking, speculation and interest, which are sometimes at odds with both Western economic theory and business practice. Since the Sharia, the Islamic law, is a case law, one has to look at its sources and methods in order to understand the basis of Islamic economics and finance.

---

[78] See for instance Nienhaus (1982), Nienhaus (1983), Kuran (1986)

[79] Vogel and Hayes, III (1998), p. 19.

2.2.1.1 Sources, Methods and Schools of Law

The two bases of the Sharia are the Qur'an, the holy book of the Muslims, and the Sunna, the traditions of the Prophet Muhammad.[80] Both represent the perfect, immutable divine law itself, with the Qur'an being regarded as revealed by God, although they were compiled as written texts only after Muhammad's death: The former was written up under the caliphate of Uthman (644-656 A.D.); the latter was collected over several centuries through a sophisticated authentication process of conveyed reports of Prophet Muhammad's acts and words. The Qur'an is a highly complex scripture, containing religious admonitions, eschatologic scenarios, salvific histories, instructions and even precise legal regulations. Numerous Qur'an commentaries give guidance as to how to interpret the different text passages and how they are related to each other. Both the Qur'an and the Sunna lend themselves in principle to differing interpretations.

The human apprehension of the divine law – called *fiqh* – is carried out by learned scholars, the ulema. These scholars use an idiosyncratic methodology (*usul al-fiqh* or "sources of law") to derive from the texts specific rules of behavior, governing all spheres of human life. Apart from the Qur'an and the Sunna, which are regarded as primary sources of law, *fiqh* distinguishes three major secondary sources of law: consensus of all Islamic scholars (*ijma'*), deduction by analogy (*qiyas*) and independent reasoning drawing on the primary sources only (*ijtihad*). Of these three, analogy is by far the most widely used. The prerequisites for *ijma'* are stringent, leading to a very small number of rules based on this methodology. *Ijtihad*, although metaphysically the most pristine technique, is used only if the other methods fail to establish a legal ruling. Moreover, its use was controversial since the tenth century A.D. when the idea developed that the most important questions of law were answered, so that scholars were no longer qualified to practice *ijtihad* but should rather follow their predecessors' views. This "closing of the door of *ijtihad*" would constrain scholars to pure imitation (*taqlid*), hindering the development of new concepts within Islamic law. Nowadays, however, there is general agreement that the "door of *ijtihad*" is not closed and never was, as eminent scholars continued to make use of it in every age. Besides, a modern interpretation of the Sharia has become a serious issue among Muslim scholars and intellectuals affecting inter alia the foundations of Islamic economics.[81] *Ijtihad* is particularly expedient in cases, which have never been considered before. Therefore, it is increasingly being used in Islamic banking and finance, where novel financial instruments such as options need to be evaluated from a religious viewpoint.

When faced with different existing judicial views on a legal problem or a novel situation that no legal ruling has addressed yet, Islamic scholars can also make use of

---

[80] For a good introduction into Islamic law cf. Schacht (1964), for a view on the modern applications of Islamic law cf. Ende and Steinbach (1996), for Islamic law and economics – especially banking and finance – cf. Nienhaus (1991), Saeed (1996), Vogel and Hayes (1998), El-Gamal (2000), Lewis and Algaoud (2001), Archer and Abdel Karim (2003).

[81] See next paragraph on "Principles of Islamic Economics and Finance"

three adaptive mechanisms that even allow for deviations from existing norms: local custom (*'urf*), the public interest (*maslaha*) and necessity (*darura*).[82] Especially in the early days of Islam during the time of rapid geographical expansion, Islamic jurisprudence took into account and adopted existing customs and laws of newly conquered territories. Public interest comes into play when Islamic scholars need to choose among rival legal viewpoints: they are advised to pick the one which serves best the general good or *maslaha*. Finally, overriding necessity permits even the forbidden, i.e. rulings that contravene a categorical Sharia rule.

Over the course of time, Islamic scholars have compiled a large corpus of legal rulings and – within Sunni Islam – have established four schools of thought (*madhhab*, pl. *madhahib*), which progressively narrowed their positions on legal issues. These schools are the Hanafi, Maliki, Shafi'i and Hanbali, which are predominant in different geographical regions throughout the Islamic world.[83] It is important to note that not only differ these schools in hermeneutics, but also in doctrine. "Thus, on a proposition of Islamic (Sunni) law one can usually list four positions, taking the most accepted one from each school."[84] What is more, there may be differing views on the same issue even within one school.

This diversity of opinion is reflected in the way an issue is evaluated. Islamic legal rulings can be categorized into five values that not only impact the legal validity of an action but also its moral appraisal: prohibited (*haram*), reprehensible (*makruh*), indifferent (*mubah*), meritorious (*mustahabb*) and obligatory (*wajib*). In general[85], prohibited acts are sins and legally invalid, obligatory acts morally virtuous and legally valid, enforceable and compulsory. All acts falling under any of the other categories are legally valid and permissible, but may have additional moral consequences left to the hereafter. To illustrate doctrinal differences across the four schools, one can use the example of legal artifices (*hila*, pl. *hiyal*), which classical Islamic law has extensively employed – in particular for business purposes.[86] *Hiyal* can be characterized as follows:

> "The foundation of this method is a formalistic approach to contract, in the sense of a concern for the external form of transactions instead of the parties' substantive intentions. (…) A famous example is the ancient doublesale (…). In this deal a borrower and a lender arrange to sell and then resell between them a trivial object, once for cash and once for a greater sum on credit, with the net result being a loan with interest."[87]

While these *hiyal* are deemed acceptable when they are merely clever uses of law to achieve legitimate ends, schools vigorously differ on the subversive artifices. On the

[82] Cf. Warde (2000), p. 42-44.

[83] For a short overview of the schools of thought cf. Antes (1991).

[84] Vogel and Hayes, III (1998), p. 33.

[85] For a more detailed exposition, in particular with regard to exceptions, see Vogel and Hayes, III (1998), p. 41-42.

[86] For extensive expositions on *hiyal* cf. Rodinson (1971), p. et sqq., Saeed (1996), p. 37 et sqq.

[87] Vogel and Hayes, III (1998), p. 39.

one hand, the Hanafis and Shafi'is at worst view them as immoral, on the other hand the Malikis and even more so the Hanbalis forbid them altogether.

Islamic legal reasoning results in a casuistic law rather than a rational or hierarchical system of rules. When, in the following, principles of Islamic economics and finance are presented, this can only be done with a grain of salt. As Vogel explains:

> "Westerners studying the classical law may feel perplexed by its multiplicity, and conclude that behind the details there must be some fixed system that instead is 'the law'. They are wrong; such a system does not exist."[88]

2.2.1.2 Principles of Islamic Economics and Finance

Despite all the reservations outlined above, it is possible to establish a set of principles that can help to understand the basics of Islamic economics and finance, and which are also invoked by practitioners in a similar manner. There is a large number of instructions and legal rulings – both in the primary sources as well as in the literature of the various schools of law – dealing with issues such as business ethics, wealth creation, property rights, contract law, interest and usury or gambling and risk taking. The exposition of these principles will make frequent reference to the sources and methods of Islamic law to illustrate its complexity. In any event, it should not be regarded as an attempt to define some fixed system, but rather as rules of thumb, that – for matters of practicability – are widely followed by the Islamic finance community.[89]

Business ethics. Justice, honesty and fairness are at the heart of Muslim business ethics. Both the Qur'an and the Sunna invoke these principles several times, e.g.: "Give full measure whenever you measure, and weigh with the true balance; this will be [for your own] good, and best in the end. [17:35]."[90] Consequently, monopolistic practices, abusing the ignorance of an inexperienced partner or commercial exploitation are repudiated.[91] Moreover, there is a strong recognition of a free market economy in the Sunna with the interaction of supply and demand as the basic market-clearing and price-setting mechanism:

> "God is the one who sets prices, who takes, who amply gives sustenance, who makes provision. I do not wish that I meet God Most High and anyone have against me a claim of injustice in either blood [life] or property."[92]

Wealth creation. Economic activity, industriousness and entrepreneurship are greatly encouraged in Islam, while fatalism, idleness and rejection of the world are denounced. Labor and effort are regarded as the primary means of wealth creation.[93]

---

88 Vogel and Hayes, III (1998), p. 44.

89 See for instance Nienhaus (1991), p. 251-254, Nienhaus (1999), p. 621-622, van Schaik (2001), p. 46-48, Bahrain Monetary Agency (2002).

90 Vogel and Hayes, III (1998), p. 65.

91 van Schaik (2001), p. 46.

92 Vogel and Hayes, III (1998), p. 65.

93 CIBEDO (1980), p. 13.

Commerce and entrepreneurship have a particular significance in Islam as Muhammad himself used to be a trader and caravan leader.[94] Thus, the Qur'an allows to do commercial transactions during pilgrimages or calls on the believers to engage in commercial activities even on Fridays after the collective prayer in the mosque: "When the prayer is ended, disperse through the earth and seek something of God's bounty… [62:10]."[95] In short, wealth creation is in line with Islamic precepts if an effort is performed or a financial liability accepted, the venture was productive and the profit was made in an honest manner.[96]

Property rights. While it is widely held in *fiqh* statements that God is the sole owner of all property and man as his agent only holds the right of use and enjoyment, in practice private property is acknowledged.[97] Even disparities in the distribution of goods are accepted. However, the Sharia places special emphasis on the rightful acquisition and usage of property. Wrongful taking is for example associated with usurpation, usury, gambling, theft, perjury or deception. Property rights should be used in a productive and socially beneficial way; hoarding and wasting are condemned.[98]

Contract law. The Sharia rulings on fulfillment and freedom of contract are ambiguous. While the Qur'an strongly emphasizes the moral obligation to fulfill contracts and the Sunna condemns promise-breaking, the latter also sets specific obstacles to free contracting. A famous *hadith* "(…) suggests that the very terms of contracts, not to mention contracts themselves, must be prescribed by God's writ. Unless a term is positively allowed by revelation (…), it is nugatory, the parties' agreement notwithstanding."[99] The various schools of law differ considerably in their positions regarding new contracts and contract stipulations.[100] Modern Islamic banking and finance, however, generally follows the view of Ibn Taymiyya, a 14th-century Hanbali scholar:

> "The underlying principle in contracts and stipulations is permissibility (*ibaha*) and validity. Any [contract or stipulation] is prohibited and void only if there is an explicit text [from the Qur'an, the Sunna or the consensus] or a *qiyas* [analogy] (for those who accept *qiyas*) proving its prohibition and voiding."[101]

Accordingly, objects and creatures that are unclean or forbidden cannot be the item of a legal transaction – contracts or stipulations dealing with them would be void. An

---

94 Paret (1991), Rodinson (1971), p. 41 et sqq.

95 Vogel and Hayes, III (1998), p. 56.

96 van Schaik (2001), p. 46-47.

97 Nienhaus (1982), p. 62, Cummings et. al. (1980), p. 36.

98 CIBEDO (1980), p. 13, Ghaussy (1994), p. 28 et sqq.

99 Vogel and Hayes, III (1998), p. 67-68.

100 For a detailed exposition see ibid., p. 97-128.

101 Ibid., p. 98.

example for the former are pigs, for the latter fortune telling books based on astrology.[102]

Interest and usury. The prohibition of *riba* (interest or usury) is often viewed as the cornerstone of Islamic economics and finance. Although the prohibition itself is unequivocal, there is some disagreement over the meaning of *riba*.[103] The Qur'an mentions the ban on *riba* several times, but remains vague in the definition of the term:

> "Those who devour *riba* do not stand except as one stands whom Satan has confounded with his touch: for they say, 'Buying and selling [*bay'*] is like *riba*' – the while God has made buying and selling lawful and *riba* unlawful. One who becomes aware of his Lord's admonition and desists, may keep his past gains, and his affair is for God [to judge]; (...) Give up what remains of *riba*, if you are believers; for if you do it, take notice of war from God and His Apostle. But if you repent, then you shall be entitled to your principal: you will do no wrong, and neither will you be wronged. [2:275-79]."[104]

In the pre-Islamic era, *riba* applied to the increase of debt principal at maturity – usually doubling it – in exchange for an extension of the term.[105] It is sometimes argued that the Qur'an only refers to this usurious practice, which is called *riba al-jahiliyya*. The Sunna is more outspoken on the meaning of *riba*, but still leaves ample room for interpretation. It is mostly concerned with *riba* in sales of certain goods, where it distinguishes two types of *riba*: *riba* of excess (*riba al-fadl*) and *riba* of delay (*riba al-nasi'a*).[106] The former occurs, when *riba* goods of the same genus are exchanged in different amounts (i.e. number, weight or value). The latter when one *riba* good is exchanged for another and the counter-values are not exchanged at the same time. As gold and silver are among the *riba* goods, most schools of law have extended the prohibition of these two types of *riba* to money, based on analogy (*qiyas*).[107] On loans, a highly influential *hadith* states: "Every loan that attracts a benefit is *riba*."[108] The majority view holds that not only this saying bans profit on loans, i.e. interest, but also the other sources have to be interpreted as a prohibition of interest altogether. There are, however, minority deviations to this opinion based on two grounds: First, the taking of interest is acknowledged due to the requirements of the modern economy – or the principles of *darura* and *maslaha*. Second, there are

---

[102] van Schaik (2001), p. 46.

[103] Cf. Kuran (1995), p. 205.

[104] Vogel and Hayes, III (1998), p. 62. *Riba* is also mentioned in the following verses: 3:129-30, 4:161 and 30:39.

[105] At-Tabari (Reprint 1954), p. 90.

[106] See van Schaik (2001), p. 47-48. For a detailed exposition see Vogel and Hayes, III (1998), p. 74-77, Lewis and Algaoud (2001), p. 35. Among *riba* goods are certain foodstuffs, precious metals and money.

[107] El-Gamal (2000), p. 3.

[108] Vogel and Hayes, III (1998), p. 77. The authenticity of the *hadith* is disputed.

several *fatwas* – the most famous issued by the *sheikh al-azhar* Tantawi – declaring bank interest legal.[109] The issue therefore remains controversial.

Gambling and risk taking. The Sharia prohibits *maysir* and *gharar*. The former means gambling or games of chance that are clearly banned in the Qur'an.[110] The latter denotes a concept, which is – like *riba* – somewhat vague, and is associated with risk. The prohibition of *gharar* stems only from the Sunna, as the word is not mentioned in the Qur'an. Examples of *gharar* prohibited in the Sunna include the sale of fish in the sea, unripe fruit, and foodstuff, which is not in the possession of the seller or not weighed. The *gharar* transactions listed in *hadiths* implicate pure speculation, uncertain outcome, unknowable future benefits or inexactitude. In fact, "(...) the majority of classical scholars as a general rule void sales of nonexistent or uncertain objects without any consideration of the degree of risk involved."[111] Modern scholars of Islamic banking and finance have adopted the opinion of Ibn Taymiyya. In his view, *gharar* is "(...) that which 'hesitates between soundness and destruction'"[112] and therefore a matter of risk. The prohibition of *gharar* affects the validity of contracts depending on the extent of risk involved: minor uncertainty or contracts contingent on future events can be acceptable. However, even this view precludes certain modern financial transactions such as derivatives, insurance or pure speculation.

2.2.2 Islamic Financial Products

Islamic financial instruments have to perform a double task: on the one hand, they have to meet the economic requirements of investors and capital seekers; on the other hand, they have to abide by the precepts of the Sharia. Over the course of time, various instruments have been developed and are now commonly used by Islamic financial institutions – although they sometimes may not be accepted universally by Islamic scholars, as will be pointed out. Some of these products are quite similar to their conventional counterparts, others vary substantially. In the following exposition, these products are organized according to their economic and financial characteristics into debt-like instruments, equity-like instruments, derivative-like instruments, hybrid instruments and other transactions and services.[113] It should be noted that the presentation does not claim to be exhaustive: although the major Islamic financial products are covered, product innovation plays an ever-increasing role in Islamic finance so that every listing is in danger to be incomplete.

---

[109] Cf. Müller (1996), p. 48 et sqq., for an exposition of the public debate in Egypt stirred by Tantawi's *fatwa*. For a list of other learned scholars who do not believe that all transactions involving interest are usurious cf. Zaman and Movassaghi (2001), p. 37.

[110] Verses 2:219 and 5:90-91.

[111] Vogel and Hayes, III (1998), p. 91.

[112] Ibid., p. 92-93.

[113] This is a similar approach to the one followed in ISO 10962 (classification of financial instruments). For a good introduction into the scope of Islamic financial products cf. Nienhaus (1991), Nienhaus (1994), El-Gamal (2000), Warde (2000), Zaher and Hassan (2001), Lewis and Algaoud (2001). For a more technical discussion cf. Vogel and Hayes (1998).

2.2.2.1 Debt-like Instruments

Debt financing is characterized by the borrower's obligation of fixed repayments to the lender, usually in installments, irrespective of the economic success of the financed project or the solvency of the borrower. Debt-like Islamic financial instruments match this economic characteristic, but differ in their legal design from conventional products. In the following, *bay' mu'ajjal*, *murabaha*, *'ina*, and *ijara* will be detailed. Some of these instruments are quite ingenious, while others are very similar to conventional finance products.

Bay' mu'ajjal. This transaction is a credit sale or sale with deferred payment and therefore a close substitute to a conventional line of credit or interest financing. The price for such a sale is determined by mutual consent and can be set to whatever the parties agree to. For example, it can be tied to the credit period, as is the usual practice of Islamic banks. It is often reported that financing terms based on this instrument closely emulate the prevailing market interest rate for similar conventional transactions.[114]

Murabaha. In the *murabaha* transaction or mark-up financing scheme, a bank buys a good on behalf of its client and – after adding a profit margin – resells this good to its client at a higher price.[115] Usually, the resale is by deferred payment, using the *bay' mu'ajjal* credit sale instrument. The added profit margin "(...) can cover anything which the seller chooses to incorporate in it, with no questions asked or justification required."[116] This can include transaction costs, charges for credit risk, currency risk and the bank's opportunity cost. It has often been argued that this financing technique is pure window-dressing and nothing but interest in disguise.[117] However, *murabaha,* along with *bay' mu'ajjal,* is a trade transaction and *not* a financial transaction, and therefore would be governed even in Western countries by trade law and not the banking act. In theory, the bank takes ownership and possession of the good before the resale to its client, thereby assuming the risk that the goods are destroyed, deteriorate or are rejected by the client as unsatisfactory or defective. Nevertheless, in practice, the bank's client usually contractually commits to accepting the good, assuming the transportation risk and waiving all claims on the bank as a seller. Moreover, the contracts frequently provide for their enforcement under a non-Islamic law. Consequently, the bank's risk is greatly reduced and the transaction closely resembles a purely financial transaction.[118]

'Ina. This transaction is another form of double sale, similar to *murabaha*. In contrast to *murabaha*, the original seller and final buyer of the good is the same party, with the bank acting as a liquidity provider. For example, a business sells its inventory in exchange for immediate cash payment to a bank and then buys back the inventory on

---

[114] Vogel and Hayes, III (1998), p. 139.

[115] For a detailed exposition of this instrument, cf. Usmani (2002), p. 37-68.

[116] Vogel and Hayes, III (1998), p. 182.

[117] Cf. Zaman and Movassaghi (2001), p. 36.

[118] Bälz (2002), p. 381.

an installment basis. The way that *'ina* sometimes is employed is also a perfect illustration for a *hila*:

> "A variation on this *'ina* deal is for a party in need of funds to find a transaction and then insert itself into the loop. For example, if A needs money, he identifies B, who is intending to buy a good, such as cement, for cash from cement producer C. Party A gets an Islamic bank to buy the cement and sell it to A on a *murabaha* installment basis. A then immediately sells the cement to B for cash. A then has the use of the cash until it is depleted by the *murabaha* installment payments to the bank."[119]

However, *'ina* is not a generally accepted Islamic financial instrument. While it is widely used in Malaysia, it is considered invalid in the Middle East.[120]

Ijara. *Ijara* is the Islamic leasing mode and is defined as the sale of usufruct (*manfa'a*).[121] The practice of *ijara* is virtually identical to a conventional lease. Similar to its conventional counterpart, the Islamic lease is offered in two forms: operational lease and full-payout financial lease – the latter is known as *ijara wa-iqtina'*. There are, however, some theoretical differences between Islamic and conventional leases. First, Islamic law "(...) views some benefits and burdens of the property as belonging naturally and unchangeably to the lessee, and others as belonging to the lessor."[122] The duty to repair and the linked repair costs, for instance, always fall on the lessor. Second, as the usufruct is a stream of use extending into the future, and therefore risky and uncertain, issues of *gharar* arise. The lessee is therefore given leeway regarding his rights to cancel the lease if the usufruct turns out to be less valuable than expected. Third, financial leases are once more affected by *gharar* considerations. The residual value of the leased goods at the end of the term is – as a future event – uncertain and often made contingent on conditional agreements. Such stipulations are regularly regarded as void in Islamic law. As mentioned before, the Islamic leasing practice closely follows conventional rules and largely ignores these Islamic regulations.[123]

Empirical research on the use of Islamic financial products has consistently shown the prevalence of debt-like Islamic products on the asset side of Islamic banks' balance sheets.[124] *Bay' mu'ajjal* and *murabaha* products are the most widespread modes of financing: in a study of Aggarwal and Yousef, these products captured approx. 40% of total financing. Debt-like Islamic financial products are often deemed "(...) less Islamically-approved modes of financing"[125] and their widespread use is greatly

---

[119] Vogel and Hayes, III (1998), p. 183.

[120] For a discussion of this instrument, citing the views of various schools of thought, cf. Rosly and Sanusi (1999).

[121] For a detailed exposition cf. Usmani (2002), p. 69-82.

[122] Vogel and Hayes, III (1998), p. 144.

[123] Usmani (2002), p. 115.

[124] Cf. Nienhaus (1994), Mills and Presley (1999), Aggarwal and Yousef (2000), Zaher and Hassan (2001)

[125] Lewis and Algaoud (2001), p. 153.

lamented by Muslim scholars.[126] As was evidenced in the example of *'ina,* the attitude towards these instruments varies across the Islamic world – this will also be highlighted in the subsequent chapter on current practices in Islamic finance. Their prevalence can be explained on theoretical grounds, though, as "(...) debt contracts are often optimal transacting vehicles because they minimize the costs associated with asymmetric information or unobserved actions"[127]. For Islamic banks, the problems associated with *not* using debt-like instruments become crucial in the competitive financial environment of mixed financial systems, where Islamic and conventional banks operate in parallel. Predominant use of equity-like instruments would put them at a competitive disadvantage, as will be discussed in the following.

2.2.2.2 Equity-like Instruments

Equity instruments are generally defined by two main characteristics: first, they warrant ownership rights of an asset. Second, the equity holder has residual claims to the profit generated by a venture or an asset as well as the duty to bear losses. Equity-like Islamic financial products are identical in this to their conventional counterparts and hence very similar to conventional equity instruments. This section will detail *mudaraba* and *musharaka.* These two, which are direct profit-and-loss sharing schemes, are often considered to be the model form of Islamic finance and most consistent with its principles.[128] In view of the afore-mentioned similarity to conventional products, specific attention will be given to the idiosyncratic features of the Islamic instruments.

Mudaraba. In this form of equity investment, one partner – the *rabb al-mal* – provides capital to a venture, while the other partner - the *mudarib* – contributes his time and effort to manage it. This financing scheme can be applied to a whole company as well as to a single project. The share of profits between the two parties must be pre-determined and proportional. In case of losses, only the *rabb al-mal* is financially liable, up to his investment. While all assets are in his exclusive possession, he is not entitled to participate in managing the enterprise. However, he may have a say in choosing the particular business to invest in – this is known as a restricted *mudaraba* (*mudaraba al-muqayyada*). The instrument is called unrestricted *mudaraba* (*mudaraba al-mutaqala*), if this decision is completely delegated to the *mudarib. Fiqh* opinion differs as to the timing of profit sharing: Hanafis and Hanbalis argue that the profit can only be shared after completion of the activity and reimbursement of the financier's principal, while Malikis and Shafiis permit this even

---

126 Cf. ibid, p. 154-156, Usmani (2002), 113-115.

127 Lewis and Algaoud (2001), p. 72. For detailed expositions of the principal-agent problems related to profit-and-loss sharing financial instruments and the consequences for Islamic banking cf. ibid., p. 65-86, Aggarwal and Yousef (2000), Iqbal and Llewellyn (2002), in particular p. 7-14 for a good overview. While the widespread usage of these instruments is generally accounted for along these lines, Hassan et.al. (2002) use the dividend signaling hypothesis as an alternative approach; Yousef holds systemic forces of law, institutions and politics responsible (Henry and Wilson (2004)).

128 For a review of profit-and-loss sharing Islamic financing schemes cf. Nienhaus (1991), Mills and Presley (1999), Aggarwal and Yousef (2000), Dar and Presley (2000), Iqbal (2001), Hasan (2002).

before.[129] Incidentally, this scheme is also at the heart of the set-up of an Islamic bank, in the form of a two-tier *mudaraba*:

> "A first-tier *mudaraba* is created when investors (we shall call them 'depositors') place their capital with an Islamic bank, fund, or other financial institution, which here acts as the *mudarib* or working partner. The financial institution or *mudarib* in turn invests these funds with entrepreneurs (the equivalent of a conventional bank's borrowers) by means of second-tier *mudarabas*, in which the Islamic financial institution now has the role of capital investor. Such a practice is possible since classical law permits a *mudarib* to choose not to perform the productive work himself but to invest the partnership capital with other *mudaribs*."[130]

In theory, an Islamic bank should have a lower liquidity risk than a conventional bank, as the "depositors" as *rabb al-mal* have to bear all losses and the bank as *mudarib* only looses time and effort. In practice, however, Islamic banks often explicitly guarantee the capital invested, since they have to face competition with conventional banks.[131] Moreover, principal-agent-theory suggests that Islamic banks are at a competitive disadvantage when using *mudaraba* as an investment vehicle: this profit-and-loss sharing scheme is likely to attract more risky projects and provides an incentive to the project manager to understate profits, thus lowering the bank's return.[132]

Musharaka. This finance instrument is very similar to *mudaraba*, with the major difference being that here, two or more parties contribute both capital and management effort. Voting rights typically are commensurate with paid-in capital; the liability of all partners is normally unlimited.[133] *Musharaka*, which was originally employed for limited duration projects – such as the financing of a trade caravan – closely resembles a conventional joint venture or private equity financing. Participation in a *musharaka* can either be in a new project or in an existing one. Variations of the basic *musharaka* include constructs where one party only provides labor while the other brings in both labor and capital. Another variation is the diminishing *musharaka* where one party's capital is progressively reimbursed until full redemption of her share – this adaptation can be found likewise in the *mudaraba* scheme. Another similarity between these two is that the *musharaka* instrument is exposed to moral hazard. It therefore requires special joint venture or private equity expertise by an Islamic bank to engage in this type of enterprises. As the bank participates in managing the venture, further industry-specific know-how is desirable.

---

[129] Warde (2001), p. 136.

[130] Vogel and Hayes, III (1998), p. 130-131.

[131] In Malaysia, for instance, the central bank has introduced a deposit insurance system, which is also covering Islamic deposits.

[132] For a detailed discussion see Nienhaus (1991), Dar and Presley (2000). See also footnote 127 above.

[133] Citicorp (no date), p. 5. For some cases highlighting the use of *musharaka* cf. Al-Harran (1999). Ibrahim and Vijaykumar (1998) compare *musharaka* with conventional partnership modes of finance and find no major differences.

In a study of Aggarwal and Yousef, equity-like profit-and-loss-sharing schemes (*mudaraba* and *musharaka*), combined only approx. 20% of total financing.[134]

2.2.2.3 Derivative-like Instruments

A derivative is commonly defined as a financial instrument that derives its value from the price or rate of some underlying item and is usually settled at a future date. Conventional derivative financial instruments include forward contracts, futures and options, whose pricing and underlying item can imply issues of *riba* and *gharar*. Derivative-like Islamic financial instruments match certain characteristics of conventional derivatives, but differ in their legal design and implications as well as in their actual usage, as they can sometimes be used as a substitute for debt-financing. In the following, *salam*, *istisna'*, *'arbun* and *khiyar al-shart* will be detailed. Special emphasis will be given to the presentation of the possibilities of using these instruments as a substitute or replication of conventional derivatives.

Salam. This transaction is defined as a forward purchase of generically described goods – which at the time of contract closing have to be non-existent – for full advance payment.[135] Along with *istisna'*, it is the only exception to the general Sharia principle that goods that do not exist at the time of sale cannot be sold. *Salam* resembles a conventional forward contract with the major difference being the immediate payment settlement. It was originally construed for the financing needs of farmers and is generally used as a substitute for debt financing of the cost of labor and material necessary to produce the good. Islamic banks normally use this instrument in the form of back-to-back *salam*:

> "After buying goods of a certain description from a seller and paying the full purchase price (*salam* sale 1), but before the seller is due to deliver on that contract, the bank, in a separate and formally unconnected *salam* contract (*salam* sale 2), sells goods of exactly the same description and with the same due date to a third party, receiving full advance payment from that buyer. The net result is that the bank has reversed its position, fixed the profits it will earn from the two trades, and assured a purchaser for its goods."[136]

Besides the risk of price changes of the underlying asset, which *salam* shares with a conventional forward, there is another problem associated with *salam* that is aggravated by the fact of advance payment: the risk of non-fulfillment by the seller, which is usually contained by taking security from the seller such as a pledge or a guarantee.

Istisna'. This financial instrument is a commissioned manufacture, where one party buys goods that the other party undertakes to manufacture according to specifications

---

[134] Aggarwal and Yousef (2000).

[135] For a detailed exposition cf. Usmani (2002), p. 83-88.

[136] Vogel and Hayes, III (1998), p. 146.

given in the contract.[137] Originally, this transaction type was designed for the sale of unique manufactured goods as opposed to *salam* which can be effected on anything, as long as the quality and quantity can be specified exactly. *Istisna'* offers great flexibility with regard to payment terms, allowing for full payment on the spot, deferred payment or payment in instalments. Moreover, the time of delivery does not require to be fixed, which is another marked difference to *salam*. As most goods manufactured today are mass-produced and therefore of a generic, fungible nature, forward sales of these goods should actually be effected as *salam* sales. In practice, however, it is generally accepted to apply the more liberal rules of *istisna'* if the transaction involves any type of manufacture. Consequently, *istisna'* can be seen as the closest replication of a conventional forward contract, albeit with a much more limited choice of tradable underlying assets. Similarly to *salam*, Islamic banks normally use this instrument in the form of a back-to-back *istisna'*, one for the purchase from a manufacturer and the other for the sale to a client in need of financing. In this way, *istisna'* can be used as a substitute for debt financing, e.g. for project financing.

'Arbun. In this transaction, the buyer makes an immediate down payment for a good, stipulating that the remaining balance will be paid at a specified future date of delivery or to forfeit the advance payment if he decides not to take the good. The seller commits himself to deliver the good until contract expiration. Thus, *'arbun* is a close analogy to a conventional call option. On theoretical grounds, the instrument could even be used to create a "reverse *'arbun*" or put option.[138] However, all schools with the exception of the Hanbalis void this transaction. In particular, it is forbidden in *salam* contracts, i.e. the forward sale of fungible goods. The use of *'arbun* therefore is controversial.[139] The contract has found application in the structuring of capital-protected funds.[140]

Khiyar al-shart. This stipulated option gives to one or all parties an unconstrained right to withdraw from an otherwise binding contract. The stipulation may be tied to movements in the underlying asset price as well as to events that are completely unrelated to the underlying asset. If, for example, the seller of a good holds such an option, it can be used as a put option[141]. However, the party granting the option is not allowed to receive any compensation: the option cannot be sold. Its usefulness for the creation of Islamically valid derivatives therefore remains questionable.

Obviously, Islamic financial institutions are much more restricted in their degree of freedom to develop and market derivative instruments than conventional banks. In particular, viable alternatives to conventional options have yet to be conceived. This can put both Islamic banks and their clients in a competitive disadvantage towards

---

[137] For a detailed exposition cf. Usmani (2002), p. 88-91. For a discussion of various application areas cf. Al-Amine and Al-Bashir (2001).

[138] Vogel and Hayes, III (1998), p. 162-163 and 253-260.

[139] Cf. Bacha (1999) and the Discussion Forum on Islamic Financial Derivatives in the same journal.

[140] Archer and Abdel Karim (2002), p. 139 and p. 187.

[141] Ibid., p. 188.

conventional banks: The former, as they cannot offer the same spectrum of financial products as their conventional counterparts and cannot use the same set of tools for their own risk management. The latter, if they dispense with the use of conventional derivatives, as they are deprived of some hedging instruments as a consequence. At the same time, this situation strongly illustrates a need for creative financial innovation in Islamic finance.[142]

2.2.2.4 Hybrid Instruments

Financial arrangements that are a combination of debt-like instruments, equity-like instruments and/or derivative-like instruments are treated in this section. In the following, *sukuk* and Islamic mutual funds will be detailed.

Sukuk. The *sukuk* or Islamic bonds are securitized financial instruments. Securitization is defined as the process of pooling assets, packaging them into securities and making them marketable to investors. Assets backing the *sukuk* can be related to debt-like instruments or derivative-like instruments used as a substitute for debt financing or they can be related to equity-like instruments. Examples for the former are *murabaha sukuk*, *ijara sukuk*, *salam sukuk* or *istisna' sukuk*. Here, the underlying assets yield deterministic receivables and thus warrant predictable, fixed returns for the investor. Examples for the latter are *mudaraba sukuk*[143] and *musharaka sukuk*. In accordance with language usage in Islamic finance, these instruments are also referred to as *mudaraba* bonds and *musharaka* bonds, despite the implication of a debt-like instrument. The certificate holders, however, own the underlying assets, share in the profits and bear potential losses. Analogous to a conventional revenue bond, the *muqarada* financing arrangement (*mudaraba sukuk*) is backed by the revenues of a specific money-making project or function separable from the rest of the issuer's activities. It closely resembles a *mudaraba* transaction, with the issuer acting as *mudarib* and the investors acting as *rabb al-mal*. Similarly to this, the profits are split according to pre-determined percentages; investors have no say in managing the project and bear the risk of losses. In practice, however, the issuer often guarantees the face value of the *muqarada* bonds. Like *mudaraba*, the bond can also be structured as a diminishing *muqarada*. *Musharaka* bonds differ from *mudaraba sukuk* in that the issuer of the certificate is providing capital himself and therefore sharing in the ownership of the underlying assets. In both cases, the return on investment is clearly linked to the profitability of the financed projects or ventures. In addition to this, combinations of these basic *sukuk* types are also marketed.

The pricing of all *sukuk*-instruments reflects both asset ownership related risks and issuer related risks (rating or credit worthiness of the issuer). While some of these securitized products have been generally accepted as being in compliance with

---

[142] The need for financial innovation in Islamic finance is widely discussed in the literature and among practitioners, in particular with regard to derivative instruments. Cf. Bacha (1999), Noman (2002), Salehabadi and Aram (2002), Archer and Abdel Karim (2002), p. 57-59 and p. 176-196, Dadabhoy (2004).

[143] This instrument is also known as *muqarada*.

Islamic principles and can be traded in the secondary market, other remain controversial, e.g. *murabaha sukuk*. The usage of this certificate representing a monetary obligation arising from a *murabaha* transaction differs in particular between Malaysia and the Middle East: while in the former, they can be freely traded and are very popular, in the latter they can be traded at face value only, as any difference to this is regarded as *riba*.[144] There is no disagreement on others such as *ijara sukuk*, which are freely tradable at par, premium or discount. *Sukuk* not only allow corporate clients access to another means of Islamic refinancing, but in principle offer Islamic financial institutions a tool to manage their liquidity. However, the set-up of a well-functioning international interbanking market is hindered by the lack of international standards on the permissible products.[145]

Islamic mutual funds. Conventional mutual funds are professionally managed pooled investments in various instruments: currencies, commodities, bonds and most commonly stocks. Islamic mutual funds have to abide by the tenets of Islamic law and therefore differ from their conventional counterparts in the choice of investment instruments available and, in the case of bond and stock investment, in the choice of appropriate companies to invest in. First, investments in currencies or bonds may raise issues of *riba*, and are therefore avoided, although zero-coupon bonds are usually deemed acceptable.[146] Second, companies whose products and services or financial structure violate Islamic law are regularly ruled out as investment targets. Although Islamic mutual funds can be of a hybrid nature, with investments in debt-like as well as equity-like instruments, in practice, Islamic mutual funds often are equity funds. Various Islamic stock market indices have been created, the two key indices being the Dow Jones Islamic Market Index and the FTSE Global Islamic Index.[147] These indices are used as a benchmark for both the performance of Islamic mutual funds and the selection criteria for Islamically appropriate companies. The FTSE Global Islamic index, for instance, excludes stock whose core activities are related to banking or any other *riba*-activity, alcohol, tobacco, gaming, arms manufacturing, life insurance, pork production, sectors or companies significantly affected by the afore-mentioned and companies whose ratio of gross interest bearing debt to total assets exceeds 33%. The Dow Jones Islamic Market Index list of excluded businesses is very similar to this and even more detailed in the financial ratio selection criteria, employing ratios of total debt to market capitalization, sum of cash and interest bearing securities to market capitalization and accounts receivable to total assets.[148]

As in the case of derivative-like instruments, Islamic financial institutions are more restricted in their degree of freedom to develop and market hybrid instruments than

---

[144] Cf. Bahrain Monetary Agency (2003) and No Author (2002), p. 43-44. For a detailed discussion about the Middle Eastern view on *murabaha sukuk* cf. Rosly and Sanusi (1999).

[145] Cf. also section on liquidity management and secondary markets below.

[146] Warde (2001), p. 142.

[147] For the Dow Jones Islamic Market Index cf. www.djindexes.com/jsp/imiMethod.jsp. For the FTSE Global Islamic Index cf. FTSE International Limited (2001).

[148] Companies are excluded if any of the first two ratios exceeds or is equal to 33% or if the last ratio exceeds or is equal to 45%.

conventional banks. Moreover, similarly to the situation of debt-like instruments, there are marked differences in product acceptance between Malaysia and the Middle East. In both instances, rules in Malaysia are more liberal, allowing for a wider product spectrum.

2.2.2.5 Other Transactions and Services

Apart from the financial instruments presented above there is a number of other transactions and services that an Islamic commercial or investment bank can offer: corporate advisory (including mergers and acquisitions, initial public offerings and structured finance), private wealth management and advisory, letters of credit, guarantees, account management, credit and other cards, electronic bill payment, safekeeping or remittances, to name but a few. Most of these services are – in principle – analogues to their conventional counterparts, and will therefore not be detailed here. However, there are two services that merit a closer look, as they can obviously be affected by issues of *riba*: on the one hand account management, on the other hand credit cards and the like.

Account management. Islamic banks usually offer two types of accounts: current accounts and investment accounts. The former is akin to a conventional checking account, where customers can withdraw their funds on demand at any time. Islamic banks are, however, prohibited from paying interest on these accounts, as conventional banks sometimes do.[149] Because of this, they are sometimes accused of "(...) accepting free money and making profits for themselves out of virtually risk free operations"[150] – hence, a high share of current accounts in customer deposits could potentially explain a high bank profitability. Investment accounts are a unique Islamic form of account, in the form of a *mudaraba* investment. It exhibits features similar to a conventional savings account, as it earns a profit and withdrawal usually is restricted. Theoretically the profit is determined ex post, based on the profitability of the bank's investments, as opposed to the interest paid on a conventional savings account. However, in markets where Islamic banks operate alongside conventional banks, in practice the rate of profit often reflects the prevailing, comparable interest rate – which is a clear indication that Islamic banks compete with conventional banks. In fact, several studies have shown that besides religious aspects, competitive returns are a major selection criterion for Islamic banking customers.[151] Investment accounts are the dominating deposit form with approx. 50% of total funds, followed by current accounts with approx. a 30% share of total funds.[152]

---

[149] Al-Deehani et. al. (1999), p. 248.

[150] Archer and Abdel Karim (2002), p. 33. According to Islamic law, they are entitled to the returns generated from investing the funds deposited in current accounts if they guarantee the accounts and consequently bear the risk of an investment loss. Cf. ibid., p. 115.

[151] Haron and Ahmad (2000), Zaher and Hassan (2001), p. 181, Lewis and Algaoud (2001), p. 132-156, Kaleem and Isa (2003).

[152] Based on author's own calculations, using annual report data from a subset of 27 banks.

Credit and other cards. There are three types of cards usually offered by conventional banks: credit cards, charge cards and debit cards. As the name implies, the first is used to buy products or services on credit, i.e. the balance due is charged on the customer's account some time after he receives the statement. The charge card is similar to a credit card, except that the balance must be paid in full when the statement is received. A debit card, finally, allows customers to access their funds immediately, electronically and directly debits their account. The debit card therefore appears to be most appropriate for use by Islamic banks, as all issues of *riba* are avoided. It is noteworthy, however, that also the other two types of cards are offered by some Islamic banks and deemed acceptable by some Islamic scholars. Moreover, for both types of cards, clients usually incur late payment fees – a practice, which is lamented by some Islamic scholars.[153] Credit cards are just another example of differing views on Islamic financial products among Islamic scholars, illustrating the current lack of universally accepted product standards in the industry.

2.2.3 Islamic Finance Markets

It is often held that modern, non-governmental Islamic banking came into existence with the creation of Dubai Islamic Bank in 1975.[154] In the following years, a considerable number of private, profit-oriented Islamic financial institutions was set up in various Islamic and non-Islamic countries, amounting to over 180 today.[155] In this section, current practices of these Islamic banks will be detailed. It starts with an overview encompassing market size, regional scope and major market types in Islamic finance. Subsequently, the institutional framework – the regulatory and supervisory environment, as well as the framework for liquidity management and secondary markets – is presented. Finally, Islamic finance practices in the GCC area and Malaysia will be depicted – including the description of major players, marketed products and the regulatory environment – as these regions can be considered to be the most important ones for profit-oriented, free-market Islamic financial institutions.

2.2.3.1 Overview

Islamic financial institutions operate under three different banking systems: fully "Islamised" banking systems, dual banking systems, and conventional banking systems. It is often claimed that Iran, Pakistan and Sudan constitute cases of a fully "Islamised" banking system, as their respective governments assert to have introduced or to be in the process of introducing interest-free banking systems as the rule. However, the effectiveness of these systems remains largely questionable. In fact, in the case of Iran, "(…) many observers outside Iran have doubts about its Islamic banking credentials"[156]: According to the principles of Islamic banking in Iran, *riba* is

[153] Usmani (2002), p. 115.

[154] For a detailed exposition of the evolution of Islamic banking cf. Warde (2001), p. 73-87, Zaher and Hassan (2001)

[155] Archer and Abdel Karim (2002), p. 205-208.

[156] Archer and Abdel Karim (2002), p. 38.

only created if the borrower has an identity independent from the lender. As all banks in Iran have been nationalized and are state-owned, central government as well as fully government-owned agencies and corporations are thus financed using traditional borrowing methods.[157] Within a gradual Islamisation process, the banking system in Pakistan was required to operate on an interest-free basis from 1985 onwards, with the exceptions of foreign currency deposits, foreign loans and government debts.[158] However, in 2002, Pakistan's Supreme Court reversed its own previous ruling banning interest[159] and sent the case back to the Federal Shariat Court – for the time being, the case remains unresolved. What is more, Pakistani government claimed that modern, interest-based banking was not against Islamic principles.[160] Pakistan therefore effectively runs a dual banking system rather than a fully "Islamised" one. It is also important to note, that the banking sector in Pakistan was largely government-owned and –controlled until fairly recently, and that the country's economy as a whole is regarded as mostly unfree in the 2005 Index of Economic Freedom.[161] Sudan comes closest to a truly fully "Islamized" banking system.[162] However, it is also dominated by a few government-owned banks, with extensive political interference in the banks' operations, and a highly regulated economy in general.[163] Dual banking systems are characterized by two distinct regulatory environments for Islamic and conventional banks. The two most notable examples of dual banking systems are Bahrain and Malaysia, two free-market oriented economies. In conventional banking systems, finally, there is no separate regulation of Islamic banks: the same conventional rules apply. A major example is Saudi Arabia, again a free-market oriented economy. It is these Islamic banks in free-market oriented economies for which strategic management theories can be tested.

As the original idea behind Islamic finance is to cater to Muslim banking clients who want to reconcile Islamic principles and their financial requirements, it seems fair to claim that the global Muslim population as well as Muslim corporations and governments can be considered as the target group for Islamic banks. The largest Muslim populations can be found in Indonesia, India, Pakistan, Bangladesh, Turkey and Iran – outside the Arab world (see Exhibit 1). Major Muslim communities exist also in Western countries in the US, Great Britain, Germany and France. Banking assets in major Muslim countries are currently concentrated in Malaysia, followed by Saudi Arabia (see Exhibit 2). In total, the banking market size represented by Muslim private and corporate clients amounts to an estimated 250 million Muslim households

157 Lewis and Algaoud (2001), p. 103.

158 Ibid., p. 111.

159 In 1999, the Supreme Court outlawed interest in every form and called by whatever name and laid down specific guidelines for a completely interest-free economy by 2001. The Pakistani government argued for a five-year delay in implementing the law on riba-free banking, but the Supreme Court granted a one-year delay only. Cf. Lewis and Algaoud (2001), p. 114-115, Archer and Abdel Karim (2002), p. 39.

160 Cf. Warde (2001), p. 112-120 and http://news.bbc.co.uk/2/hi/business/2062679.stm.

161 Heritage Foundation (2005), Lewis and Algaoud (2001), p. 132.

162 Lewis and Algaoud (2001), p. 104-107.

163 Heritage Foundation (2005)

and US$ 1,238 billion in domestic banking assets.[164] It should be noted, however, that the domestic banking assets referred to in Exhibit 2 do not comprise the substantial amounts of private wealth held abroad by nationals from the Gulf states: in 2001, it was estimated at US$ 1,194 billion, about the same magnitude as total domestic banking assets in the OIC countries.[165] Nor does it contain the banking assets held by Muslims living in Western countries. At any rate, there is a considerable potential market for Islamic banks, even when taking into account that compliance to Islamic law may not be the primary selection criterion of all Muslims in their financial dealings.

Exhibit 1: Global Muslim population in major countries

Country	Population size (2003; millions)	Share of Muslims (%)	Muslim population (2003; millions)
Indonesia	219.9	88%	193.5
India	1,065.5	14%	149.2
Pakistan	153.6	97%	149.0
Bangladesh	146.7	88%	129.1
Turkey	71.3	99%	70.6
Iran	68.9	99%	68.2
Egypt	71.9	94%	67.6
Nigeria	124.0	50%	62.0
Ethiopia	70.7	50%	35.4

Source: United Nations Population Division, www.islamcpopulation.com

Compared to this market potential, the actual market size is minimal. Although reliable numbers are hard to compile on a worldwide level, as many Islamic banks do not disclose financial information and official Islamic banking statistics often are available to a limited extend only, at the beginning of 2004 the Islamic finance market is estimated at US$ 250 billion globally.[166] It remains unclear, however, what this number refers to: First, it is not broken down geographically. Second, it is not stated

---

[164] The number of Muslim households worldwide is estimated as follows: the global Muslim population, approx. 1.5 billion in 2003, divided by 6 number of people per household. Domestic banking assets are of member countries of the Organization of Islamic Conferences (OIC) in 2002.

[165] Henry and Wilson (2004), p. 135.

[166] Various press articles that appeared during the last two to three years estimate the Islamic finance market size at approx. US$ 200 billion. According to IAIB, Islamic banking assets totaled US$ 137 billion in 1996. Assuming a 10% annual market growth, the above-mentioned figure would seem reasonable. It should be noted, however, that there is still much speculation about the size of the Islamic banking market. Cf. also Bahrain Monetary Agency (2004), p. 1.

whether it relates to on-balance sheet or also to off-balance sheet items, as the latter can make up a substantial part of Islamic banks' invested funds.[167]

Exhibit 2: Banking assets in major Islamic countries

Country	Domestic banking assets (2002; US$b)
Malaysia	249
Saudi Arabia	133
Indonesia	103
Turkey	94
United Arab Emirates	90
Egypt	88
Lebanon	76

Source: IMF International Financial Statistics

According to statistics dating back to 1997, on-balance sheet Islamic banking assets are concentrated in the Near and Middle East, followed by Southeast Asia. In the rest of the world, only minor Islamic banking assets can be found.[168] The single most important countries for Islamic finance operating as free-market economies are Saudi Arabia, Malaysia, Kuwait, the United Arab Emirates and Bahrain.[169] There is also a relatively high number of Islamic financial institutions in these markets. The biggest number can be found in Malaysia, followed by Bahrain, Saudi Arabia, Kuwait and the United Arab Emirates.[170] As national banks in the GCC countries are allowed to open branches in other member states, the countries mentioned above can be clustered into GCC countries and Malaysia.

Islamic banks either operate as full-fledged financial institutions or as Islamic windows of conventional banks. The former can be fully independent entities or subsidiaries of conventional banks. The latter are secluded Islamic departments or in the form of personnel working in conventional banking with additional training in Islamic banking. Examples for full-fledged Islamic banks are Al Rajhi Banking & Investment Corp. in Saudi Arabia, an independent entity, or Noriba in Bahrain, a subsidiary of UBS. Examples for Islamic windows are the Islamic banking activities of Burgan Bank in Kuwait or of Deutsche Bank, globally. It should be noted that Islamic banks are rather small compared to their conventional counterparts – at least on a global level. As an example, Al Rajhi Banking & Investment Corp., one of the

[167] Cf. Archer and Abdel Karim (2002), p. 116.
[168] Warde (2001), p. 7.
[169] Author's own calculations based on central banks' reports, annual reports of individual banks.
[170] Archer and Abdel Karim (2002), p. 205-208.

largest full-fledged Islamic banks, has the size of a large German regional savings bank with approx. US$ 16 billion in assets and would not even be part of the top 50 German banks. In Saudi Arabia, however, it ranks fourth with the largest bank having assets of approx. US$ 20 billion.[171]

Exhibit 3: Islamic equity funds

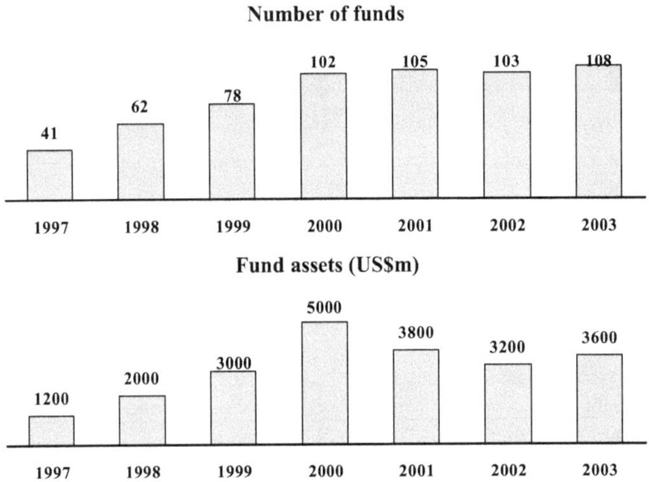

Source: Failaka

A niche market and maybe an area where Western financial institutions in general are most active in Islamic finance are Islamic equity funds.[172] The market size is estimated at US$ 3.6 billion in 2003, with over 100 Islamic equity funds available (see Exhibit 3). Many major US and European fund managers are active in the field, including AXA, Brown Brothers Herriman, Citibank, Commerzbank, Deutsche Bank, HSBS, Merrill Lynch, Pictet et Cie, and UBS. The largest Islamic equity fund manager is Wellington Management in Boston with US$ 727 million under management, the largest fund sponsor National Commercial Bank of Saudi Arabia.

2.2.3.2 Institutional Framework

The financial industry is generally viewed as a highly sensitive economic sector. Therefore, the institutional framework is of particular importance, as is illustrated by

[171] No Author (2003)

[172] For the following exposition cf. www.failaka.com/Library/Articles/World%20Islamic%20Funds%20 Workshop-T%20AlRifai.pdf

economic as well as business considerations.[173] In the following, the regulatory and supervisory environment as well as the framework for liquidity management and secondary markets are presented. Some of the institutions depicted have only been founded recently, while others are already well established. As will become apparent, the Islamic finance industry can still be considered as an emerging market. The exposition must therefore remain tentative.

Regulatory and supervisory environment. Rating the adequacy of the regulation and supervision of financial institutions in the Arab world for a survey of the World Economic Forum on a scale between "inadequacy for financial stability" and "among the world's most stringent", Arab business leaders recently put their countries at an above-average position.[174] While this assessment might be even enhanced for the conventional banking industry by closer adherence to the rules and regulations developed by the Basle Committee, the situation is more complicated for the Islamic financial industry, as the very nature of their operations suggests that, for them, the standards and best practices developed for conventional banking are not necessarily adequate. Given that the sources of funds are mainly investment accounts and used for asset-related investments or trades, the regulatory framework "(...) needs to place greater emphasis on the management of operational risks and information disclosure issues than is normally the case in conventional banking."[175] Moreover, their products need to be in conformity with Islamic law, the assurance of which is regarded as the most fundamental corporate governance issue in Islamic finance. What further complicates the situation is that, as outlined in a previous section, Islamic law is not a fixed system but a casuistic law, which lends itself to various interpretations. Therefore it is not surprising that the regulatory environment of the Islamic financial industry varies according to the approaches employed by the national regulators, i.e. central banks or monetary agencies. Some countries have developed specific prudential and supervisory rules to regulate Islamic banks or Islamic windows of conventional banks, while other countries apply the same rules for both conventional and Islamic banks.[176] Examples of the former among the free-market oriented Islamic finance markets are Bahrain and Malaysia, an example for the latter is Saudi Arabia.

The resulting lack of uniformity mainly affects three areas: accounting standards, Sharia assurance and product or transaction standards. As the – conventional – international or national accounting standards do not cater for the specificities of Islamic financial transactions, Islamic banks originally had to interpret them individually, leading to a lack of transparency and comparability of financial statements as well as inadequate corporate disclosure.[177] Sharia assurance is also tackled unevenly in the various countries, although it is generally done by means of a

---

[173] See for example Dudley (2004), p. 38, Sundararajan and Errico (2002), Dar et. al. (2001), Errico and Farahbaksh (1998)

[174] Cornelius et. al. (2003), p. 364.

[175] Errico et. al. (1998), p. 3.

[176] The prudential and supervisory rules will be looked at in further detail below in the chapters on Islamic banking in the GCC area and in Malaysia.

[177] Archer and Abdel Karim (2002), p. 111-113.

Sharia supervisory or advisory board, usually comprised of specially trained Islamic scholars.[178] Some countries have established their own Sharia boards to advise the respective central banks or securities commissions on Sharia related issues, some (additionally) obligate the Islamic financial institutions to have their own, others still leave the establishment of Sharia boards discretionary.[179] The functions that these Sharia boards perform – albeit to varying degrees – are the ex ante review of the contract templates for the various transactions, the ex post review of a sample of the transactions performed and the issuance of a report on Sharia compliance. Both the review and the reporting process are not standardized. As the Sharia rulings of these boards are based on their interpretation of the underlying Sharia principles, the same Islamic financial instrument can be rejected by one board and approved by another. This leads to multiple and various standards regarding the marketability and acceptability of products.[180] As was illustrated above, there are in particular marked differences in product acceptance between Malaysia and the Middle East.[181] Obviously, Sharia rulings can have a considerable impact on the competitive situation of an Islamic bank, as they directly influence the spectrum of financial products the banks can offer as well as the related costs.

The diversity of opinion might be mitigated by the fact that a relatively small number of recognized Sharia scholars is present in the Sharia boards of many different Islamic financial institutions.[182] Besides, a number of measures has been taken by scholars, the industry and regulators to address the need for standardization. First, various *fiqh* academies have been established, the most important of which is presumably the Islamic Fiqh Academy founded by the Organization of Islamic Conferences in 1981. Its objective is inter alia "to achieve the theoretical and practical unity of the Islamic Ummah"[183] and "to study contemporary problems from the Sharia point of view and to try to find the solutions in conformity with the Sharia through an authentic interpretation of its content"[184]. In the course of the 1990s, it has concentrated on Islamic finance and banking issues, and has therefore provided ample reference possibilities for the rulings of the individual Sharia boards.[185] Second, the Islamic finance industry established in 1991 a self-governing body, the Accounting and Auditing Organization for Islamic Financial Institutions (AAOIFI) with the objective to prepare accounting, auditing, governance, ethics and Sharia standards for Islamic financial institutions. In particular, it aims at the implementation of these standards and guidelines by approaching the concerned regulatory bodies, Islamic financial

---

178 For good overviews on issues related to Sharia boards cf. Lewis and Algaoud (2001), p. 179-183, Archer and Abdel Karim (2002), p. 74-88.

179 Examples for the first are Bahrain, Indonesia, Malaysia and Sudan, for the second Kuwait, Malaysia, Qatar and the UAE.

180 Cf. Zaman and Movassaghi (2001), p. 37.

181 Archer and Abdel Karim (2002), p. 87-88.

182 Nienhaus (2004).

183 Cf. http://www.oic-oci.org/

184 See above.

185 Vogel and Hayes, III (1998), p. 48. Vogel has based a great part of his exposition on rulings of this academy.

institutions, other financial institutions that offer Islamic financial services, and accounting and auditing firms. Its accounting standards are mandatory in Bahrain, Jordan, Sudan and Qatar and are used as guidelines in Saudi Arabia.[186] Last, in 2002 a number of regulatory and supervisory authorities, inter-governmental international organizations as well as financial institutions have established the Islamic Financial Services Board (IFSB) in order to promote, disseminate and harmonize best practices in the regulation and supervision of the Islamic financial services industry and to develop a prudent and transparent industry, including banking, capital markets and insurance. It pledges to follow a cross-sectional approach, addressing the specificities of Islamic finance and taking international standards on banking, securities and financial conglomerates into consideration.[187] Among its members are the Bahrain Monetary Agency, the Central Bank of Egypt, the Bank Negara Malaysia, the State Bank of Pakistan, the IMF and the World Bank, to name but a few. The IFSB has started work on prudential standards for capital adequacy and risk management – exposure drafts were issued in early 2005 – and is planning to prepare standards on corporate governance as well as transparency and market discipline. For the time being, the work-in-progress status of the efforts of AAOIFI and IFSB illustrates again the highly diverse current regulatory and supervisory environment of Islamic financial institutions across countries, which may have a considerable effect on the competitive situation of Islamic banks located in different jurisdictions.

Liquidity management and secondary markets.

> "The most vulnerable weakness of Islamic banks is the limited tools available for their liquidity management and the lack of an active secondary market. One of the major weaknesses in this domain is caused by the predominance of debt-based modes of financing such as *murabaha* (...). Once a debt has been created, it cannot be transferred to anyone else except at par value. This renders the whole structure of an Islamic financial market highly illiquid. (...) Steps need to be taken to establish and/or strengthen secondary markets."[188]

Despite recent efforts by central banks, governments and financial institutions from Islamic countries to develop these markets, this statement still largely holds true, at least on an international scale. This will be highlighted in the following exposition of the institutional framework of liquidity management and secondary markets in a national as well as international context.

Obviously, Islamic banks cannot use the conventional, interest-based instruments for liquidity management, which are available in the conventional money and interbanking markets. Traditionally, Islamic banks had to address the liquidity issue by holding large portions of cash, short-term commodity *murabaha* and other liquid assets, thus matching the maturities of most of their assets with the predominantly

[186] Presentation by Prof. Rifaat Ahmed Abdel Karim at the Institute of Development Research and Development Policy, Ruhr-University, Bochum, Germany, on 13 December 2003.

[187] As set out by the Basle Committee on Banking Supervision and the International Organization on Securities Commissions.

[188] Archer and Abdel Karim (2002), p. 167-168.

short-term maturities of their deposits.[189] Malaysia was among the first countries to tackle this issue with the introduction of its Islamic Interbank Money Market (IIMM) in 1994. The IIMM covers two aspects: interbank trading of Islamic financial instruments and *mudaraba* interbank investments. The former allows eligible banks to trade in the designated financial instruments such as Islamic accepted bills, bankers' acceptances and securities among themselves. The latter allows Islamic banks in need of liquidity to obtain investments from surplus Islamic financial institutions based on *mudaraba*. The period of investment is from overnight to 12 months.[190] With the creation of the Liquidity Management Centre (LMC) in 2002, Bahrain is going even one step further, as the LMC seeks to facilitate "(...) the creation of an Islamic interbank money market enabling Islamic Financial Services Institutions (IFSIs) to manage their liquidity as effectively as their non-Islamic counterparts"[191] on an international scale. On the one hand, the LMC is issuing *sukuk* created by securitisation of pooled assets acquired from governments, financial institutions and corporates. These *sukuk* are offered to financial institutions to invest their surplus liquidity. On the other hand, the LMC is creating a secondary market for the trading of these instruments so that Islamic financial institutions can manage their liquidity. However, the effectiveness of the LMC remains to be proven.[192]

Islamic financial products such as *sukuk* are usually traded at national stock exchanges: major examples are the Bahrain Stock Exchange, the Labuan International Financial Exchange or the Luxembourg Stock Exchange. In analogy to conventional practices, there are often primary and secondary listings of Islamic securities at various exchanges. However, *sukuk* are a relatively new invention: as a consequence, the value of *sukuk* outstanding is still relatively low and the market remains rather shallow and illiquid.

Accordingly, the absence of an effective money and interbanking market for the global Islamic finance industry is still widely acknowledged and liquidity regarded as inadequate.[193] Recognizing the need to develop a cross-border secondary market for Islamic financial instruments, the Islamic Development Bank, the Bahrain Monetary Agency, the Labuan Offshore Financial Services Authority, the Bank of Sudan, the Bank of Indonesia, and the Ministry of Finance Brunei set up the International Islamic Financial Market (IIFM), which became operational in 2002. IIFM's objectives are to develop a market for independent Sharia enhancement of existing or new Islamic financial instruments through increasing the number of issuance and participants, to provide guidelines for the issuance of new Islamic financial instruments, to enhance cooperation amongst market participants by encouraging product development and trading of instruments in the secondary market, and finally to undertake research for

---

[189] Cf. Montagu-Pollock and Wright (2002), p. 32, Archer and Abdel Karim (2002), p. 163-169, Adil (2004).

[190] Cf. http://www.bnm.gov.my

[191] Bahrain Monetary Agency (2002), p. 79.

[192] Edwardes (2003), p. 3-5.

[193] Cf. OICV-IOSCO (2004), p. 67.

the development of Islamic financial markets.[194] It offers three services to reach these objectives: Sharia endorsements for Islamic financial products, issuance of guidelines for Islamic financial instruments, and the facilitation of cross-border listings and secondary market trading. In spite of these far-reaching goals, the look at its accomplishments are sobering: in the first three years after its inception, the IIFM has endorsed five *sukuk* issues: the Malaysia Global Sukuk issued on behalf of the Government of Malaysia (US$ 600 million), the first sovereign global *sukuk*; the Islamic Development Bank Sukuk, the first global *sukuk* issued by a multilateral institution through a Special Purpose Vehicle (US$ 400 million); the Qatar Global Sukuk, the second sovereign global *sukuk* (US$ 700 million); the BMA International Sukuk (US$ 250 million); and the Tabreed Trust Certificate (US$ 100 million), which is the first global corporate *sukuk* based on *ijara* and *istisna'*contracts.[195]

In view of the rather low volume of intentionally global *sukuk* issues and given that *sukuk* are often held until maturity, in particular in the Middle East[196], it seems fair to claim that the development of viable secondary and interbanking markets remains a challenge for the global Islamic finance industry. However, there are notable differences between Malaysia and the GCC countries. In the former, far more instruments for liquidity management are available and deemed acceptable than in the GCC countries, which were also introduced at an earlier stage. Moreover, secondary markets are more evolved, as *sukuk* are readily traded, many of which are however not accepted in the GCC countries.[197]

2.2.3.3 Islamic Banking in the GCC area

On-balance sheet Islamic finance assets in the Gulf Cooperation Council (GCC) area amounted to an estimated US$ 40 billion in 2002, a bit more than 10% of total on-balance sheet banking assets in the region (see Exhibit 6). With the exception of Oman, all GCC countries are major markets for Islamic finance.[198] This section presents stylized facts about Islamic finance in this region. It starts with an economic and socio-demographic overview, followed by the depiction of the banking sector and financial markets – with an emphasis on Islamic banking – and the regulatory environment.

Economic and socio-demographic overview. In 2002, the GCC countries without Oman gained a combined GDP of approx. US$ 386 billion. GDP per capita varies between approx. US$ 11,000 in Saudi Arabia and approx. US$ 22,000 in the United Arab Emirates, splitting the GCC countries into two segments: relatively high-income countries – United Arab Emirates, Qatar and Kuwait – and relatively low-income countries – Bahrain and Saudi Arabia (see Exhibit 4). Over the period from 1987 to 2002, all countries showed increasing GDP per capita, albeit with varying growth

---

[194] Cf. http://www.iifm.net/profile-objectives.php

[195] Cf. http://www.iifm.net/edge-endorsements.php

[196] No Author (2002), p. 44, Edwardes (2003), p. 3.

[197] No Author (2002), p. 44-45.

[198] For the following exposition, GCC is meant to cover all official GCC countries except for Oman.

rates.[199] It seems fair to claim that demand for more diverse and more sophisticated financial products increases with wealth. One could expect, then, to see a wider use of differentiation strategies in richer countries, and – as product differentiation is at the heart of Islamic finance – even a greater penetration of Islamic banks in wealthier countries. In fact, a recent study showed some correlation between market share of Islamic banks and per capita GDP.[200]

Exhibit 4: Major economic and socio-demographic indicators

Indicator	Bahrain	Kuwait	Qatar	Saudi Arabia	United Arab Emirates	Malaysia	Germany
GDP (2002; $b)	9.9	36.9	15.9	268.9	53.9	198.4	2,160.0
GDP per capita (2002; $)	14,837	16,902	19,460	11,069	21,692	8,591	26,214
Exports per GDP (2002; %)	82%	60%	62%	41%	76%	104%	36%
Imports per GDP (2002; %)	65%	41%	24%	23%	64%	90%	32%
Fiscal balance (2001; % of GDP)	-6%	23%	10%	-4%	-6%	-6%	-2%
Population size (2003; thousands)	667	2,183	817	24,293	2,484	23,092	82,398
Median age	29	26	31	19	28	24	41
Population growth rate (2003; %)	1.6%	3.3%	2.9%	3.3%	1.6%	1.9%	0.0%
Education index (2002)	0.85	0.81	0.83	0.71	0.74	0.83	0.95
Internet users (2002; % of population)	21%	9%	9%	6%	36%	25%	39%
Telephone main lines per 1000 capita (1997)	228	189	174	161	368	199	618

Note: Germany is included for comparison purposes.

Source: Arab World Competitiveness Report, Heritage Foundation, IMF Country Reports, International Labour Office, ITU Statistics, Moody's, United Nations Development Program, United Nations Population Division, U.S. Department of State

[199] Cf. http://www.imf.org/external/pubs/ft/med/2003/eng/fasano.

[200] Henry and Wilson (2004), p. 9.

All countries are strongly oil-dependent, yet to varying degrees – in terms of the share of petroleum production and refining in GDP, export receipts and government revenues. Oil income makes up between 30% in Bahrain and 55% in Qatar of GDP, 47% in the United Arab Emirates and 95% in Kuwait of export revenues and 57% in the United Arab Emirates and 80% in Kuwait of government revenues (see Exhibit 5). All GCC countries have been and still are implementing policy reforms to accelerate non-oil growth and reduce vulnerability to oil price shocks. According to the IMF, following the sharp drop in oil prices in 1998-99 and the associated financial pressures, governments in the GCC have reinforced structural reform programs along the lines of fiscal consolidation and sustainability, legal and institutional reforms to expand the private sector, privatization of state enterprises, liberalization of foreign capital inflow restrictions and labor market reforms. Privatization of utilities and related services has been strongly pursued by many GCC countries. "Oman, Qatar and the United Arab Emirates are presently relying on the private sector and foreign direct investment to fund and manage infrastructure projects in the energy and water sectors, while Saudi Arabia has moved aggressively to privatize telecommunications."[201] Structural reforms to attract foreign direct investment have recently been adopted, allowing for 100 percent foreign ownership of companies in most non-hydrocarbon sectors. The manufacturing sector (especially petrochemicals, construction material, plastics) has been strengthened in Saudi Arabia, trade and related activities have been growing in the United Arab Emirates, the banking and insurance sector is by far the single most important sector in Bahrain and in Qatar, natural gas is becoming the key sector in the economy, bypassing oil.[202] In all GCC countries, trade makes up an important part of economic activity. This is reflected in both the relation of export value to GDP and import value to GDP, which hovers between 41% and 82% for exports, and 23% and 65% for imports (see Exhibit 4). This translates into significant corporate banking business opportunities across the GCC countries, as privatization, the economic diversification and the trade activities must be funded.

Exhibit 5: Importance of oil income in GCC countries except for Oman

Indicator	Bahrain	Kuwait	Qatar	Saudi Arabia	United Arab Emirates
Share of oil income in GDP (2002; %)	30%	50%	55%	45%	33%
Share of oil income in export revenue (2002; %)	60%	95%	85%	90%	47%
Share of oil income in government revenues (2002; %)	60%	80%	70%	75%	57%

Source: IMF

[201] Cf. http://www.imf.org/external/pubs/ft/med/2003/eng/fasano.

In 2001, Bahrain, Saudi Arabia and the United Arab Emirates had an overall budget deficit, while Qatar and Kuwait had a budget surplus (see Exhibit 4). As was also evidenced above in some examples of sovereign global *sukuks*, there clearly is demand for Islamic banking products related to government funding in the GCC countries.

All countries have experienced a high population growth in the past two decades, with current population growth rates between 1.6% and 3.3%. This is also reflected by the median age of the population in the GCC countries, which lies between 19 in Saudi Arabia and 31 in Qatar (see Exhibit 4). Together with the rising participation of women in the labor force, the population growth is translating into a growing national labor force. At the same time, "GCC countries are highly dependent on a large expatriate labor force, reflecting the small (but rapidly growing) size of the domestic workforce and the limited domestic supply of adequate skills."[203] The United Nations education index suggests that, while the ranking is relatively high compared globally, it is still relatively far away from the most developed countries, such as Germany (see Exhibit 4). Saudi Arabia and the United Arab Emirates rank particularly low, in relative terms. While expatriate workers account in most GCC countries for about three-quarters of the total workforce, most of the national labor force is employed in the government sector.[204] As a consequence, skilled labor is relatively scarce across all GCC countries, granting a relatively high bargaining power to HR suppliers in the banking sector. This is particularly true for the Islamic finance sector, as employees have to have special Islamic finance know-how alongside conventional banking knowledge. Moreover, the growing population implies growing demand for retail banking products, in particular consumer finance and mortgages.

Communication indicators, which are particularly important for the potential use of modern delivery channels, point to a relative backwardness of all GCC countries except for the United Arab Emirates (see Exhibit 4). As an example, Internet use varies between 6% in Saudi Arabia and 36% in the United Arab Emirates, compared to 39% in Germany as a benchmark. Therefore, with the exception of the United Arab Emirates and, to some extent, Bahrain, there is a relatively unfavorable framework for online or telephone banking to become an effective substitute for a branch network in the GCC retail banking sector.

Banking sector and financial markets. In 2002, the banking sector of the GCC countries without Oman comprised combined assets of approx. US$ 369 billion. Saudi Arabian banks had the highest share, with approx. US$ 133 billion in assets, followed by the United Arab Emirates, Bahrain, Kuwait and Qatar. This picture is substantially altered on a per capita level, with Bahrain ranking first, followed by the United Arab Emirates, Kuwait, Qatar and Saudi Arabia (see Exhibit 6). The leading position of Bahrain is heavily influenced by the importance of its offshore banking operations -

[202] Ibid.

[203] Ibid.

[204] Ibid.

offshore banking assets make up more than three-quarters of Bahrain's total banking assets.[205] This suggests that the banking sector is relatively more developed in Bahrain, Kuwait, the United Arab Emirates and Qatar, while Saudi Arabia is lagging behind.

Exhibit 6: Banking sector and financial markets indicators

Indicator	Bahrain	Kuwait	Qatar	Saudi Arabia	United Arab Emirates	Malaysia	Ger-many
Banking sector: assets (2002; $b)	74.0	55.6	16.9	132.7	89.9	248.7	4,359.5
Islamic finance: assets (2002; $b)	2.9	9.5	2.1	19.0	7.5	18.3	-
Banking sector assets per capita (2002; $)	110,905	25,468	20,684	5,462	36,180	10,770	52,908
Islamic finance assets per capita (2002; $)	4,346	4,351	2,570	782	3,018	792	-
Market share Islamic finance	4%	17%	12%	14%	8%	7%	0%

Source: Al-Iktissad Wal-Aamal, Annual Reports, Arab World Competitiveness Report, World Federation of Exchanges

In the five GCC countries covered, Islamic finance assets ranged in 2002 between approx. US$ 19 billion in Saudi Arabia and approx. US$ 2 billion in Qatar (see Exhibit 6). On a per capita basis, Islamic finance assets are highest in Kuwait, followed by Bahrain, the United Arab Emirates, Qatar and finally Saudi Arabia. With market shares between 4% and 17%, Islamic finance remains in all countries a niche market. In conformity with the situation of the overall banking and financial markets sector, Kuwait, Bahrain, the United Arab Emirates and Qatar dispose of a relatively more developed Islamic finance market, while Saudi Arabia is again lagging behind. As was evidenced above in the chapter on Islamic financial products, Islamic banks operating alongside conventional banks often set the financial conditions of their financial instruments such that they match their conventional competitive offerings. It is argued in the literature that this holds true for all Islamic banks in mixed systems, even though a study of bank customers in Bahrain showed religion as the main factor for customer choice of Islamic banks.[206] Therefore, Islamic banks in the GCC are most likely in competition with conventional banks.

[205] Cf. BMA Annual report 2002, p. 27.

[206] Lewis and Algaoud (2001), p. 149-150; Metawa and Almossawi (1997).

Exhibit 7: Major Islamic finance institutions in the GCC countries except Oman

Company	Assets (2002; US$ millions)	Country	Share of total GCC Islamic banking assets (%)
Al Rajhi Banking & Investment Corp.	15,784	Saudi Arabia	38%
Kuwait Finance House	8,527	Kuwait	21%
Dubai Islamic Bank	5,336	UAE	13%
Abu Dhabi Islamic Bank	2,161	UAE	5%
Bank Al Jazira	1,519	Saudi Arabia	4%
Qatar Islamic Bank	1,408	Qatar	3%
Shamil Bank	1,047	Bahrain	3%
Bahrain Islamic Bank	557	Bahrain	1%
First Islamic Investment Bank	523	Bahrain	1%

Source: Al-Iktissad Wal-Aamal

Exhibit 8: Profitability indicators for selected GCC Islamic finance institutions

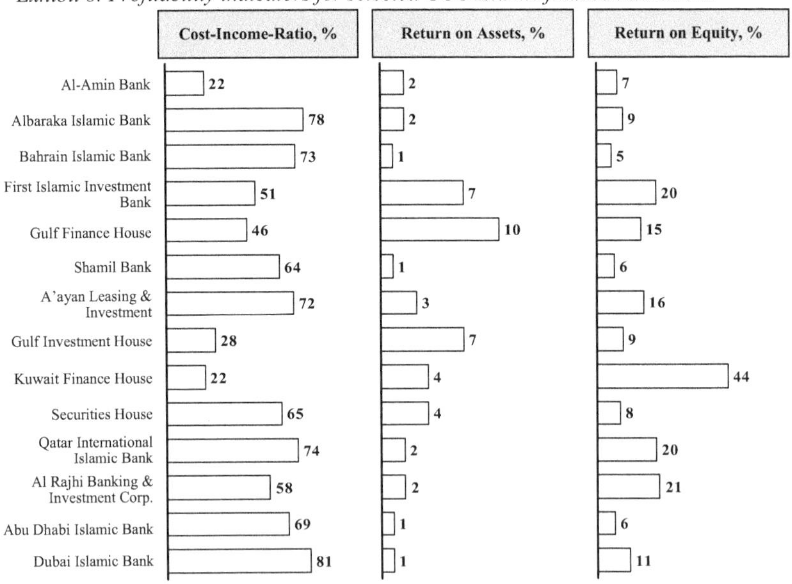

Source: Annual reports 2002 and 2001

There are approx. 60 Islamic financial institutions and Islamic windows of conventional banks in the five GCC countries covered. Concentration in the industry is high: the top three companies combine almost three-quarters of total GCC on-balance sheet Islamic banking assets, the top nine companies hold about 90% of total GCC on-balance sheet Islamic banking assets (see Exhibit 7). Three companies out of the top nine are based in Bahrain, one in Kuwait, one in Qatar, two in the United Arab Emirates and two in Saudi Arabia. The largest Islamic bank in the GCC region is Al Rajhi Banking & Investment Corp. from Saudi Arabia, followed by Kuwait Finance House and Dubai Islamic Bank. Despite this high concentration, Islamic banks in the GCC countries do not enjoy monopolies, which is in stark contrast to the situation in the 1970s and 1980s. Starting in the 1990s, many conventional banks opened Islamic windows or subsidiaries – as an example, most conventional banks in Saudi Arabia today have Islamic windows – and many new Islamic banks were created – such as the Qatar International Islamic Bank.[207] Consequently, there are at least three Islamic banks, windows or financing companies in operation in every GCC country considered.

Exhibit 9: Consolidated balance sheets of Islamic banks, % share of total

Balance sheet item	GCC and Malaysia	GCC	Malaysia
Cash and cash equivalent	9%	9%	10%
Advances to other financial institutions	3%	0%	8%
Murabaha/ Al-Bai'Bithaman Ajil	48%	55%	32%
Ina	0%	0%	1%
Salam/ Istisna	4%	5%	0%
Ijara	6%	3%	13%
Mudaraba/ Muqarada	1%	1%	0%
Musharaka	1%	1%	0%
Investment in securities/ companies	12%	5%	27%
Other	17%	20%	10%
Total assets	**100%**	**100%**	**100%**
Deposits from other financial institutions	4%	3%	7%
Current accounts	28%	35%	13%
Investment/ savings accounts	47%	37%	70%
Shareholders' equity	11%	13%	7%
Other	9%	12%	3%
Total liabilities & shareholders equity	**100%**	**100%**	**100%**

Source: Annual reports

[207] Archer and Abdel Karim (2002), p. 34.

The reported profitability of many Islamic banks is relatively high, in particular compared internationally. In a subset of 14 GCC Islamic banks covering 90% of total GCC on-balance sheet banking assets, in 2002 the cost-income-ratio ranged between 22% and 81%, return on assets between 1% and 10%, return on equity between 5% and 44% (see Exhibit 8). However, due to the above-mentioned lacking standard of accounting and business practices, and, potentially, reserve requirements across countries, these figures have to be interpreted with caution. As an example, high profitability might reflect a high share of current accounts in customer deposits, or a high proportion of off-balance sheet assets.

Islamic financial institutions operating in the GCC area cover a wide array of financial services. These include retail and wholesale banking, investment banking, corporate banking, investment funds and leasing. While the larger Islamic financial institutions tend to be universal banks – eight out of the nine companies listed in Exhibit 7 are universal banks, one is an investment bank – the smaller Islamic financial institutions tend to specialize in specific customer segments – such as high net worth individuals – or product offerings – such as investment banking. This observation also holds true at the country level. The financial services portfolio is partly reflected in the consolidated balance sheet of Islamic banks in the GCC.[208] On the asset side, *murabaha* and *al-bai'bithaman ajil* are by far the most widely used financing instruments – markedly more so than in Malaysia (see Exhibit 9). The use of all other Islamic finance schemes is extremely limited. On the liabilities and shareholders equity side, current accounts are with a 35% share in total liabilities and shareholders equity noticeably more in use than in Malaysia, and have almost the same share as investment accounts. However, current accounts' share in total liabilities and shareholders equity of Islamic banks is in a comparable range with the one of conventional banks in the region.[209] Islamic financial institutions in the GCC countries therefore seem to be better positioned to boost their profits by using current accounts for investments without compensating depositors than their Malaysian equivalents.

Regulatory environment. In 2003, an IMF study about the financial development in the Middle East and North Africa stated that the relative strength of the countries assessed, as a group, include regulation and supervision as well as financial openness.[210] Room for improvement is seen in the institutional environment and the promotion of the non-bank financial sector. Based on IMF's measurement, "(...) the MENA region performs better than most other developing country regions, but ranks far behind the industrialized countries and East Asia."[211] The IMF study also points out that "(...) within the MENA region there is substantial variation in the degree of

[208] Based on a subset of 15 GCC Islamic banks comprising approx. 90% of total GCC Islamic finance assets and 12 Malaysian Islamic banks comprising 80% of total Malaysian Islamic finance assets.

[209] Author's own calculations.

[210] Cf. http://www.imf.org/external/pubs/ft/med/2003/eng/creane/index.htm

[211] Ibid. MENA is defined by the IMF for this study as Algeria, Bahrain, Djibouti, Egypt, the Islamic Republic of Iran, Jordan, Kuwait, Lebanon, Libya, Mauritania, Morocco, Oman, Pakistan, Qatar, Saudi Arabia, Sudan, the Syrian Arab Republic, Tunisia, the United Arab Emirates, and Yemen.

financial development; some countries have advanced financial sectors, while for others progress in this area has been limited."[212] Among those MENA countries rated highest in terms of their financial development are all GCC countries. The IMF finds that the highest-rated countries have strengthened banking supervision and regulation, established up-to-date procedures to collect prudential information, set up bank inspection and audit mechanism, and taken steps to conform to international Basel standards by increasing capital adequacy ratios and reducing non-performing loans. It also acknowledges that in many of the GCC countries, the banking sector is well developed, profitable and efficient. However, the quality of the institutional environment, such as the judicial system, bureaucracy, law and order, and property rights, is rated as relatively poor even for the best-performing countries. It is important to note in this context that all but one of the five GCC countries considered are members of the World Trade Organization (WTO), the exception being Saudi Arabia, which is an observer government in the process of accession. As a consequence, all countries are expected to open their banking sectors to foreign competition, although some restrictions apply for the time being.[213] The GCC countries have already opened up their markets to banks from GCC member states.[214]

The 2002 Executive Opinion Survey conducted by the World Economic Forum largely corroborates IMF's assessment.[215] Rating institutional environment (administrative regulations, legal framework, intellectual property protection), financial sector openness, and financial regulation and supervision, respondents rated the GCC countries largely between 4 and 6, where the highest possible value 7 denotes global best practice (see Exhibit 10). Notable exceptions are Kuwait and Saudi Arabia, which ranked low in administrative regulations and financial sector openness. Overall, financial regulation and supervision came off particularly well.

With the exception of Saudi Arabia and Oman, all GCC countries have an Islamic banking law in place.[216] Bahrain, which has the highest number of licensed Islamic financial institutions in the GCC area, has probably also the most elaborate legal framework for operations of Islamic banks in the region. In 2002, it introduced the Prudential Information and Regulatory Framework for Islamic Banks (PIRI) in order to monitor the operations of the banks and to help identify any signs of the

---

[212] Ibid.

[213] For example, the UAE stopped granting licenses to foreign banks in 1982 and limited the number branches to eight. Cf. Islam (2003a), p. 67. In Saudi Arabia, foreign banks are not allowed to operate branches; in the early 1980s, existing foreign banks were turned into joint-venture banks with a minimum of 60% Saudi ownership. Cf. Islam (2003b), p. 24. However, the UAE has also set up a financial free zone in 2002 – the Dubai International Financial Centre (DIFC) – as an onshore banking centre for foreign financial institutions. Here, 100% foreign ownership is possible, whereas banks incorporated in the UAE outside the DIFC must be majority-owned by UAE nationals. Cf. Islam (2003a), p. 60.

[214] Islam (2003a), p. 62.

[215] Cf. Cornelius et. al. (2003), p. 322-380. The survey records the perspectives of business leaders within the Arab world, asking them to compare aspects of their local business environment with global standards. The survey results for the GCC countries except for Oman are based on 112 responses.

[216] Cf. http://www.gasandoil.com/goc/news/ntm32413.htm

deterioration of a bank's performance.[217] At the heart of PIRI is a CAMEL rating system adapted to an Islamic environment as a tool for management of operational risks.[218] The BMA has developed criteria that require Islamic banks to maintain an adequate level of capital, maintain assets of a sound quality, safeguard the interests of the profit sharing investment account holders, maintain a consistent level of quality earnings, and monitor their liquidity mismatch positions.[219]

Exhibit 10: Selected 2002 Executive Opinion Results

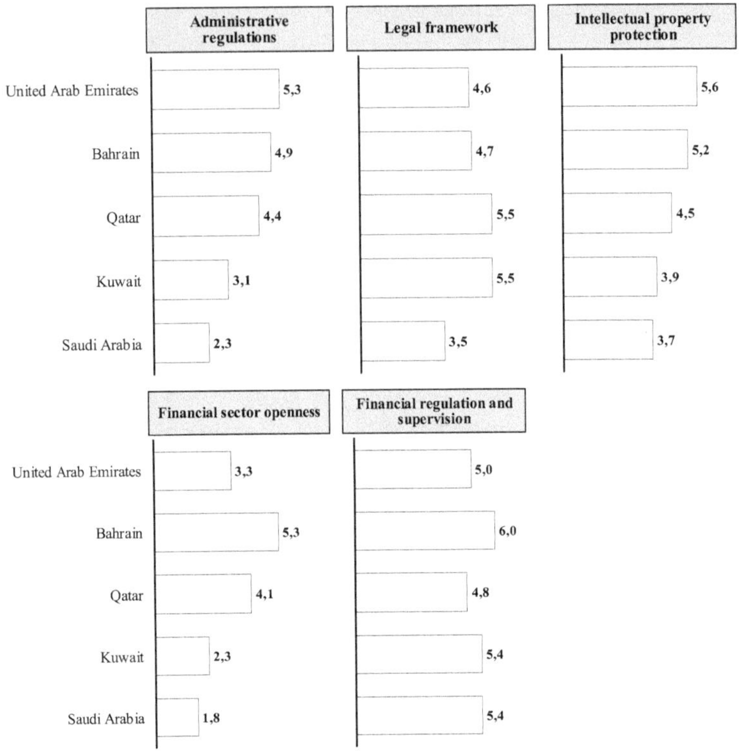

Note: Rating from 1 to 7 (1=Poor … 7=Meets global best practice)
Source: World Economic Forum

[217] For the following depiction of PIRI cf. Bahrain Monetary Agency (2002), p. 59-68.

[218] CAMEL rating is a measure of the relative soundness of a bank frequently used by financial supervisory and regulatory bodies across the globe. The acronym stands for capital, assets, management, earnings, and liquidity. These are the five critical dimensions of a bank's operations. They reflect in a systematic fashion a bank's financial condition, compliance with supervisory regulations, and overall operating soundness. Cf. Errico and Farahbaksh (1998) and Sundararajan and Errico (2002).

[219] These regulations are broadly in line with IMF recommendations on banking supervision and management of operational risks in an Islamic framework. Cf. Errico and Farahbaksh (1998) and Sundararajan and Errico (2002).

Besides, the BMA has also taken steps to enhance corporate governance of Islamic banks. It requires Islamic banks to regularly submit a statement of strategy and objectives for a minimum period of three years, details of their organizational structure, highlighting the qualifications and relevant industry experience of key management personnel, and details on how they maintain an independent function for risk management and internal audit. The internal Sharia review should be carried out in accordance with AAOIFI's governance standard; all Islamic financial institutions are also required to adhere to the standards issued by the Sharia board of the AAOIFI.

The Islamic bank-specific legal framework in Kuwait, Qatar and the United Arab Emirates is by far not that elaborate. The Islamic banking laws in these countries mostly deal with the set-up of an Islamic bank, the establishment of Sharia boards, and capital requirements.[220] As was evidenced above in the overview section already, the regulatory and supervisory framework clearly differs across countries, which might also have an impact on the performance of Islamic banks.

2.2.3.4 Islamic Banking in Malaysia

On-balance sheet Islamic finance assets in Malaysia amounted to approx. US$ 18 billion in 2002, about 7% of total on-balance sheet banking assets in the country. As before for the GCC countries, this section presents stylized facts about Islamic finance in Malaysia, covering the economic and socio-demographic environment, the banking and sector financial markets, and finally the regulatory environment.

Economic and socio-demographic overview. In 2002, Malaysia gained a GDP of approx. US$ 198 billion. GDP per capita was approx. US$ 8,600 and thus significantly lower than in the five GCC countries covered (see Exhibit 4). If demand for more diverse and more sophisticated financial products increases with wealth, there should be more demand for basic banking products in Malaysia than in the GCC countries – at least in the retail sector. From 1971 to the late 1990s, Malaysia transformed itself from a producer of raw materials into an emerging multi-sector economy. Growth was almost exclusively driven by exports, particularly of electronics. The country is heavily dependant on the economic conditions in the US and Japan, its top export destinations and key sources of foreign investment. The importance of trade is also reflected in the relation of export value to GDP (104% in 2002) and import value to GDP (90% in 2002) (see Exhibit 4). All this implies significant demand for corporate banking products.

Malaysia's economy was harshly impacted by the Asian crisis 1997-1998 and the global economic recession and the downturn in the IT sector in 2001. In the wake of the 1997-1998 Asian crisis, the Malaysian government put into practice comprehensive policy measures relating to fiscal and monetary policies, capital controls and exchange rate regimes, financial sector reforms, and corporate reforms.

---

[220] For the laws governing Islamic financial institutions in Kuwait, Qatar and the UAE respectively, cf. www.cbk.gov.kw/www/law.html, www.qcb.gov.qa/pages/English_Site/Ta3lemat/index.htm, www.uaecb.gov.ae/LawNo6-1985-IslaminBanks.pdf

In particular, a bank consolidation program – aimed at creating larger and more efficient financial institutions ready to compete globally as new foreign competition was allowed – was introduced, and prudential supervision and regulation was strengthened.[221] Interestingly enough, Islamic banks were reported to have weathered the Asian financial crisis better than most of the conventional banks.[222] Malaysia's economy rebounded in 2002.[223]

In 2001, Malaysia had a budget deficit, just like Bahrain, Saudi Arabia and the United Arab Emirates (see Exhibit 4). As was also evidenced above, there clearly is demand for Islamic banking products related to government funding in Malaysia, as the Malaysian government issued the first global sovereign *sukuk* ever.

Just like the GCC countries, Malaysia faces a high population growth, with a growth rate of 1.9% in 2003. The median age of the population is 24, which is on a comparable level to the median age in the GCC countries (see Exhibit 4). However, Malaysia has an estimated 8% of the population living below the poverty line, and a highly unequal income distribution, with the poorest 10% of the population receiving only 2% of the income while the richest 10% receive almost 40%.[224] In the United Nations education index Malaysia ranks at levels comparable with the GCC countries, which are relatively high compared globally, yet still relatively far away from the most developed countries, such as Germany (see Exhibit 4). Thus the bargaining power of HR suppliers in the banking sector should also be at comparable levels with the GCC countries, in particular in the Islamic finance sector, where employees have to have special Islamic finance know-how alongside conventional banking knowledge. Despite the unequal income distribution, the growing population implies growing demand for retail banking products, in particular for consumer finance.

As is the case for most of the GCC countries, communication indicators point to a relative backwardness of Malaysia. Internet use stood at 25% compared to 39% in Germany. Telephone main lines per 1000 capita were at 199, about a third of the telephone diffusion in Germany (see Exhibit 4). Therefore, there is a relatively unfavorable framework for telephone banking to become an effective substitute for a branch network in the Malaysian retail banking sector, but better conditions exist for online banking.

Banking sector and financial markets. In 2002, the banking sector of Malaysia comprised assets of approx. US$ 249 billion, which is more than the banking assets of any single one of the five GCC countries covered in the previous section. On a per capita level, however, Malaysia's banking sector is outshone by all GCC countries except for Saudi Arabia (see Exhibit 6). This is in line with the relatively smaller GDP per capita in Malaysia compared to the GCC countries, suggesting that there are fewer funds available for the financial sector. Similar in this to Bahrain, Malaysia disposes

---

221 Meesook et. al. (2001), p. 7-10.

222 Cf. Lewis and Algaoud (2001), p. 87 (footnote 12).

223 Cf. Central Intelligence Agency (2004).

224 Cf. ibid.

of a prominent offshore banking sector (Labuan International Offshore Financial Center – Labuan IOFC), which held total assets of approx. US$ 19 billion in 2002, making it significantly smaller than Bahrain's offshore banking sector, which stood at approx. US$ 59 billion that year.[225]

Islamic finance assets in Malaysia made up approx. US$ 18 billion in 2002 of total banking assets, leading to a market share of 7% (see Exhibit 6). On a per capita basis, Islamic finance assets are at the level of Saudi Arabia and thus significantly lower than in all other GCC countries covered in the previous section. Although the size of Islamic assets in the Labuan IOFC is not published, the small number of licensed Islamic financial institutions suggests that Islamic finance activities are minimal.[226] What is more, the Labuan Offshore Financial Services Authority (LOFSA) highlights the role of Labuan IOFC for the issuance of Islamic bonds and Islamic insurance, both of which are not reflected in terms of banking assets. LOFSA also acknowledges that it is only on the way of becoming an active center for Islamic banking and finance. The Islamic finance market therefore seems to be less mature or less successful than in most GCC countries. The lower market share may also be an indication of stronger competition of Islamic banks with conventional banks in Malaysia. As was evidenced above in the chapter on Islamic financial products, a good indication for this competition are the financial conditions of Islamic banks' financial instruments. Profits paid to investors by Bank Islam Malaysia – one of the largest Islamic banks in the country – are generally comparable to those of conventional banks, indicating the competitive relationship between the two segments.[227]

Malaysia's government is actively promoting Islamic finance as outlined in the Financial Sector Masterplan (FSMP), issued in 2001. The plan envisages an expansion of the Islamic finance sector to a 20% market share until 2011. One could expect, then, that the regulatory framework is particularly attractive for Islamic banks. Out of a total of 30 banking institutions belonging to 10 banking groups in 2002, 19 were involved in Islamic finance activities. Concentration in the industry is high with the top three companies combining 45% of total Islamic banking assets. However, the industry is less concentrated than in the GCC countries (see Exhibit 11). Most of the players in the market are Islamic windows of conventional banks, with only two full-fledged Islamic banks existing in 2002. The largest Islamic bank in Malaysia is the Islamic window of Maybank, followed by the full-fledged Islamic financial institutions Bank Islam and Bank Muamalat.

As is the case with the Islamic banks in the GCC area, many Malaysian Islamic banks report to be highly profitable, in particular compared internationally. In a subset of 12 Malaysian Islamic banks or Islamic windows covering three-quarters of total Islamic banking on-balance sheet assets, in 2002 the cost-income ratio ranged between 5% and 89%, return on assets between 0.3% and 3%, and return on equity between 5%

[225] Cf. Labuan Offshore Financial Services Authority Annual Report, BMA Annual Report.

[226] In 2002, there were three Islamic investment banks and two full-fledged Islamic banks out of a total of 54 licensed banks. Cf. Labuan Offshore Financial Services Authority Annual Report.

[227] Lewis and Algaoud (2001), p. 138.

and 36% (see Exhibit 12). These figures, however, have to be regarded with caution: it is striking that the cost income ratio of the only full-fledged Islamic banks in the selection – Bank Islam and Bank Muamalat – are much higher than the ratio of most Islamic windows, which are at exceptionally low levels. In the same vein, their return on equity is much lower than the one of most Islamic windows. A potential reason for this are accounting practices, which may give a lot of leeway to conventional banks as to the allocation of cost items and equity to their Islamic windows.

Exhibit 11: Major Islamic finance institutions in Malaysia

Company	Assets (2002; US$ millions)	Share of total Malaysian Islamic banking assets (%)
Maybank - Islamic window	3,433	19%
Bank Islam	3,154	17%
Bank Muamalat	1,706	9%
Public Bank - Islamic window	1,235	7%
RHB Bank - Islamic window	1,117	6%
Affin Bank - Islamic window	1,110	6%
Hong Leong Bank - window	921	5%
EON Bank - Islamic window	745	4%
AmBank - Islamic window	419	2%
OCBC Bank - Islamic window	285	2%
Southern Bank - Islamic	198	1%
Alliance Bank - Islamic window	188	1%

Source: Annual reports, BNM

Similarly to the Islamic banks in the GCC countries, Islamic banks in Malaysia offer a broad array of services, targeting all kinds of customer segments. Both the full-fledged Islamic banks as well as the Islamic windows generally are universal banks, engaged strongly in both retail and corporate banking activities. The Islamic financial institutions in Malaysia rely less than their counterparts in the GCC area on *murabaha* and similar instruments as a mode of financing. They only make up 32% of total assets in the consolidated balance sheet of Islamic banks in Malaysia (see Exhibit 9). Apart from that, investment in securities with a share of 27% and *ijara* with a share of 13% of total assets are the next most important financing schemes. The use of all other Islamic financial instruments is limited. On the liabilities and shareholders equity side, investment accounts are the dominating item and current accounts used to a very limited extent only, which is in stark contrast to the situation in the GCC countries.

Exhibit 12: Profitability indicators for selected Malaysian finance institutions

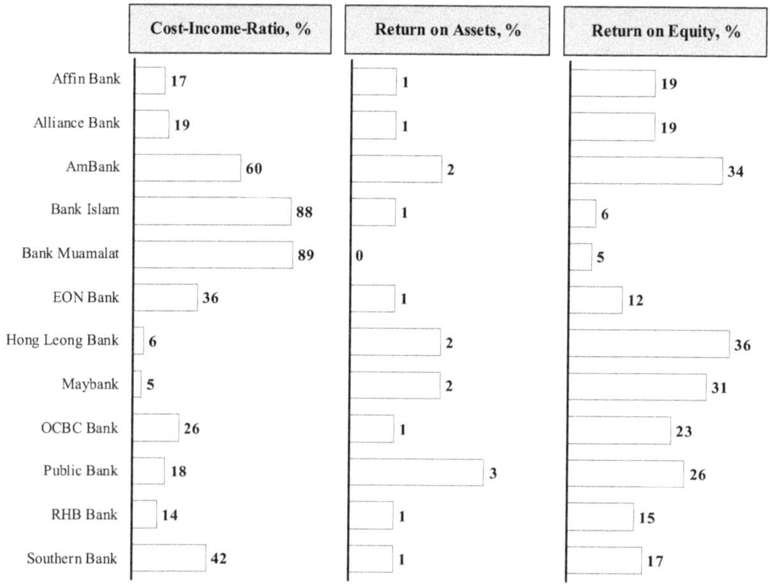

Note: Figures always relate to their Islamic finance activities
Source: Annual reports 2002

Regulatory environment. According to the IMF, Malaysia has well-developed legal and regulatory frameworks, that helped facilitate the recovery process of the country after the two recent recessions in 1997-1998 and in 2001.[228] Compared to other Asian countries, the IMF recognizes Malaysia's relatively strong banking culture and accounting and prudential supervision systems. Malaysia's tight control over the banking system – use of a CAMEL-based approach, public disclosure requirements, on-site examinations, and other measures – was acknowledged in the wake of the 1997-1998 Asian crisis already.[229] In 2004, the IMF again honored Malaysia's significant progress in reforming the financial sector, leading to improved bank soundness.[230] The current supervisory activities of Bank Negara Malaysia (BNM), Malaysia's central bank, focus on promotion of the stability of the banking system and the evolving financial industry, using a risk-based supervisory approach. "The overall thrust of this approach is to identify and assess key risks encountered by

228 Cf. http://www.imf.org/external/np/sec/pn/2004/pn0427.htm; Meesook et. al. (2001), p. 7; International Monetary Fund (2000), p. 282-283; International Monetary Fund (1999), p. 71-72.

229 IMF (1999), p. 67-71.

230 http://www.imf.org/external/np/sec/pn/2004/pn0427.htm

banking institutions and their capacity to manage these risks."[231] Besides credit risk, financial institutions' market and operational risk management practices, corporate governance practices, anti-money laundering measures, and IT infrastructure integrity are supervised.[232] BNM is also working on meeting international best practices while implementing the New Basel Capital Accord. It is important to note in this context that Malaysia is a member of the WTO. Therefore, it is expected to open its banking sectors to foreign competition, although some restrictions apply for the time being: In 2001, the Bank Negara Malaysia blocked competition from new foreign banks until after 2007. Moreover, foreign participation in commercial banking is limited to 30 percent of equity in any single institution.[233]

Similar in this to the majority of the GCC countries, Malaysia has an Islamic banking law in place, which was reviewed in 2003. In the course of that year, a number of measures was introduced to improve the legal and regulatory framework of Islamic banking in Malaysia. The Sharia Advisory Council at BNM has become the sole authority to decide on Sharia matters on Islamic banking and finance falling under the purview of BNM, the framework for the computation of the rate of return in Islamic banking operations was enhanced, and guidelines describing minimum requirements of the financial statements of Islamic banks issued.[234] Consequent to the first measure, a rationalization of the role of individual Islamic banks' Sharia boards was announced and guidelines on their role, scope of duties and responsibilities were issued in December 2004.[235] As was outlined above already, rules concerning Islamic financial products in Malaysia are more liberal than in the GCC countries, allowing for a wider product spectrum.

2.3 Empirical Literature Review

Factors influencing company performance have attracted some attention in empirical research – markedly so in the strategic management literature, and to a lesser degree also in the Islamic finance literature. This section presents major empirical studies dealing with influencing factors on company performance. It starts with a review of general studies that analyze the importance of the various factors brought forward in strategic management theories, followed by the depiction of Islamic finance studies, which so far adopted economic rather than strategic management approaches.

---

231 BNM Annual report 2003, p. 119.

232 Ibid., p. 119-121.

233 Heritage Foundation (2005)

234 BNM Annual report 2003., p. 146-147.

235 BNM Annual report 2004, p. 163-164. Among the duties and responsibilities of the Sharia boards are to advise the board of directors on Shariah matters on the bank's business operations to ensure that they comply with Shariah principles at all times, to endorse the Shariah Compliance Manuals, and to endorse and validate relevant documentations.

2.3.1 General Studies

Over the past 20 years, a number of studies has investigated the interrelation of firm performance and various influencing factors developed in the strategic management literature (see Exhibit 13). Among those influencing factors generally are firm effects, corporate effects, and industry effects, or a selection of these three.[236] So far, the empirical research has reported contradictory findings and remains inconclusive.

In his seminal paper, Schmalensee finds that industry effects are the major factor explaining firm performance, while market-share effects are negligible, and corporate effects even non-existent. However, this diagnosis is not corroborated by later research. In their studies, Brush et. al., and Ruefli and Wiggins observe that there is a sizable corporate effect, which moreover is a better predictor of business performance than industry factors. Other researchers – namely Rumelt, Mehra, and Spanos et. al. – find that firm effects are more important in predicting firm performance than industry factors, and that resource-based strategic groups yield better results in explaining intraindustry performance variations than market-based strategic groups. They do acknowledge, however, that industry effects exist. This assertion is strongly supported in studies by Buzzell and Gale[237], McGahan and Porter, and Spanos and Lioukas: they observe that both industry and firm effects are important in explaining firm performance. McGahan and Porter also find large differences in the importance of these effects across industries. Mauri and Michaels, and Hawawini et. al. present a more differentiated view of industry and firm effects in their studies. Mauri and Michaels observe that firm effects are more important than industry effects in explaining firm performance, yet industry effects are the major influence on core strategies on R&D and advertising. Finally, Hawawini et. al. find that firm-specific assets matter more than industry factors for value leaders and losers, while the reverse is true for the vast majority of firms.

Most of the studies employ a variance decomposition methodology and do not further break down the independent variables. Moreover, most do not offer causal or structural explanations for profitability differences across industries, corporations, or business units, but simply affirm differences in return associated with these categories. Spanos and Lioukas are the most notable exception. In their study, they develop a comprehensive composite model to test the causal logic of rent generation: they distinguish firm assets effects, strategy effects, and industry effects, which directly and indirectly determine market performance and profitability as indicators for a firm's performance. Except for dimensions of industry structure, all constructs are made up by multiple items. As noted above, their study confirms on the one hand that firm performance depends on direct and indirect industry effects – Porter's five

[236] Corporate effects are those attributable to the membership of a firm in a corporate group.

[237] Buzzell and Gale have based their study on the PIMS (Profit Impact of Market Strategies) research program, which was initiated in 1972 already. It reflects their views about the most important lessons to be drawn from the PIMS-based research. PIMS was probably the first large-scale empirical analysis of firm performance and its influencing factors, which according to the PIMS competitive strategy paradigm are market structure, competitive position, and strategy and tactics.

forces; on the other hand that it depends on direct and indirect effects stemming from available resources and capabilities – namely organizational and managerial, marketing, and technical firm assets.

Exhibit 13: Overview of important general studies

Author(s)	Sample	Independent Variable(s)	Dependent Variable(s)	Key Findings
Spanos et. al. (2004)	928 Greek firms in time period 1995-96	▪ Industry variables ▪ Firm strategy variables ▪ Industry controls ▪ Firm controls	Firm performance	While both firm and industry factors significantly contribute to firm profitability, firm-specific factors are more important. Hybrid strategies yield better performance results than pure ones.
Hawawini et. al. (2003)	562 firms across 55 industry classifications over a 10 year period	▪ Firm effects ▪ Industry effects ▪ Year effects ▪ Industry-year effects	Firm performance	Firm-specific assets matter more than industry factors for value leaders and loser. To the vast majority of firms, industry effects are more important than firm-specific factors.
Ruefli and Wiggins (2003)	Up to 5964 business units in time period 1980-1996	▪ Industry effects ▪ Corporate effects	Business performance	Corporate factors are a better predictor of business performance than industry factors.
Spanos and Lioukas (2001)	147 Greek firms	▪ Firm assets ▪ Strategy ▪ Industry forces	▪ Market performance ▪ Profitability	Both industry and firm assets together with strategic activities contribute to firm success.
		▪ Firm assets	▪ Strategy	
		▪ Strategy	▪ Industry forces	
Brush et. al. (1999)	535 three-segments corporations and 173 four-segments corporations for time period 1986-1995	▪ Corporate ROA ▪ Industry ROA	Segment ROA	There is a sizeable corporate effect on business segment performance, which appears to be greater than the industry effect.
Mauri and Michaels (1998)	264 single-business companies using 5- and 15-year periods	▪ Firm effects ▪ Industry effects	▪ R&D intensity ▪ Advertising intensity ▪ ROA	Firm effects are more important than industry effects on firm performance, but not on core strategies.

Exhibit 13 (continued): Overview of important general studies

Author(s)	Sample	Independent Variable(s)	Dependent Variable(s)	Key Findings
McGahan and Porter (1997)	5196 business segments over a 14 year period	▪ Year effects ▪ Industry effects ▪ Corporate-parent effects ▪ Business-specific effects	Business segment performance	There are important industry and business-specific effects on business segment performance. Moreover, there are large differences in the importance of these effects across industries.
Mehra (1996)	45 US bank holding companies	▪ Market-based strategic groups ▪ Resource-based strategic groups	Firm performance	Resource-based strategic groups yield better results in explaining intraindustry performance variations than market-based strategic groups.
Rumelt (1991)	Sample A: 1774 business units for time period 1974-76 Sample B: 2810 business units for same time period	▪ Industry effects ▪ Corporate effects ▪ Year effects ▪ Industry-year effects ▪ Business-unit effects	Firm performance	There are significant business-unit effects that strongly outweigh industry and corporate membership as predictors of profitability.
Buzzell and Gale (1987)	Nearly 3000 business units for periods ranging from 2 to 12 years	▪ Market structure ▪ Competitive position ▪ Strategy	Firm performance	Both industry and firm assets together with strategic activities influence firm success.
Schmalensee (1985)	1775 business units in 1975	▪ Industry effects ▪ Corporate effects ▪ Market-share effects	Firm performance	Industry effects are the major factor explaining firm and industry performance, market-share effects are negligible, corporate effects non-existent.

2.3.2 Islamic Finance Studies

The determining factors of firm performance in Islamic finance have received scant quantitative empirical study, despite the relatively big number of case studies about Islamic banks.[238] In an early exploratory study, Nienhaus reviews the performance of

[238] This observation holds also true when widening the scope and looking at empirical studies about the performance of Islamic banks without analysis of its determining factors. Examples are Nienhaus

Islamic banks in "(...) an attempt to summarize facts and figures (...) and to give a preliminary assessment of notable trends and cases."[239] While he finds that "(...) Islamic banking can be operational and profitable"[240] he does not explain the influencing factors of Islamic banks' performance, and does not apply any statistical model. Later studies close this research gap, but use economic rather than strategic management approaches to identify the determining factors of Islamic bank performance (see Exhibit 14).

Exhibit 14: Overview of important Islamic finance studies

Author(s)	Sample	Independent Variable(s)	Dependent Variable(s)	Key Findings
Hassan and Bashir (2003)	Up to 39 banks for time period 1994-2001	Bank characteristics: ▪ Fund source management ▪ Fund use management ▪ Leverage ▪ Liquidity External factors: ▪ Macroeconomic environment ▪ Financial market structure ▪ Taxation	Bank performance	Bank performance is impacted by capital and loan ratios, regulatory tax factors, the financial market structure, and the macroeconomic environment.
Bashir (2000)	14 banks for time period 1993-1998	▪ Bank characteristics ▪ Macroeconomic indicators ▪ Taxation indicators ▪ Financial structure indicators	Bank performance	Bank performance is positively impacted by capital and loan ratios, customer and short-term funding, ratio of non-profit earning assets, overhead, foreign ownership, and favorable macroeconomic environment. It is negatively impacted by taxes.
Haron (1996)	14 banks for time period 1984-1994	▪ Competition ▪ Market share ▪ Scarcity of capital ▪ Money supply ▪ Inflation ▪ Bank size	Bank performance	Bank performance is positively impacted by interest rate, inflation, and size, negatively by market share, and money supply. Competition has no significant impact.

(1988), Hassoune (2002), Brown (2003). Nienhaus' study will be presented above, as it is one of the earliest studies addressing Islamic bank performance.

239 Nienhaus (1988), p. 129.

240 Ibid., p. 165.

Haron finds that bank performance is positively impacted by the prevailing interest rate, inflation, and size, and negatively impacted by market share, and money supply. In his study, competition has no significant impact. A study by Bashir identifies various factors related to bank characteristics, macroeconomic indicators, taxation indicators, and financial structure indicators, which impact the performance of Islamic banks. In particular, high returns are partly explained by a high ratio of non-profit earning assets, which somehow supports the claim presented earlier that high bank profitability can partly be accounted for by a high share of current accounts in customer deposits. Hassan and Bashir test different independent variables and find that capital and loan ratios, regulatory tax factors, the financial structure, and the macroeconomic environment impact bank performance. Although all three studies draw only to a limited extent on the strategic management literature, they do include factors such as competition or market structure. Hassan and Bashir even distinguish bank characteristics and external factors – including market structure – as the major building blocks of the independent variables, which is somehow in analogy to firm and industry effects in the strategic management research.

2.4 Conceptual Model and Hypotheses

Drawing on the previous expositions of Islamic finance, strategic management theories, and empirical research on factors influencing company performance, this section develops a conceptual model and hypotheses about strategic management in Islamic finance. It starts with an overview of the model, depicting its various building blocks. Next, detailed hypotheses regarding the building blocks of the model and their interrelation will be presented. Finally, a summary will complement the exposition. The intended purpose of this model and its subsequent empirical analysis is twofold: on the one hand, general theoretical propositions of the strategic management literature shall be tested; on the other hand, the concrete Islamic finance-specific manifestations of company strategy and performance and its various influencing factors shall be examined.

2.4.1 Overview

The conceptual model is composed of external factors, internal factors, and company strategies as explanatory factors, and company performance as *explanandum* (see Exhibit 15).

As has been shown in the chapter on strategic management theories, the market-based view and the resource-based view offer rivaling explanations for variations in company performance. Although in the case of both approaches, the line of argument includes company strategy as a relay in between external factors and internal factors, respectively, and company performance, it can be argued that external and internal factors also have a direct impact on company performance. All else being equal, more favorable external factors – which make an industry or market segment more attractive – can lead to higher returns for the companies operating in this industry as compared to others. As was shown above, this is also corroborated by some empirical studies. Moreover, better endowment with resources and capabilities may also have a direct influence on company performance, as in the case of special manufacturing capabilities leading to a relatively low cost position. Again, as discussed in a previous chapter, this is supported by some empirical research. Moreover, as was detailed in the section on strategic management theories, both regard company strategies as an explanatory element, without however thoroughly explaining the causal relationship between an actual set of external or internal factors, respectively, and the right choice of company strategies. Therefore, all three factors will be scrutinized in the empirical study. While the expected impact of the three explanatory factors on Islamic bank performance will be detailed in the next section, the building blocks themselves are illuminated in the following, starting with external factors.

Exhibit 15: Conceptual model

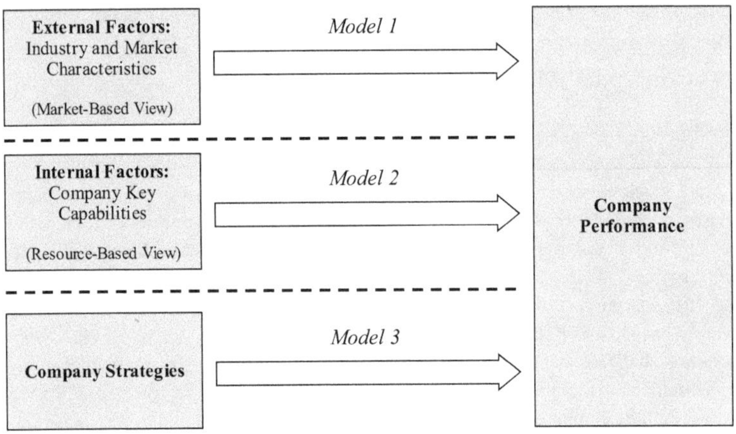

External factors comprise the global environment and the industry structure (see Exhibit 16). As outlined in chapter 2.1, the former includes a company's macro-economic, socio-cultural, technological, and political/legal environment. For reasons of complexity reduction, this study will focus on (re)financing opportunities as a proxy for the macro-economic environment, and on the regulatory framework. Due to the inadequate actual state of Islamic secondary, money, and interbanking markets as well as the lack of uniformity in regulatory and supervisory issues in Islamic finance – which was depicted in chapter 2.2.3 – this seems to be of particular importance for the Islamic finance industry. The latter mainly consists of Porter's five forces: the threat of new entrants, the power of suppliers, competition, the power of customers, and the threat of substitutes, with one refinement: the power of suppliers has been decomposed into power of HR suppliers and power of technology suppliers, as both are the major inputs for banking services.

Exhibit 16: External factors

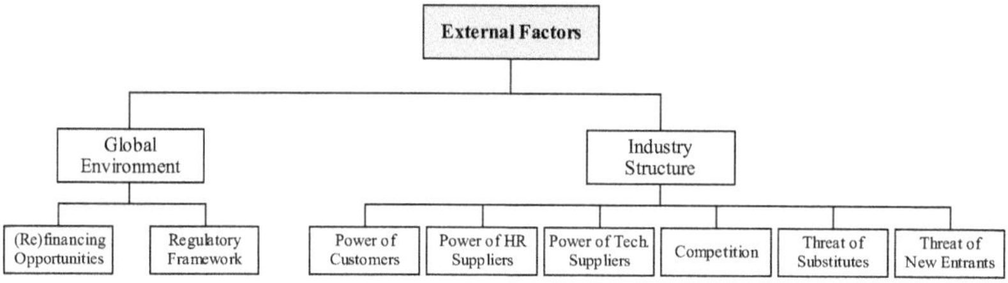

While the decomposition of the external factors is rather straightforward and largely undisputed in theory, internal factors – core competencies of the company – are harder to postulate because of their intangible character.[241] Moreover, core competencies that offer potential competitive advantages need to be distinguished from basic competencies, which are merely prerequisites for being active within an industry. However, this distinction cannot easily be predicted, but boils down to an empirical question. As was demonstrated in the section on strategic management theories, internal factors can be subdivided into market-access core competencies, functionality-related core competencies, and integrity-related core competencies. These categories encompass further refinements brought forward in the theoretical and empirical literature.[242] Two internal factors – reputation as Islamic company and Sharia board efficiency and effectiveness – that can be attributed to market-access core competencies and functionality-related core competencies, respectively, have been singled out for analytical purposes. On the one hand, Western banks active in Islamic finance might have a comparative disadvantage concerning the reputation as Islamic company. On the other hand, as Sharia boards might have considerable power on operational decisions of Islamic banks, their influence merits a closer look.

Exhibit 17: Internal factors

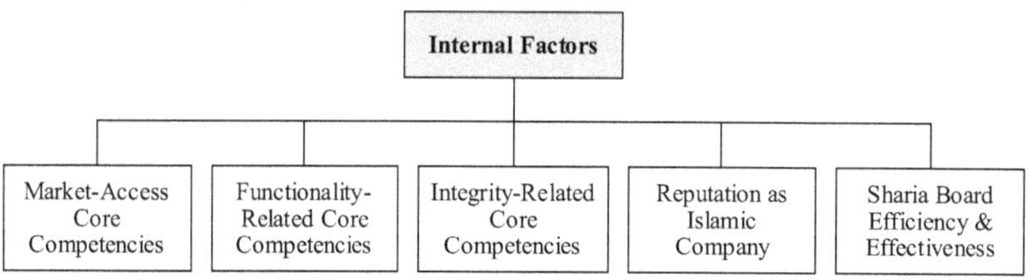

---

[241] Cf. chapter 2.1

[242] Cf. Mehra (1996), p. 311-312, Knaese (1996), p. 82-91, Delley (2001), p. 84-147, Spanos and Lioukas (2001), p. 915. These refinements will be the basis for the subsequent operationalisation of these constructs.

Porter's set of generic strategies has been further refined for use in this study. First, as is frequently done in empirical research, differentiation is subdivided even more: we distinguish product differentiation and marketing and sales differentiation.[243] Second, we differentiate price leadership and cost leadership. Porter's generic cost leadership strategy postulates that the company pursuing it sets its prices at levels, which are customary in the particular market.[244] Therefore, price leadership – i.e. a strategy where a company sets its prices at substantially lower levels than customary in the market – needs to be distinguished. Third, emulation of conventional products and emphasis on gaining and maintaining a reputation as an Islamic company have been added for analytical purposes. On the one hand, as Islamic banks are in competition with conventional banks, one can expect that they be under pressure to be at par with their service offerings. On the other hand, as some Islamic banks are subsidiaries or departments of conventional banks, full-fledged Islamic banks might be inclined to underscore their Islamic character.

Exhibit 18: Company strategies

Company performance is subdivided into market share, profitability, and customer loyalty, which can all be considered to be fundamental elements of a company's success. The importance of market share is reflected in its use for the evaluation of corporate strategies, profitability is an important item for shareholder value, and there is a vast body of literature about customer loyalty as essential objective in strategic management[245]. Moreover, a loose relationship between these three performance indicators can be established: customer loyalty is one of the prerequisites for both maintenance and growth of market share, especially in saturated markets. Market share, in turn, is often seen as one of the prerequisites for profitability.[246]

[243] Cf. Spanos and Lioukas (2001), Gerbach (2002).
[244] Porter (1986), p. 154-156.
[245] Cf. Welge and Al-Laham (1999), p. 119-182.
[246] Cf. Hinterhuber et.al. (1997), p. 7.

Exhibit 19: Company performance

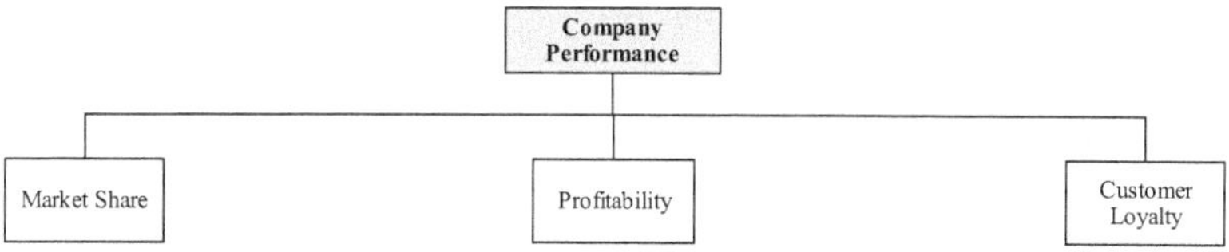

2.4.2 Hypotheses

The interrelation of the building blocks of the conceptual model depicted above will be detailed in the following. Based on the observations made in the analytical framework section, for each of the three potential explanatory factors, expected observations and dependencies will be presented. As has been done in the section on current practices in Islamic finance, this will be done with special focus on Islamic banks in the GCC and Malaysia, as these are the most important markets for profit-oriented, free-market Islamic financial institutions.

2.4.2.1 Model 1: Impact of External Factors on Performance

In the conceptual model, external factors are made up of the global environment and the industry structure. While the former largely depends on the geographical market segments looked at, the latter can additionally depend on the product and customer segments of the industry.

Global environment. In view of the macro-economic, regulatory and legal differences described above between the GCC area and Malaysia, and even across GCC countries, the two global environment factors taken into consideration – (re)financing opportunities and regulatory framework – are expected to differ in the geographic markets covered. As outlined in chapter 2.2.3, GDP per capita – which can be regarded as an indicator for economic development – varies substantially across the GCC countries covered and Malaysia. Moreover, as was explained, there are substantial differences in the industrial structure of all countries considered. Therefore, one would expect differences in the financing opportunities. Besides, the development of viable secondary, money, and interbanking markets remains a challenge for the Islamic finance industry globally, as was argued in chapter 2.2.3.2. However, the issue is tackled unevenly across the countries considered – marked differences exist in particular between Malaysia, where liquidity and secondary markets are quite well developed, and the GCC countries, where this is not the case. As for the regulatory framework and standardization issues, the lack of uniformity in accounting standards, Sharia assurance, and product standards affecting all countries has been evidenced in chapter 2.2.3. As was demonstrated, notable differences exist in particular between the GCC countries and Malaysia, with more liberal rules in the latter, and generally more constraints in the former. Consequently, given the differences of the global environment, which can be more or less favorable for the operations of Islamic banks, the global environment is expected to have an impact on Islamic bank performance.

Industry structure. As Islamic finance is a single industry, and already a niche segment within the wider realm of finance, one can expect that no differences exist in the individual factors – the refined set of Porter's forces. This view is corroborated if one takes a closer look at the occurrence of the forces in the case of Islamic banks in the GCC countries and Malaysia. As for the bargaining power of customers, Islamic banks in the GCC (at least the big ones) and Malaysia typically target a broad spectrum of customers, as was evidenced in chapter 2.2.3 above: corporate clients ranging from small to large companies, and private clients ranging from mass customers to high net worth individuals. These clients generally have a choice of several potential suppliers. Consequently, their bargaining power is expected to be largely the same across the industry. Concerning HR suppliers, both the Islamic banks in the GCC countries and Malaysia will face a resembling bargaining power, as the educational level as well as the unemployment rate are at largely similar levels, despite the fact that the expatriate workforce alleviates the scarcity of skilled labor in the GCC countries. In the same vein, the power of technology – mostly IT – suppliers is expected to be similar, as these suppliers are global players, which are present in all geographical markets concerned. As for competition, the Islamic finance industry in both the GCC countries and Malaysia is highly concentrated, even though to a bit lesser extent in the latter than the former. Therefore, Islamic banks will face a resembling degree of competition in both geographic areas. Likewise, the threat of substitutes is expected to be similar across the GCC countries and Malaysia, as conventional banks are active in all markets considered, which are typically regarded as potential competitors. Finally, the threat of new entrants will be largely similar across the GCC countries and Malaysia. All countries covered are in the process of opening up their financial markets, as all are members of the WTO with the exception of Saudi Arabia, which is an observer government. For the time being, however, some restrictions apply in all countries, as was shown in chapter 2.2.3 above. Consequently, no impact of the industry structure on Islamic bank performance is expected. This also implies that there are no market-based strategic groups in Islamic finance, as Islamic financial institutions already are a strategic group within the greater realm of finance.

All things together, the hypotheses about external factors can be summarized as follows:

Proposition 1: *External factors have an uneven impact on Islamic bank performance. While the industry structure does not explain intra-industry performance differences in Islamic finance, a more favorable global environment leads to better performance.*

2.4.2.2 Model 2: Impact of Internal Factors on Performance

Given the firm-specific development of resources and core competencies, differences in the endowment with internal factors across companies can be expected. Nevertheless, there can be groups of firms deploying resembling configurations of strategic resource bundles because of similar backgrounds or simply due to benchmarking activities. One potential group criterion for Islamic financial institutions is the organizational background of the bank: whether it belongs to a conventional bank or not, and, in the former case, where the corporate headquarters are located. This leads to three different groups: Islamic subsidiaries of conventional banks whose corporate headquarters are located in the West, Islamic subsidiaries of conventional banks whose corporate headquarters are located in the GCC countries or Malaysia, and Islamic banks that are either stand-alone or belong to another Islamic bank.[247] Due to the complexity of core competencies and their underlying components, it is hard to predict any specific strategic groups. Yet, as will be argued broadly along the lines of the above-mentioned group criterion for each individual internal factor, it is possible to highlight potential differences in core competencies, which can in turn lead to differences in the banks' performance.

Market-access core competencies. The market-access core competencies of Islamic banks are expected to vary considerably. For example, brand image and reputation might vary substantially across Islamic financial institutions. Subsidiaries of Western conventional banks might come off well in the reputation as a financial services provider, but might lag behind in the reputation as an Islamic company or the image of their Sharia board, while the reverse might be true for full-fledged Islamic finance companies without affiliation to a conventional bank. Another example is the access to and control of distribution channels, such as branch networks, ATM networks, Internet banking, and call centers. Here, subsidiaries of Western conventional banks might shy away from establishing their own branch and ATM networks and rather rely on Internet banking and call centers in those countries which dispose of a modern communication infrastructure, while other Islamic banks might be well endowed with branches and ATMs. Consequently, market-access core competencies should have an impact on Islamic bank performance.

Functionality-related core competencies. An example of an area where these competencies are relevant is product development. It can be argued that Western banks with their broad expertise in financial engineering are well positioned in this area. Yet, Malaysian Islamic financial institutions, which are well reputed for being innovators in the Islamic finance industry, might even outperform their Western competitors. Finally, GCC Islamic banks, which were among the first active in the market, might have a competitive edge due to their knowledge of market

---

[247] This rather odd segmentation is preferable over a simple geographic segmentation (e.g. location of corporate headquarters: West, GCC country, Malaysia), as the latter would attribute several Islamic banks belonging to the Geneva-based Dar al-Maal al-Islami Trust (DMI) to Western banks, even though they could rather be seen as GCC banks, given the origin of DMI's owner and the focus of their operations.

requirements. Another area is transaction processing. It can be argued that Western banks with their broad technological expertise are well positioned in this field. Yet, information technology, which is a cornerstone of transaction processing, is equally accessible to GCC and Malaysian Islamic banks, potentially leading to them possessing the same capabilities as their Western competitors. Yet another is supporting processes. This rather broad area encompasses various capabilities and competencies, such as HR processes, risk management capabilities, or knowledge and data management. It can be argued that Islamic subsidiaries of Western banks with their extensive know-how in conventional banking might come off particularly well in all those competencies, which are not Islamic finance-specific. As a consequence of all having been said, functionality-related core competencies should have an impact on Islamic bank performance.

Integrity-related core competencies. These competencies are made up of areas such as co-operation, management quality, and firm culture. An example of co-operation is the easiness of communication across hierarchies, which may depend on the cultural background of the employees or management. Regarding management quality, knowledge and skills of managers as well as their quality of work clearly depends on various factors, such as their educational background, their talent, or their experience. Rigorous recruitment and promotion policies as well as formal, regular evaluations can lead to the workforce of a firm meeting certain unified standards. It seems obvious that the factors determining management quality can vary across companies. The way that people interact within a company, and the attitude of the company towards the achievements of its employees are examples of firm culture. It can be argued that differences in firm culture exist across companies due to various reasons such as firm size (small firms may be more "personal" than large, hierarchical companies), type of management (owner as CEO vs. an employed CEO), and the like. Hence, integrity-related core competencies should have an impact on Islamic bank performance.

Reputation as Islamic company. As has been argued before, Islamic subsidiaries of conventional banks might have a smaller reputation as Islamic company than full-fledged Islamic finance companies without affiliation to a conventional bank. As the Islamic character of the financial service is a unique selling proposition of an Islamic bank, this might have an effect on the image of the bank. Consequently, it is expected that it also has an impact on Islamic bank performance.

Sharia board efficiency and effectiveness. As has been argued before, Sharia boards might have considerable power on operational decisions of Islamic banks. At the same time, there are considerable differences in the extent of Sharia board functions and opinions voiced. Hence, it is expected that Sharia board efficiency and effectiveness has an impact on Islamic bank performance.

All of the above leads to the following propositions:

Proposition 2: *Internal factors have an impact on Islamic bank performance. Better endowment with resources and capabilities (core competencies) leads to better performance.*

Proposition 3: *Company performance depends on the adherence to resource-based strategic groups with the following group criterion: Islamic subsidiaries of conventional banks whose corporate headquarters are located in the West, Islamic subsidiaries of conventional banks whose corporate headquarters are located in the GCC countries or Malaysia, and Islamic banks that are either stand-alone or belong to another Islamic bank*

2.4.2.3 Model 3: Impact of Company Strategies on Performance

As strategy is a long-term oriented behavior to gain competitive advantage[248], it seems consequential to assume that company performance also depends on company strategies.

Cost leadership. As was presented before, the cost leadership strategy is often viewed as less relevant for the banking industry than the differentiation strategy. Moreover, it also implies that there is a single company in the industry pursuing it instead of a large group of companies. As we see no reason why this should be different for the Islamic finance industry, we expect no correlation between the cost leadership strategy and bank performance.

Price leadership. As price leadership implies an efficient application of a cost leadership strategy, the same arguments brought forward above apply. Moreover, prices can also be used as a signaling instrument. As banking services can be qualified as experience goods, firms use high prices to signal the quality of their goods and services.[249] Consequently, no correlation or even a negative correlation between the price leadership strategy and bank performance is expected.

Product differentiation. Looking at the overall banking industry, product differentiation lies at the heart of Islamic finance, as the supply of non-conventional finance products defines this niche market. It can be argued, however, that product differentiation is also used to compete within the Islamic finance industry. First, differentiation strategies are often viewed as highly relevant for the banking industry, as was presented before. Second, given the restrictions set by the precepts of the Sharia, Islamic banks are under particular pressure to develop ingenious products, which meet the economic requirements of investors and capital seekers. Therefore, a

---

248 Cf. chapter 2.1

249 Tirole (1995), p. 111.

positive correlation between the product differentiation strategy and bank performance is expected.

Marketing and sales differentiation. Marketing and sales is another area of differentiation, which is often viewed as highly relevant for the banking industry. This can affect the bank's customer orientation, distribution strategy, or brand and image. As an effective customer interaction is a basic requirement for all banking services, this area appears to be an obvious playing field for differentiation efforts. Moreover, the arguments brought forward above concerning market-access core competencies can analogically be applied for marketing and sales differentiation strategies. Therefore, we expect that there is a positive correlation between the marketing and sales differentiation strategy and bank performance.

Focus. As was argued above, the question of what correlation to expect between the use of niche strategies and financial performance depends on the characteristics of the industry. It was shown that the Islamic finance industry in the GCC countries and Malaysia is rather strongly concentrated, with a small number of banks dominating the market. Therefore, a positive correlation is expected, as most Islamic banks should – as rational entities – be focusing on lucrative niches within Islamic finance. However, this relation is expected for profitability and customer loyalty as performance indicators only, as a niche will by definition only represent a small share of the market.

Emulation of conventional products. Islamic banks are in competition with conventional banks. Therefore, one can expect that they need to be at par with conventional banks' service offerings and have an incentive to emulate the financial conditions of conventional products. However, as this applies to all Islamic banks present in the market place, this seems to be a necessary, but not a sufficient condition for bank performance. Therefore, no impact of this strategy on bank performance is expected.

Reputation as Islamic company. As there are subsidiaries of conventional banks as well as full-fledged Islamic banks without affiliation to a conventional bank present in the Islamic finance industry, the Islamic character of the bank might be an important factor of the buying decision of customers. If this is so, good performance might partly be attributed to a strategy, which puts an emphasis on building reputation as an Islamic company. Consequently, a positive relation between this strategy and bank performance is expected.

All taken together, we posit the following:

Proposition 4: *Company strategies have an uneven impact on Islamic bank performance. While no correlation is expected between cost leadership strategy, price leadership strategy, and emulation of conventional products on bank performance, a positive correlation is expected between product differentiation strategy, marketing and sales differentiation strategy, focus strategy, as well as reputation as Islamic company and Islamic bank performance.*

2.4.3 Summary

As was shown above in the section on strategic management approaches, the market-based view and the resource-based view can be seen as complementary in explaining the causal logic of companies' income generation. Consequently, across various industries, both external and internal factors are expected to have an influence on company performance. Within a single industry, however, external factors related to the industry structure are largely the same for all companies. Consequently, variations in performance should not be attributable to such external factors, but only to the remaining explanatory elements. From a theoretical perspective, the exact interrelation between – on the one hand – a combination of external and internal factors, and – on the other hand – the selection of individual strategies, remains unresolved: in the literature, mainly heuristics supporting the strategy selection process are discussed. This is especially true for emerging, strongly growing industries such as the Islamic finance industry, where industry rules are in the course of formation. Despite the vagueness left by theoretical considerations about the "right" set of strategies under specific external and internal circumstances, it can be expected that firms acting in the same industry will adopt different company strategies. This is first suggested by conventional wisdom and supported by everyday observations across a wide array of industries. Moreover, it can also be assumed on theoretical grounds, as firms will most likely differ in internal factors, which in turn should influence the strategies chosen. Moreover, both the market-based view and the resource-based view predict a causal relationship between company strategies and company performance. As has been demonstrated for the case of Islamic finance, not all strategies are expected to impact company performance. On the one hand, there are statistical reasons for this: provided that companies are acting rationally, a correlation will not be established if a strategy can only be deployed by a single company. On the other hand, the pursuance of a strategy is sometimes expected to be a necessary, but not a sufficient condition for bank performance.

3 Empirical Study

This chapter draws on the previously developed analytical framework for the empirical analysis of strategic management and competitive strategy in Islamic finance. It is organized in two sections. First, the research methodology is described. Then, the research findings derived from the empirical analysis of the conceptual model and hypotheses presented above are discussed.

3.1 Research Methodology

In the following, the research methodology is presented. This section will give special emphasis to the exposition of data measurement, as the operationalisation of theoretical constructs is a crucial step for the subsequent empirical analysis of the links between them. Before that, data collection and sampling as well as the data analysis methods will be detailed.

3.1.1 Data Collection and Sampling

3.1.1.1 Data Collection Tool

As data collection tool, a standardized questionnaire that was faxed or emailed to the potential participants was developed.[250] The questionnaire contains four sections:

- **Industry and market environment:** In this section, respondents were asked to select first the geographical focus of their company and then to indicate their evaluation of a number of factors and trends affecting the Islamic finance industry in that geographic area. In detail, they were asked to assess metatrends of the industry (disintermediation, deregulation, etc.); the attractiveness of various market segments as well as the major reasons for that; the relative position of Islamic banks as compared to conventional banks; the industry forces (Porter's five forces) and selected other external global environment factors; and potential measures to compete effectively against conventional banks.

- **Company key characteristics:** Here, respondents were asked first to provide general information about the firm, such as the organizational set-up (full-fledged Islamic banks vs. Islamic window of conventional bank); the scope of banking activities (corporate and government financing, personal financing, etc.); the ownership structure; the usage of management tools; the principal company goals (maximizing the shareholder value, promoting social welfare, etc.); customer segments served; information on their Sharia board (number of people, scope of functions, etc.); and financials (balance sheet, sources of income). In addition to that, they were asked to assess their company's strength relative to competition with regard to several internal factors such as organization structure and communication, management quality, firm culture, marketing and sales, transaction processing, as well as steering and supporting functions.

- **Strategy:** Respondents were asked first about their company's preferred growth strategy, and the usage of external resources. The major part of this section, however, calls for a detailed assessment of the strategies used by the respondent's company to effectively compete in the market place, such as price leadership, cost leadership, product differentiation, or marketing and sales differentiation.
- **Performance data:** In the last section respondents were asked to provide both quantitative and qualitative performance data. The former comprises market share; economic value created (i.e. net operating profit after tax minus equity times cost of equity); and net profit after tax as percentage of total assets as well as net profit after tax as percentage of shareholders' equity and reserves. The latter consists of statements concerning the respondent's company's standing relative to other Islamic banks in terms of market share; profit margin and return; and customer retention and satisfaction.

The questionnaire was set up in a way as to allow respondents an easy starting point in order to increase the motivation to answer it.[251] All questions were of one of the following three types: tick-marking questions allowing for a single answer only; tick-marking questions allowing for multiple answers; or questions asking for quantitative data, mostly in the form of tables to be filled in. Most of the tick-marking questions allowing for a single answer only were asking the respondent to provide his assessment on a seven point Likert scale, thus enabling him to clearly differentiate and to express a neutral opinion due to the odd number of points. The questions are designed such that the empirical analysis of the questionnaire is possible without answers being given to the quantitative data questions, as it was presumed that these are often considered confidential and, accordingly, that many companies would not answer them.[252] However, the quantitative questions can be used to double-check some of the qualitative statements asked for. Moreover, many of the questions were included only because they were intended to be used in a benchmark report distributed to the respondents as a thank-you for participation.

Before the final version of the questionnaire was sent out to potential participants, it was pre-tested in telephone interviews (n=4) with Islamic bank representatives and academics, checking the appropriateness and answerability of questions. These interviews lasted between 40 minutes and one and a half hours. As a consequence, modifications of minor importance had to be made. On the one hand, some questions

[250] The questionnaire is documented in the appendix.

[251] Cf. Schnell et. al. (1999), p. 319.

[252] This was actually the case.

had to be rephrased or eliminated due to redundancy. On the other hand, some aspects were added due to the input of the experts.

3.1.1.2 Data Generation

The data generation process was carried out between February 2004 and July 2004, involving the following steps: company selection, approach of potential participants, and data documentation.

As was outlined previously, the GCC countries and Malaysia can be considered to be the most important markets for profit-oriented, free-market Islamic financial institutions. As a consequence, the empirical study is focused on these markets. A long-list of potential participants was generated using the following sources:

- The directory of Islamic financial institutions in Bahrain issued by the Bahrain Monetary Agency
- The directory of Islamic financial institutions in Kuwait issued by the Central Bank of Kuwait
- The directory of Islamic financial institutions in Malaysia issued by Bank Negara Malaysia
- The list of member Islamic banks and financial institutions issued by the GCIBFI (General Council for Islamic Banks and Financial Institutions)
- A list of Islamic banks and financial institutions issued by the IIBI (Institute of Islamic Banking and Insurance)

The information available there – in many cases simply the name and address of the financial institution – was complemented by an Internet research and, if necessary, a personal contact by telephone. As a result, a list including the names and contact details of the person responsible for strategic management decisions – i.e. the managing director in case of full-fledged Islamic banks; the head of Islamic finance in case of an Islamic "window" of a conventional bank – was established. In total, this list contained 77 Islamic financial institutions: 61 in the GCC area, 16 in Malaysia. Based on the available information, it can be assumed that the long-list comprised most Islamic financial institutions active in the GCC area or Malaysia.

The questionnaire was emailed – or, if an email address was not available, faxed – to the identified contact person, including an introductory part explaining the background of the study and instructions how to fill in the answers as well as a confidentiality declaration assuring anonymity. The potential participants were asked to return the filled-in questionnaires within two weeks. After that deadline had passed, all companies that had not returned the questionnaire nor declined their participation were contacted by phone, checking whether the questionnaire had actually reached the intended recipient. If this was the case, the phone call was used as a reminder. Otherwise, the material was sent again. In some cases, this process had to be carried out repeatedly.

Out of the 77 Islamic financial institutions contacted, 36 or 47% participated in the study. Compared to other empirical studies, this is a highly satisfactory response rate, which is mostly due to the time-intensive, personal follow-up process after the initial dispatch of the questionnaires.

The data of all returned questionnaires was continuously archived in a SPSS data file, SPSS for Windows, Version 11.5.1. In case of incomplete questionnaires, respondents were contacted and asked to hand in the missing information. All relevant data still incomplete after this process was completed through imputation using expectation maximization.[253]

3.1.1.3 Sample

The sample for the empirical analysis comprises 36 Islamic financial institutions: 25 with the major region of operations in the GCC area and 11 in Malaysia. The former represent approx. 80% of the estimated total on-balance sheet Islamic banking assets in the GCC, the latter approx. 70% of the estimated total on-balance sheet Islamic banking assets in Malaysia. Given the market concentration in these regions, this implies that all major Islamic financial institutions active in these markets are included in the study.

The organizational background of the banks included in the sample is the following: 18 are departments or subsidiaries of conventional banks. The same number of participants is a full-fledged Islamic bank, either as a self-standing unit or a subsidiary of another Islamic bank. Out of the 18 departments or subsidiaries of conventional banks, 4 have their head entity based in a Western country, the rest have their head entity based in the GCC or Malaysia.

Irrespective of whether the banks covered belong to a conventional bank or not, the majority of the banks included in the sample is a subsidiary fully owned by a parent firm (n=17). Out of the rest, 12 are privately owned, 4 are joint ventures and 3 state-owned.

Most of the Islamic banks represented in the sample are "universal" banks (n=25), i.e. they are offering corporate and institutional services such as corporate financing or institutional asset management as well as personal services such as home financing or checking. A small fraction is focusing on corporate banking (n=5) or on financing and asset management – without personal banking services (n=6). This is in line with the observation made earlier that most Islamic banks in the region are universal banks.

Before turning to the section on data analysis, the following will illustrate some of the topics included in the questionnaire that are not used in the subsequent empirical analysis of the conceptual model. In detail, the statements of the respondents on attractive market segments for Islamic finance, on the factors contributing to their attractiveness, on measures for effective competition with conventional banks, on

[253] As can be seen in the original data set presented in the appendix, only a very small number of data points was generated in this way.

their principal company goals, and on the size and functions of their Sharia boards will be depicted. This depiction serves two purposes: On the one hand, the firms included in the sample are further characterized. On the other hand, some light is shed on a few areas of discussion in the Islamic finance literature, such as the reasons for the prevalence of *murabaha* financing, the further development of Islamic financial derivatives, or the often lamented lack of involvement of Islamic banks in development banking.

Exhibit 20 shows the average rating of the attractiveness of the various Islamic finance market segments in the sample. For each segment, respondents were asked to state its perceived attractiveness on a seven point Likert scale (1=not attractive, 7=highly attractive). As is illustrated, overall home finance is viewed as the most attractive market segment, followed by trade finance and advances for personal durables. Investment banking, asset management and corporate finance take up the medium ranks, while public sector financing, advances for personal consumption and venture capital are at the tail end of the rating. Interestingly enough, all segments are regarded as at least somewhat attractive, as even venture capital is above the neutral point four of the Likert scale. The high attractiveness of segments relating to corporate and institutional banking as well as personal banking is, by the way, reflected in the above-mentioned observation that most banks in the sample are "universal" banks.

Exhibit 20: Attractive market segments, average rating

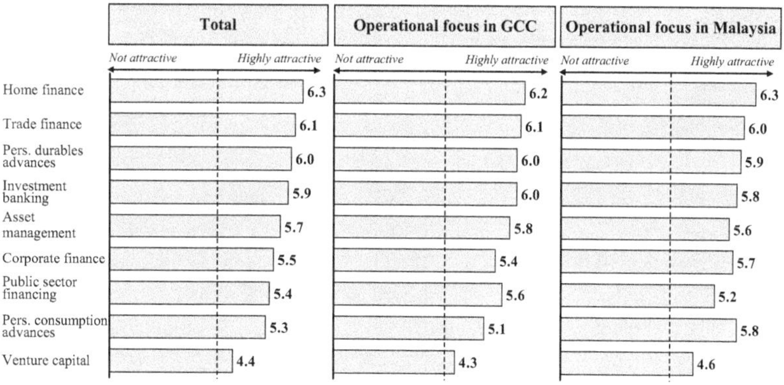

Note: Rating from 1 to 7 (1=not attractive ... 7=highly attractive)

Comparing the ratings of Islamic banks with operational focus in the GCC with those with operational focus in Malaysia, the picture remains largely unchanged. There are only slight modifications in the order of relative importance of the various segments within each of the two regional foci. The differences in average rating for the individual segments between the GCC and Malaysia – most notably in the rating of advances for personal consumption – are statistically not significant.

As was illustrated above in the background section on Islamic finance in practice, *murabaha* and *bay' mu'ajjal* are the most widely used Islamic financing instruments in the GCC and Malaysia.[254] It is often claimed in the literature that one of the reasons for the prevalence of these products is a liquidity constraint of Islamic banks. As deposits can be easily withdrawn, and viable refinancing opportunities matching those of the conventional banking market – secondary, money and interbanking markets – are hardly available[255], Islamic banks allegedly prefer short-term financings such as *murabaha* for reasons of asset-deposit maturity matching. Exhibit 21 shows the factors contributing to the attractiveness of the various market segments mentioned above, as stated by respondents of the survey. Overall, the segments are regarded as attractive due to high margins, high growth potential, high demand, and, to a certain degree, low risk. Asset-deposit maturity matching is mentioned only by a third of respondents – a bit more than that in the GCC, much less in Malaysia, which may reflect the perhaps better-developed liquidity market in Malaysia.[256] This seems to suggest that asset-deposit maturity matching may not be the driving force behind Islamic banks' investment decisions. They may simply focus on large, profitable segments with high growth potential, as is reflected in the survey, which – at least in the case of trade finance – concomitantly attenuates their liquidity constraints.

Exhibit 21: Factors contributing to attractiveness, % of respondents mentioning factor

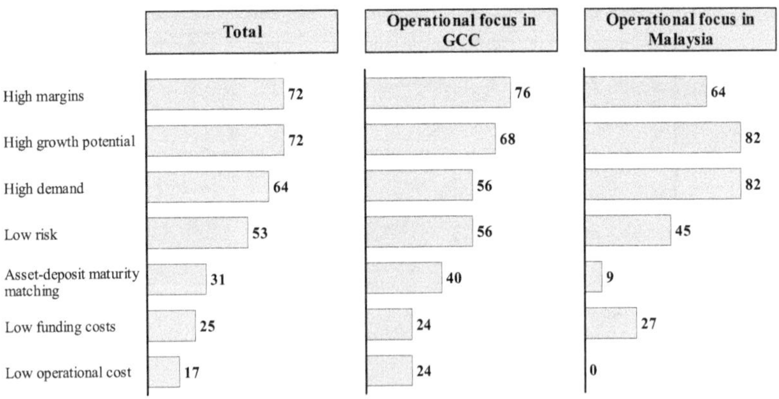

[254] The observation is in line with the stated attractiveness of trade finance, for which *murabaha* is a typical instrument.

[255] See section above on liquidity management and secondary markets.

[256] The difference is statistically significant.

Exhibit 22: Measures for effective competition with conventional banks, average rating

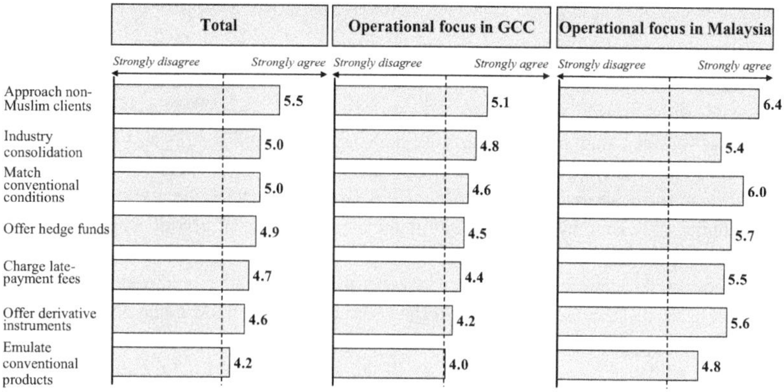

Note: Rating from 1 to 7 (1=strongly disagree … 7=strongly agree)

As indicated several times previously, Islamic financial institutions in the GCC and Malaysia are in competition with conventional banks, as these are also active there. In order to compete effectively, Islamic banks need to address several problems, most notably in the area of financial instruments that can be made available to clients[257]. This also relates to their self-conception, i.e. whether they restrict themselves to a niche market within the broader realm of finance which is defined by religious adherence or whether they intend to cater to all clients – irrespective of their religion. Exhibit 22 illustrates the measures deemed necessary by the firms participating in the study to compete effectively with conventional banks. For each measure, respondents were asked to state their agreement or disagreement on its use on a seven point Likert scale (1=strongly disagree, 7=strongly agree). Islamic banks view the approach of non-Muslim clients as the most important measure – markedly more so in Malaysia than in the GCC, where it nevertheless still ranks first.[258] Overall, the respondents also see a need for industry consolidation. The competition with conventional banks is underlined by the appraisal that Islamic financial products must match conventional conditions. Respondents also acknowledge a need to offer derivative financial products. However, there are notable differences between the statements of Islamic banks with operational focus in the GCC and those with operational focus in Malaysia. The latter are much more in favor of offering hedge funds and derivative instruments as well as matching conventional conditions – at statistically significant levels. The former are just slightly above the neutral point four of the Likert scale in

[257] Islamic banks are always at a competitive disadvantage compared to conventional banks, as their set of available financial instruments – both on the asset and the liability side – is always smaller than the one of conventional banks: Conventional banks can imitate all products of Islamic banks, while the reverse is no true.

[258] The difference between the GCC and Malaysia is statistically significant.

their average rating. This seems to support the conventional wisdom that Islamic banks in Malaysia are much more innovative and willing to experiment with new product ideas than their more conservative counterparts in the GCC.

Exhibit 23 shows the principal company goals of the firms represented in the sample. As becomes easily apparent, Islamic banks in the GCC and Malaysia are business-driven entities, with maximizing shareholder value, providing highest-standard banking services and maximizing profits at the heart of their goals. As can be expected for mostly private firms, other, more social and economic policy-related goals such as encouraging people to save and invest, promoting the precepts of Islam, developing the economy, and promoting social welfare are of secondary importance, if at all. Comparing the statements of Islamic banks with operational focus in the GCC with those with operational focus in Malaysia, the picture remains largely unchanged. There are only slight modifications in the order of relative importance of the various goals for companies with operational focus in the GCC. The differences between the GCC and Malaysia – with the exception of the goal "developing the economy" – are statistically not significant.

Exhibit 23: Principal company goals, % of respondents mentioning goal

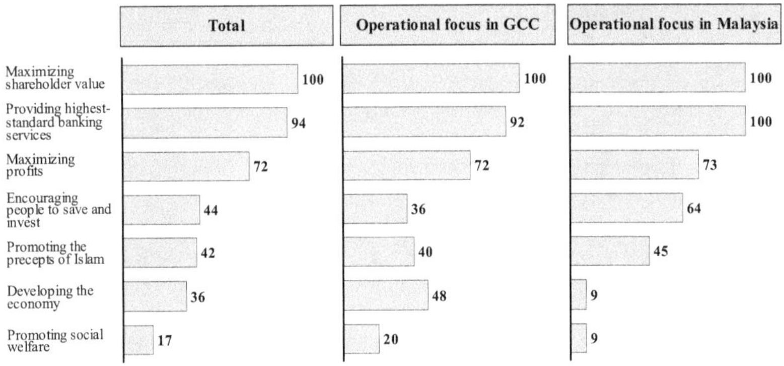

As was illustrated in the previous section on the institutional framework of Islamic finance, there is a lack of uniformity in the regulatory and supervisory environment across the various GCC countries and Malaysia. This is especially true for the existence and the role of Sharia boards. Exhibit 24 shows that the mere existence as well as the composition of Sharia boards varies greatly among the firms represented in the sample. Some firms do not have a Sharia board, most have three or four people on their Sharia boards, a significant number yet has even more than five people in their Sharia boards. While this uneven picture largely holds true for companies with operational focus in the GCC, those with operational focus in Malaysia appear to be more uniform, with 60% of the firms having three people on their Sharia boards. The variety of approaches is also illustrated by Exhibit 25, which shows the scope of

Sharia board functions. The ex ante approval of new products is the only function performed by all Sharia boards. All boards do not even issue a compliance report.

Exhibit 24: Number of people on Sharia board, % share of respondents

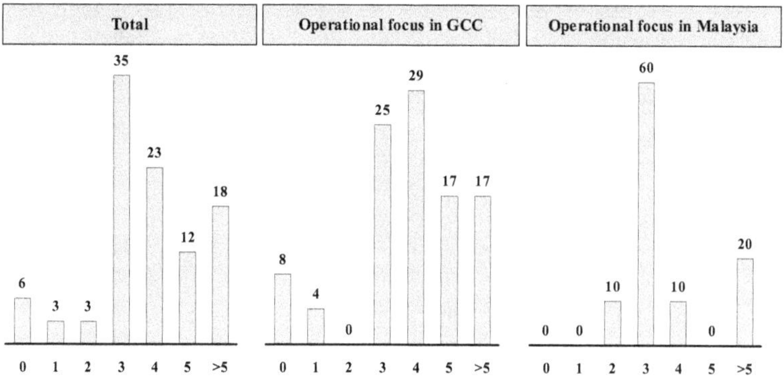

Exhibit 25: Scope of Sharia board functions, % of respondents mentioning function

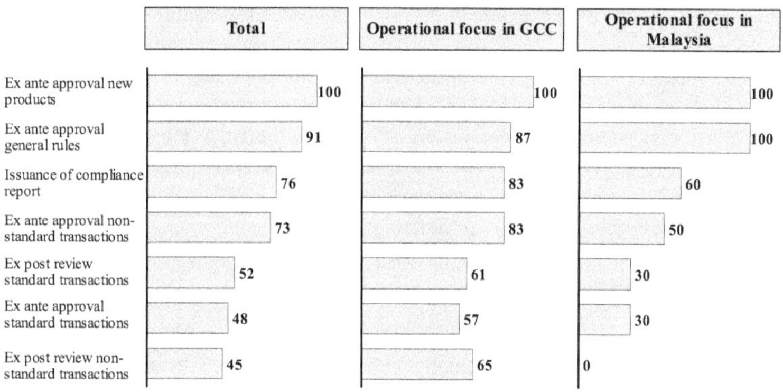

3.1.2 Data Analysis

The empirical data analysis follows a two-step approach. First, the reliability and validity of the measurement model is tested. Then, the hypothesized relationships between the constructs are analyzed. Both steps are described below. All statistical analyses have been computed using the software package SPSS 11.5.1.

The conceptual model developed previously in the analytical framework section consists of the assumed relationships between theoretical constructs. These theoretical constructs or latent variables are abstract, non-observable entities, which cannot be measured directly, but have to be represented by one or more indicators.[259] Hence the need for operationalisation of these constructs. In the course of this operationalisation, the number of variables used for the subsequent statistical examination is greatly reduced, as for each data set variables related to the same theoretical constructs are grouped by applying factor analysis. Factor analysis can be differentiated into exploratory and confirmatory factor analysis. While the former, also known as the classical approach of factor analysis[260], is commonly used to discover patterns of redundancy and identify theoretical constructs, the latter is used to "(...) examine whether a prior expectation of the variable grouping is consistent with the data (...)"[261]. Confirmatory factor analysis requires an *a priori* determination of the number of latent variables and their allocation to indicators. Even though, in this study, the number of latent variables is suggested in the conceptual model, the allocation of indicators to latent variables is not. Therefore, exploratory factor analysis is used to infer the theoretical constructs from the set of indicators and to test the reliability and validity of the measurement model.

Factor analysis can only be applied if the data matrix of the indicator variables has sufficient correlations.[262] Several methods are available to test the appropriateness of factor analysis: the anti-image correlation matrix, the Bartlett test of sphericity, and the measure of sampling adequacy. In the literature, the measure of sampling adequacy is viewed as the best instrument to test the appropriateness of factor analysis.[263] A value of the measure of sampling adequacy below 0.5 is generally viewed as unacceptable, a value of 0.8 or more as desirable.[264] Moreover, a sample size of at least 50 observations is recommended.[265] In any case, there should at least be five times as many observations as there are variables to be analyzed. Therefore, Hair et. al. suggest to "(...) do this by employing the most parsimonious set of variables, guided by conceptual and practical considerations, and then obtaining an adequate sample size for the number of variables examined"[266]. It should be noted that while this study respected the minimum cases-to-variable ratio, the number of observations falls short of the recommended minimum number of observations, which may potentially lead to distortions in the results.

The quality of the indicators chosen depends on how well they correspond to the construct they represent, and is commonly defined by the reliability and validity of the

---

259 Cf. Hair et. al. (1998), p. 585-586; Backhaus et. al. (2003), p. 334-339.

260 Herrmann and Homburg (Eds.) (2000), p. 384.

261 Lehmann et. al. (1998), p. 620.

262 Cf. Stewart (1981), p. 56-58, Hair et. al. (1998), p. 99-100, Malhotra (1999), p. 589-591, Litfin et. al. (2000), p. 283-284 ; Backhaus et. al. (2003), p. 272-277.

263 Backhaus et. al. (2003), p. 276.

264 Ibid.

265 Hair et. al. (1998), p. 98-99.

266 Ibid., p. 99.

measure.[267] Reliability is the degree to which the observed variable measures are free from random error. A measure is reliable if it leads to consistent results in multiple measurements. In other words: a high reliability means there is a low random measurement error. Validity is the extent to which a measure correctly represents the theoretical construct behind it, i.e. the degree to which it is free from any systematic or non-random error. Although many aspects of validity are discussed in the literature[268], this study focuses on content validity, convergent validity, and discriminant validity.[269] Content validity, also known as face validity, signifies the degree to which the observed variable truly represents the semantic meaning of the theoretical construct. Convergent validity is the degree to which two measures of the same concept are correlated. Discriminant validity, finally, is the degree to which two conceptually different measures differ. Exhibit 26 lists all construct tests applied in this study and the test method used.

Exhibit 26: Construct tests and test method

Construct test	Test method
Reliability	▪ Cronbach's Alpha ▪ Item-to-total correlation
Content validity	▪ Pretest
Convergent validity	▪ Factor analysis (factor loading) ▪ Correlation analysis (only performance measures)
Discriminant validity	▪ Factor analysis (factor loading)

Except for content validity, which is a subjective assessment, several statistical criteria are commonly used in order to determine reliability and validity in an exploratory factor analysis.[270] For reliability, Cronbach's Alpha is the most frequently used test method – it is a measure of internal consistency of the indicators of a factor. Besides Cronbach's Alpha, the item-to-total correlation is often used as another measure of reliability. This measure is sometimes also used to eliminate indicators in case of a low value of Cronbach's Alpha, in order to increase reliability. Finally, the factor loading is commonly viewed as a measure for convergent and discriminant validity. However, despite their frequent use, these methods have several weaknesses. There are four major concerns related to Cronbach's Alpha: first, it cannot be tested through inferential statistics. Second, its thresholds are based on rules of thumb.

---

[267] Cf. Hair et. al. (1998), p. 3-10, Lehmann et. al. (1998), p. 251-257, Hamann and Erichson (2000), p. 92-96.

[268] Cf. Jacoby (1978), p. 91.

[269] Along with nomological validity, these are the most widely accepted forms of validity used in empirical business research of theoretical constructs. Cf. Peter (1981), p. 133-145, Homburg and Giering (1996), p. 7, Hair et. al. (1998), p. 118.

[270] Cf. for this paragraph Gerbing and Anderson (1988), p. 188-190, Homburg and Giering (1996), p. 8-9, Hair et. al. (1998), p. 117-119, Litfin et. al. (2000), p,. 285-286.

Third, the value of Cronbach's Alpha increases with the number of indicators used in the factor analysis. Fourth, Cronbach's Alpha assumes that items have equal reliabilities. The first two concerns related to Cronbach's Alpha hold also true for the item-to-total correlation and the factor loadings. As a remedy for these weaknesses, confirmatory factor analysis as a subsequent step to exploratory factor analysis has been proposed in the literature, which yields quantitative measures of reliability and validity suited for inferential statistics.[271] However, confirmatory factor analysis requires a large sample size[272], and therefore has not been applied in this study.[273] It is important to note in this context, that even the 2-step approach proposed in the literature uses both Cronbach's Alpha and item-to-total correlation as reliability indicators in the exploratory factor analysis preceding the confirmatory factor analysis, despite the acknowledgement of their weaknesses.[274]

Exhibit 27 summarizes the criteria thresholds used in this study. Following Hair et. al., the minimum of the item-to-total correlation per item was defined at .50.[275] With regard to factor loading, a value of greater or equal to .30 is already considered to meet the minimum level in the literature, while other authors suggest minimum values between .40 and .50 as relevant for practical purposes.[276] We follow the suggestion of Hair et. al. and consider a factor loading per item greater or equal to .50 as practically significant.[277] However, this approach emphasizes practical significance – for a factor loading of .50 to be statistically significant, a sample size of 120 would be required.[278] The sample size of this study would even require a factor loading above .75 to be statistically significant – it should be noted, though, that such extremely high factor loadings are not typical.[279] For the measure of sampling adequacy, a minimum threshold of .50 is generally accepted in the literature, even though it is considered to yield "miserable" results, while good measure of sampling adequacy values start at or above .80.[280] As the measure of sampling adequacy increases with sample size[281], and given the small sample size of this study, the minimum of the measure of sampling adequacy was set at .50. In accordance with suggestions made by Gerbing and Anderson as well as Homburg, the lower limit of the explained variance was defined at 50%.[282] Finally, Cronbach's Alpha had to be above .60 for items to pass the reliability test.[283] While the generally agreed upon lower limit of Cronbach's Alpha is

---

271 Cf. Homburg and Giering (1996).

272 Ibid., p. 14. Hair et. al. (1998) suggest a minimum sample size of 200 observations – cf. p. 605.

273 Besides, confirmatory factor analysis is not supported by the statistical package used in this study.

274 Homburg and Giering (1996), p. 12.

275 Hair et. al. (1998), p. 118.

276 Backhaus et. al. (2003), p. 299; Litfin et. al. (2000), p. 285.

277 Ibid., p. 111.

278 Significance is based on a .05 significance level (α), a power level of 80%, and standard errors assumed to be twice those of conventional correlation coefficients. Cf. Hair et. al. (1998), p. 112.

279 Ibid., p. 111.

280 Cf. Backhaus et. al. (2003), p. 276..

281 Hair et. al. (1998), p. 99-100.

282 Cf. Gerbing and Anderson (1988), Homburg (2000).

283 McAllister (1995), p. 36.

.70, Hair et. al. suggest that "(...) it may decrease to .60 in exploratory research"[284] and Litfin et. al. observe that you find substantially lower thresholds used in the literature, suggesting that even a minimum value of .50 is sufficient in exploratory research[285], such as the study at hand. Overall, the reliability and validity criteria thresholds used in this study are broadly in line with generally used rules of thumb in factor analysis.[286]

Exhibit 27: Criteria thresholds used in this study

Criteria	>=
Item-to-total correlation per item	.50
Factor loading per item	.50
Measure of sampling adequacy	.50
Explained variance	50%
Cronbach's Alpha	.60

After testing the reliability and validity, the propositions brought forward above in the conceptual model section are examined. For this matter, several standard statistical tests are applied. The hypothesized relationships between the constructs, i.e. the impact of the various factors on the different company performance variables, are analyzed using the Spearman correlation coefficient (due to the ordinal character of the Likert scale ratings) and a linear regression analysis. It is important to note, in this context, that results of these analyses are independent of the measurement scale used for data collection (e.g. a seven point Likert scale vs. a five point Likert scale), as linear transformations cancel themselves in a correlation analysis. We refrained from using more elaborate techniques such as structural equation modeling due to the small sample size. The investigation of differences of the factors or the performance indicators across various groups or clusters – such as the hypothesized strategic groups – are performed using the t-test in the case of two clusters, and ANOVA in the case of three or more clusters.

3.1.3 Data Measurement

This chapter evaluates and documents the operationalisation of the theoretical constructs developed previously in the analytical framework. In the following, the operationalisation of external factors, internal factors, company strategies and company performance will be depicted. All measures made up by two ore more items

[284] Hair et. al. (1998), p. 118.
[285] Litfin et. al. (2000), p. 285.
[286] Cf. Hair et.al. (1998), p.111-119.

have been tested by reliability and validity tests using the criteria mentioned above. The original data set for all items is documented in the appendix.

3.1.3.1 Operationalisation of External Factors

External factors consist of eight constructs: the threat of new entrants, the power of human resource suppliers, the power of technology suppliers, competition, the power of customers, the threat of substitutes – i.e. a refined view of Porter's five forces – as well as (re)financing opportunities and the regulatory framework and standards – i.e. a selection of global environment factors. While the first six have been constructed as single-item measures, the last two are made up by four and three items, respectively. For each item, respondents were asked to state their agreement or disagreement on a seven point Likert scale (1=strongly disagree, 7=strongly agree).

The industry forces have been measured by the following statements, respectively:

- There is low barriers to enter the Islamic finance market
- There is a lack of skilled human resources
- Suppliers of state-of-the-art technology have high bargaining power (e.g. IT vendors)
- Competition in the industry is very high
- The clients have a strong bargaining position
- The threat of substitutes is high (conventional banks)

These measures have been used in previous studies in a similar fashion.[287] It is therefore assumed that they are reliable and valid.

Exhibit 28: Factor "(re)financing opportunities"

Item	**Item-to-total correlation**	**Factor loading**
The industry's liquidity market is too restricted	.63	.66
There is not enough attractive profit-and-loss-sharing investment opportunities	.54	.59
Overall, attractive investment opportunities are hard to find	.85	.92
Access to capital is limited	.66	.66
Measure of sampling adequacy	.51	
Explained variance	51.42%	
Cronbach's Alpha	.67	

[287] Cf. Gerbach (2002), p. 114, Spanos and Lioukas (2001), p. 932.

The (re)financing opportunities are operationalised as documented in Exhibit 28. The factor is made up by four items, which relate to the industry's liquidity market, profit-and-loss sharing as well as overall investment opportunities, and access to capital. In an exemplary manner, we can illustrate here the relationship between this factor and its underlying indicators: For each data set, a single numerical value of this factor replaces the four Likert-scale values of the corresponding variables in the original data set and is used in the subsequent statistical analyses. The factor satisfies all reliability and validity criteria, although it has a rather low measure of sampling adequacy and explained variance.

The operationalisation of the factor "regulatory framework and standards" is presented in Exhibit 29. The factor is composed of three items, which relate to the improvement potential of the industry's regulatory and legal framework, the standardization of Sharia opinions, and the standardization of products. All reliability and validity criteria are met with the exception of Cronbach's Alpha. However, the value of Cronbach's Alpha of .57 is very close to the necessary minimum of .60, so that the factor can be seen as reliable and valid. We therefore did not discard it and included it in the study.

Exhibit 29: Factor "regulatory framework and standards"

Item	Item-to-total correlation	Factor loading
The industry's regulatory and legal framework could improve	.62	.66
There is a lack of standardization of Sharia opinions	.83	.59
There is a lack of standardization of products (incl. documentation)	.75	.92
Measure of sampling adequacy	.52	
Explained variance	56.67%	
Cronbach's Alpha	.57	

3.1.3.2 Operationalisation of Internal Factors

Internal factors consist of five constructs, all of which are multiple-item factors: market-access core competencies, functionality-related core competencies, integrity-related core competencies – i.e. the decomposition of core competencies proposed by Hamel and Prahalad – as well as the reputation as an Islamic company and Sharia board effectiveness – i.e. the two Islamic-finance specific internal factors that have been singled out for analytical purposes. While the last two are simple multiple-item factors, the first three are complex multiple-item factors, as they are themselves composed of several multiple-item factors. For each item, respondents were asked to state their firm's strength relative to competitors on a seven point Likert scale (1=much weaker than competitors, 7=much stronger than competitors).

We begin with the exposition of the operationalisation of market-access core competencies. This factor is composed of the factor "customer relations", the factor "brand image", and the factor "distribution capabilities". As market-access core competencies is a complex factor made up by other factors, first the operationalisation of these factors has to be presented.

Exhibit 30 documents the operationalisation of the factor "customer relations". The factor is composed of four items, which relate to the firms' access to short-term capital, access to mid- and long-term capital, their current customer base, and the characterization of the relationship with their customers. As the table illustrates, all reliability and validity criteria are met for this factor.

Exhibit 30: Factor "customer relations"

Item	Item-to-total correlation	Factor loading
Access to short-term capital	.83	.82
Access to mid- and long-term capital	.80	.76
Current customer base	.75	.75
Advantageous relationships with customers	.68	.74
Measure of sampling adequacy	.68	
Explained variance	58.78%	
Cronbach's Alpha	.76	

Exhibit 31 presents the items of the factor "brand image" and the corresponding values of the reliability and validity tests. Two items relating to the reputation of the firms as financial services provider and the brand image make up the factor. Both the reliability and the validity tests are passed. The explained variance is rather high with a value of approx. 82%.

Exhibit 31: Factor "brand image"

Item	Item-to-total correlation	Factor loading
Reputation as financial services provider	.89	.91
Brand image	.90	.91
Measure of sampling adequacy	.50	
Explained variance	82.30%	
Cronbach's Alpha	.78	

The factor "distribution capabilities" is operationalised as documented in Exhibit 32. It is composed of five items, relating to the control of and access to distribution channels, the firms' branch network, ATM network, Internet banking facilities, and call center facilities. Except for the item-to-total correlation of the item "control of and access to distribution channels", all reliability and validity criteria are fulfilled. As the item-to-total correlation is very close to the necessary minimum of .50, we view it as fulfilled.[288] Overall, the factor has particularly high values in the measure of sampling adequacy and Cronbach's Alpha and a highly satisfactory explained variance.

Exhibit 32: Factor "distribution capabilities"

Item	Item-to-total correlation	Factor loading
Control of and access to distribution channels	.45	.53
Branch network	.89	.90
ATM network	.88	.91
Internet banking	.89	.87
Call center	.81	.83
Measure of sampling adequacy	.75	
Explained variance	67.26%	
Cronbach's Alpha	.88	

The factor "market-access core competencies" is made up by the factors "customer relations", "brand image", and "distribution capabilities", which were presented above. As presents Exhibit 33, it passes all reliability and validity tests.

The factor "functionality-related core competencies" is another factor that is composed of several other factors, which are: customer service, supporting processes, resource efficiency, technological capabilities and equipment, technological expertise, financial expertise, and financial processing capabilities. As before, we begin with the presentation of the operationalisation of the individual simple factors.

Response time to customer requests, marketing and sales service quality, and transaction processing service quality are the components of the factor "customer service". As Exhibit 34 illustrates, all reliability and validity criteria are met, with quite a good explained variance of approx. 76%, a good level of the measure of sampling adequacy, and a particularly high value of Cronbach's Alpha.

---

288 In fact, some studies define the necessary item-to-total correlation at levels which are lower than .50. Cf. Kumar et.al. (1993), p.12.

Exhibit 33: Factor "market-access core competencies"

Item	Item-to-total correlation	Factor loading
Factor "customer relations"	.80	.85
Factor "brand image"	.61	.65
Factor "distribution capabilities"	.79	.79
Measure of sampling adequacy	.59	
Explained variance	58.67%	
Cronbach's Alpha	.64	

Exhibit 34: Factor "customer service"

Item	Item-to-total correlation	Factor loading
Response time to customer requests	.79	.88
Marketing and sales service quality	.91	.92
Transaction processing service quality	.88	.82
Measure of sampling adequacy	.69	
Explained variance	76.14%	
Cronbach's Alpha	.84	

Exhibit 35: Factor "supporting processes"

Item	Item-to-total correlation	Factor loading
Risk management	.64	.66
Research capabilities	.85	.78
Knowledge and data management	.73	.79
HR processes and administration	.69	.74
Measure of sampling adequacy	.66	
Explained variance	55.31%	
Cronbach's Alpha	.72	

Exhibit 35 details the items of the factor "supporting processes" and the respective values of the reliability and validity tests, which are all passed. The factor is composed of risk management, research capabilities, knowledge and data management, and HR processes and administration.

The items of the factor "resource efficiency" are relating to the resource efficiency in product development, marketing and sales, and transaction processing, as shown in Exhibit 36 below. All reliability and validity criteria are satisfied, with quite a good explained variance and a particularly high value of Cronbach's Alpha. Moreover, the items are loading relatively high on the factor.

Exhibit 36: Factor "resource efficiency"

Item	Item-to-total correlation	Factor loading
Product development resource efficiency	.75	.82
Marketing and sales resource efficiency	.88	.91
Transaction processing resource efficiency	.95	.94
Measure of sampling adequacy	.67	
Explained variance	78.69%	
Cronbach's Alpha	.86	

Technological capabilities and equipment in the areas of product development, marketing and sales, and transaction processing as well as information processing capabilities are the components of the factor "technological capabilities and equipment". As Exhibit 37 documents, the factor passes the reliability and validity tests.

Exhibit 37: Factor "technological capabilities and equipment"

Item	Item-to-total correlation	Factor loading
Product development technological capabilities and equipment	.69	.75
Information processing capabilities	.71	.75
Marketing and sales technological capabilities and equipment	.91	.93
Transaction processing technological capabilities and equipment	.85	.82
Measure of sampling adequacy	.69	
Explained variance	66.48%	
Cronbach's Alpha	.83	

The factor "technological expertise" is composed of technological expertise in product development, marketing and sales, and transaction processing. Exhibit 38 presents the results of the reliability and validity tests: all criteria are met.

Exhibit 38: Factor "technological expertise"

Item	Item-to-total correlation	Factor loading
Product development technological expertise	.77	.81
Marketing and sales technological expertise	.88	.86
Transaction processing technological expertise	.90	.86
Measure of sampling adequacy	.70	
Explained variance	71.42%	
Cronbach's Alpha	.79	

Exhibit 39 shows the items of the factor "financial expertise". The components of the factor are product development innovation, know-how of both Islamic and financial market requirements, market knowledge, private equity / venture capital expertise, and financial expertise. As can be seen, all reliability and validity criteria are fulfilled.

Exhibit 39: Factor "financial expertise"

Item	Item-to-total correlation	Factor loading
Product development innovation	.73	.77
Know-how of both Islamic and financial market requirements	.65	.74
Market knowledge	.62	.70
Private equity / venture capital expertise	.83	.69
Financial expertise	.60	.72
Measure of sampling adequacy	.65	
Explained variance	52.42%	
Cronbach's Alpha	.71	

The factor "financial processing capabilities" is composed of the items placing power, deal and customer assessment, customer counseling, securitization of investment products, and trading and treasury. As documented in Exhibit 40, all reliability and validity criteria are satisfied.

As mentioned before, the complex factor "functionality-related core competencies" is made up by the seven simple factors presented above. This factor has the highest number of items among all factors used in this study. Exhibit 41 presents the respective values of the reliability and validity criteria for these items. All tests are passed. There are particularly high values of the measure of sampling adequacy and Cronbach's Alpha and a satisfactory value of the explained variance.

Exhibit 40: Factor "financial processing capabilities"

Item	Item-to-total correlation	Factor loading
Placing power	.64	.74
Deal and customer assessment	.68	.74
Customer counselling	.87	.86
Securitization of investment products	.70	.66
Trading and treasury	.56	.63
Measure of sampling adequacy	.70	
Explained variance	52.95%	
Cronbach's Alpha	.76	

Among the internal factors, the factor "integrity-related core competencies" is the last complex factor, which is composed of the following five simple factors: the factor "co-operation", the factor "management quality", the factor "firm culture", the factor "implementation capabilities", and the factor "financial standing". As before, the operationalisation of these simple factors needs to be presented first.

Exhibit 41: Factor "functionality-related core competencies"

Item	Item-to-total correlation	Factor loading
Factor "customer service"	.74	.77
Factor "supporting processes"	.80	.80
Factor "resource efficiency"	.79	.87
Factor "technological capabilities and equipment"	.87	.89
Factor "technological expertise"	.86	.86
Factor "financial expertise"	.66	.71
Factor "financial processing capabilities"	.83	.88
Measure of sampling adequacy	.86	
Explained variance	68.39%	
Cronbach's Alpha	.92	

The operationalisation of the factor "co-operation" is documented in Exhibit 42. Vertical communication, cross-functional information exchange, cross-functional co-operation, team-based approach, and coordination are the items, which make up this factor. As can be seen, all reliability and validity criteria are met.

Exhibit 42: Factor "co-operation"

Item	Item-to-total correlation	Factor loading
Vertical communication	.67	.66
Cross-functional information exchange	.86	.86
Cross-functional co-operation	.91	.93
Team-based approach	.71	.77
Coordination	.81	.83
Measure of sampling adequacy	.76	
Explained variance	66.22%	
Cronbach's Alpha	.87	

Exhibit 43 details the items pertaining to the factor "management quality": managerial competencies, quality of leadership, strategic vision, effectiveness of the resource management, and the knowledge and skills of the employees. All reliability and validity tests are passed.

Exhibit 43: Factor "management quality"

Item	Item-to-total correlation	Factor loading
Managerial competencies	.83	.83
Quality of leadership	.82	.87
Clear strategic vision	.66	.73
Effective resource management	.67	.59
Knowledge and skills of employees	.66	.68
Measure of sampling adequacy	.78	
Explained variance	55.81%	
Cronbach's Alpha	.79	

Transparency and openness across company / hierarchies, ability to attract and retain high-quality people, prevalence of a meritocracy culture, highly motivating environment, reward of creativity and innovation, and market-oriented organization are the components of the factor "firm culture". As Exhibit 44 illustrates, all reliability and validity criteria are fulfilled for this factor.

Exhibit 44: Factor "firm culture"

Item	Item-to-total correlation	Factor loading
Transparency and openness across company / hierarchies	.64	.63
Ability to attract and retain high-quality people	.79	.84
Prevalence of a meritocracy culture	.86	.85
Highly motivating environment	.86	.81
Reward of creativity and innovation	.88	.91
Market-oriented organization	.72	.77
Measure of sampling adequacy	.83	
Explained variance	64.70%	
Cronbach's Alpha	.89	

The factor "implementation capabilities" is made up of the items strategy implementation, strategic planning, controlling, compensation and reward system, and use of strategy-enforcing tools. Exhibit 45 shows that this factor passed all reliability and validity tests.

Exhibit 45: Factor "implementation capabilities"

Item	Item-to-total correlation	Factor loading
Strategy-implementation	.70	.73
Strategic planning	.71	.81
Controlling	.68	.77
Compensation and reward system	.71	.77
Use of strategy-enforcing tools (e.g. balanced scorecard)	.74	.68
Measure of sampling adequacy	.75	
Explained variance	56.79%	
Cronbach's Alpha	.79	

Exhibit 46 illustrates the items and the test values of the factor "financial standing". The factor is composed of asset quality, equity base, and financial rating. All reliability and validity criteria are satisfied, although at comparatively low levels.

Exhibit 46: Factor "financial standing"

Item	Item-to-total correlation	Factor loading
Asset quality	.72	.81
Equity base	.63	.79
Financial rating (e.g. Moody's)	.68	.54
Measure of sampling adequacy	.56	
Explained variance	52.00%	
Cronbach's Alpha	.51	

Exhibit 47 documents the test results of the complex factor "integrity-related core competencies". As can be seen, all criteria are fulfilled. There are relatively high levels of the measure of sampling adequacy, and Cronbach's Alpha. The factor loading of the factor financial standing, however, is relatively low.

Exhibit 47: Factor "integrity-related core competencies"

Item	Item-to-total correlation	Factor loading
Factor "co-operation"	.73	.82
Factor "management quality"	.88	.86
Factor "firm culture"	.78	.86
Factor "implementation capabilities"	.78	.85
Factor "financial standing"	.53	.51
Measure of sampling adequacy	.72	
Explained variance	62.56%	
Cronbach's Alpha	.84	

The factor "reputation as an Islamic company" is composed of the items reputation as Islamic company, engagement in socially beneficial activities, and Sharia board reputation. As is illustrated in Exhibit 48, the reliability and validity tests are passed.

The speed and efficiency of the Sharia-approval process in product development as well as marketing and sales, the Sharia compliance, and the effectiveness and efficiency of the Sharia board are the items of the factor "Sharia board efficiency and effectiveness". Exhibit 49 shows the results of the reliability and validity tests: all criteria are met. The item Sharia board efficiency and effectiveness has a particularly high factor loading on the identically named factor.

Exhibit 48: Factor" reputation as an Islamic company"

Item	Item-to-total correlation	Factor loading
Reputation as Islamic company	.85	.73
Engagement in socially beneficial activities	.84	.83
Sharia board reputation	.52	.75
Measure of sampling adequacy	.63	
Explained variance	59.28%	
Cronbach's Alpha	.63	

Exhibit 49: Factor "Sharia board efficiency and effectiveness"

Item	Item-to-total correlation	Factor loading
Quick and efficient Sharia-approval process product development	.75	.79
Quick and efficient Sharia-approval process marketing and sales	.74	.80
Sharia compliance	.73	.64
Effectiveness and efficiency of Sharia board	.91	.91
Measure of sampling adequacy	.67	
Explained variance	61.40%	
Cronbach's Alpha	.78	

3.1.3.3 Operationalisation of Company Strategies

Company strategies consist of seven constructs: cost leadership, price leadership, product differentiation, marketing and sales differentiation, and focus – i.e. a refined view of Porter's generic company strategies – as well as emulation of conventional products, and positioning as an Islamic company – i.e. two Islamic-finance specific company strategies that have been singled out for analytical purposes. While the first five have been constructed as multiple-item factors, the last two are made up by a single item only. For each item, respondents were asked to state the usage by their own company on a seven point Likert scale (1=not considered, 7=major emphasis).

The factor "cost leadership" is operationalised as documented in Exhibit 50. It is composed of the following items: efforts to achieve economies of scale, high capacity utilization, highly automated transaction and administrative processes, standardization and modularization of products / services, and emphasis on gaining a high or dominant market share. As is presented in the table, the factor passed the reliability and validity tests.

Exhibit 50: Factor "cost leadership"

Item	Item-to-total correlation	Factor loading
Efforts to achieve economies of scale	.86	.86
High capacity utilization	.67	.60
Highly automated transaction and administrative processes	.84	.85
Standardization and modularisation of products / services	.72	.67
Emphasis on gaining a high or dominant market share	.66	.71
Measure of sampling adequacy	.68	
Explained variance	55.30%	
Cronbach's Alpha	.80	

The factor "price leadership" is made up of the items pricing below competitors, offering the main products in lower priced market segments, providing discounts to customers, and differentiated pricing for various distribution channels, as is illustrated in Exhibit 51. All reliability and validity criteria are fulfilled.

Exhibit 51: Factor "price leadership"

Item	Item-to-total correlation	Factor loading
Pricing below competitors	.58	.46
Offering the main products in lower priced market segments	.72	.78
Providing discounts to customers	.82	.82
Differentiated pricing for various distribution channels	.76	.80
Measure of sampling adequacy	.69	
Explained variance	53.30%	
Cronbach's Alpha	.69	

The factor "product differentiation" is a complex factor, which is composed of the two simple factors "product quality and design", and "product diversification". As has been done for the other complex factors before, first the operationalisation of the individual simple factors will be presented.

The operationalisation of the factor "product quality and design" is documented in Exhibit 52. The factor has the following items: strict product and service quality control, emphasis on quick market penetration / product introduction, emphasis on design and quality of products, emphasis on product innovation, and building product-related brands. As can be seen, all reliability and validity criteria are met, although at times at relatively low levels.

Exhibit 52: Factor "product quality and design"

Item	Item-to-total correlation	Factor loading
Strict product and service quality control	.73	.77
Emphasis on quick market penetration / product introduction	.78	.78
Emphasis on design and quality of products	.72	.73
Emphasis on product innovation	.72	.81
Building product-related brands	.71	.69
Measure of sampling adequacy	.73	
Explained variance	56.91%	
Cronbach's Alpha	.81	

Exhibit 53 presents the items providing a broad variation within the product lines, refining existing products to local needs and demands, and tailor-make products according to customer specification of the factor "product diversification". All reliability and validity criteria are fulfilled, although again at times at comparatively low levels.

Exhibit 53: Factor product diversification

Item	Item-to-total correlation	Factor loading
Providing a broad variation within the product lines	.78	.74
Refining existing products to local needs and demands	.82	.86
Tailor-make products according to customer specification	.59	.57
Measure of sampling adequacy	.51	
Explained variance	53.50%	
Cronbach's Alpha	.52	

The two simple factors detailed above are the components of the complex factor "product differentiation". As Exhibit 54 documents, this factor passes all reliability and validity tests.

Exhibit 54: Factor "product differentiation"

Item	Item-to-total correlation	Factor loading
Factor "product quality and design"	.88	.89
Factor "product diversification"	.90	.89
Measure of sampling adequacy	.50	
Explained variance	79.43%	
Cronbach's Alpha	.74	

The factor "marketing and sales differentiation" is another complex factor with the simple factors "customer orientation", "distribution", and "brand and image" as components. As for all other complex factors, first the operationalisation of the simple factors will be detailed.

Exhibit 55: Factor "customer orientation"

Item	Item-to-total correlation	Factor loading
Innovation in marketing techniques and methods	.61	.66
Immediate response to customer requests	.85	.88
Acquiring high calibre work-force	.80	.85
Extensive employee training	.79	.76
Efficient internal communication channels	.78	.73
Unobstructed and quick decision making process	.78	.79
Measure of sampling adequacy	.80	
Explained variance	61.23%	
Cronbach's Alpha	.87	

Exhibit 55 shows the items and test results of the factor "customer orientation". The factor is composed of the items innovation in marketing techniques and methods, immediate response to customer requests, acquiring high caliber work-force, extensive employee training, efficient internal communication channels, and unobstructed and quick decision making process. All reliability and validity criteria are satisfied, with particularly high levels of the measure of sampling adequacy and Cronbach's Alpha, and a satisfactory explained variance.

The items pertaining to the factor "distribution" are providing extensive customer service, control over distribution channels, and emphasis on strong distribution channels. As Exhibit 56 demonstrates, the factor passed all reliability and validity tests.

Exhibit 56: Factor "distribution"

Item	Item-to-total correlation	Factor loading
Providing extensive customer service	.71	.74
Control over distribution channels	.75	.72
Emphasis on strong distribution channels	.70	.73
Measure of sampling adequacy	.63	
Explained variance	53.17%	
Cronbach's Alpha	.56	

The factor "brand and image" is made up of the items building brand identification of company, promotion / advertising expenditures above industry average, and concerted effort to build / maintain reputation in the industry. As can be seen in Exhibit 57, all reliability and validity criteria are met.

Exhibit 57: Factor brand and image

Item	Item-to-total correlation	Factor loading
Building brand identification of company	.81	.86
Promotion / advertising expenditures above industry average	.75	.56
Concerted effort to build / maintain reputation in the industry	.67	.80
Measure of sampling adequacy	.56	
Explained variance	56.63%	
Cronbach's Alpha	.57	

Exhibit 58 details the complex factor "marketing and sales differentiation", which is composed of the simple factors presented above. The factor passed all reliability and validity tests.

The operationalisation of the factor "focus" and the corresponding test results are shown in Exhibit 59. The factor is composed of the items focusing on a few main product lines, and focusing on a few customer segments. As is evidenced in the table, all reliability and validity criteria are fulfilled.

Exhibit 58: Factor "marketing and sales differentiation"

Item	Item-to-total correlation	Factor loading
Factor "customer orientation"	.82	.82
Factor "distribution"	.82	.75
Factor "brand and image"	.71	.78
Measure of sampling adequacy	.66	
Explained variance	61.20%	
Cronbach's Alpha	.68	

Exhibit 59: Factor "focus"

Item	Item-to-total correlation	Factor loading
Focusing on a few main product lines	.86	.87
Focusing on a few customer segments	.86	.87
Measure of sampling adequacy	.50	
Explained variance	76.42%	
Cronbach's Alpha	.69	

The two Islamic-finance specific strategies have been measured by the following statements, respectively:

- Closely emulating the financial conditions of conventional banking products
- Emphasis on building reputation as an Islamic company

It is assumed that these operationalisations are reliable and valid.

3.1.3.4 Operationalisation of Company Performance

Company performance consists of three constructs: profitability, customer loyalty, and market share. All are single-item factors with the exception of customer loyalty, which is a multiple-item factor. For each item, respondents were asked to what extent they agree or disagree on a seven point Likert scale (1=strongly disagree, 7=strongly agree).

The two single-item factors have been measured with the following statements, respectively:

- Compared to other Islamic banks, we gain above-average return on equity (ROE)
- Compared to other Islamic banks, the market share of our products and services is very high

These measures have been used in previous studies in a similar fashion.[289] Moreover, as a test of convergent validity, the subjective responses were correlated with the quantitative performance data requested in the questionnaire of those firms that provided this data. Net profit after tax as percent of shareholders' equity and reserves correlated significantly with the subjective measure of return on equity (.70 at a 5% significance level; n=19). Market share by assets 2003 correlated significantly with the subjective measure of market share (.55 at a 5% significance level; n=14). It is therefore assumed that they are reliable and valid. Moreover, the subjective measure of return on equity was also correlated with financial data published in annual reports for those firms where this data was available. Again, the correlation was significant (.62 at a 1% significance level; n=19).

Exhibit 60: Customer loyalty

Item	Item-to-total correlation	Factor loading
Compared to other Islamic banks, we have a high degree of customer retention	.87	.88
Compared to other Islamic banks, our customers are highly satisfied with our products and services	.88	.88
Measure of sampling adequacy	.50	
Explained variance	77.26%	
Cronbach's Alpha	.71	

The factor "customer loyalty" is operationalised as documented in Exhibit 60. The factor is composed of two items, which relate to the firms' degree of customer retention, and the satisfaction of their customers with their products and services. The factor satisfies all reliability and validity criteria. Moreover, as another test of convergent validity, the subjective responses were correlated with the quantitative market share data requested in the questionnaire of those firms that provided this data, as customer loyalty is often viewed as one of the prerequisites for both maintenance and growth of market share.[290] Market share by assets 2003 correlated significantly with the subjective measure of customer loyalty (.48 at a 5% significance level; n=14). This can only be regarded as indicative, though, as it is conceivable that a

[289] Cf. Gerbach (2002), p. 114, Spanos and Lioukas (2001), p. 932.

[290] Cf. Chapter 2.4.1.

company maintains a high market share and at the same time constantly interchanges its customer base.

3.2 Research Findings

Using the operationalisations presented above, the theoretical propositions of the conceptual model can be tested. In the following, all three models with their corresponding hypotheses are examined. The exposition starts with the analysis of the impact of external factors on performance. Next, the impact of internal factors on performance is scrutinized. Then, the impact of company strategies on performance is examined. Finally, the chapter will be wrapped up with a summary of the empirical results.

3.2.1 Model 1: Impact of External Factors on Performance

Model 1 analyzes the impact of external factors on Islamic bank performance. External factors comprise the global environment and the industry structure. In the empirical examination, the following proposition has been tested: External factors have an uneven impact on Islamic bank performance. While the industry structure is not expected to explain intra-industry performance differences in Islamic finance, a more favorable global environment leads to better performance.

Exhibit 61: Correlation analysis to proposition 1

	Profitability (ROE)	**Customer loyalty**	**Market share**
(Re)financing opportunities	-.06	-.11	-.08
Regulatory framework and standards	-.09	-.35**	-.11
Bargaining power of customers	-.17	-.09	.13
Bargaining power of HR suppliers	-.08	-.08	.01
Bargaining power of technology suppliers	.09	.18	.01
Competition	-.14	.09	-.15
Threat of substitutes	-.02	-.07	-.11
Threat of new entrants	-.10	-.05	-.01

***: 1% significance level (1-sided)
** : 5% significance level (1-sided)
* : 10% significance level (1-sided)

Exhibit 61 documents the results of the correlation analysis to this proposition. In detail, (re)financing opportunities, and regulatory framework – representing the global environment – as well as bargaining power of customers, bargaining power of HR suppliers, bargaining power of technology suppliers, competition, threat of substitutes, and threat of new entrants – representing the industry structure – have been correlated with profitability, customer loyalty, and market share, respectively. As was theoretically expected, no significant correlations between Islamic bank performance and industry structure variables were observed. However, the global environment variables do not correlate with Islamic bank performance, with the exception of the correlation between the regulatory framework and customer loyalty, which is significant at the 5% level.

The proposition was further examined using a linear regression analysis. The result of the regression analysis for profitability (ROE) is presented in Exhibit 62. As can be seen, the regression analysis explains approx. 24% of the variance of profitability (ROE). The only significant regression coefficient is the one of the factor "regulatory framework and standards", which has a negative impact on the performance indicator (Std. Beta = -.46). However, with an F-value of 1.037 at a significance level of .433, the overall regression is not significant.

Exhibit 62: Regression analysis to proposition 1 for profitability (ROE)

	Std. Beta	Sig. level
(Re)financing opportunities	-.02	.918
Regulatory framework and standards	-.46*	.026
Bargaining power of customers	-.42	.093
Bargaining power of HR suppliers	-.04	.840
Bargaining power of technology suppliers	.32	.159
Competition	-.03	.906
Threat of substitutes	.09	.628
Threat of new entrants	.02	.938
R^2	.235	
F	1.037	.433

* : value is significant

This last statement holds also true for the regression analysis for customer loyalty, as it has an F-value of .627 at a significance level of .748. Moreover, as is shown in Exhibit 63, none of the regression coefficients is significant.

Exhibit 63: Regression analysis to proposition 1 for customer loyalty

	Std. Beta	Sig. level
(Re)financing opportunities	-.03	.871
Regulatory framework and standards	-.34	.112
Bargaining power of customers	-.40	.131
Bargaining power of HR suppliers	-.01	.950
Bargaining power of technology suppliers	.33	.171
Competition	.20	.406
Threat of substitutes	-.01	.962
Threat of new entrants	.13	.550
R^2	.157	
F	.627	.748

* : value is significant

Exhibit 64 documents the regression analysis to proposition 1 for market share. Again, none of the regression coefficients is significant. Besides, as was the case in the other two regression analyses, the overall regression is not significant with an F-value of .646 at a significance level of .732.

Exhibit 64: Regression analysis to proposition 1 for market share

	Std. Beta	Sig. level
(Re)financing opportunities	-.06	.757
Regulatory framework and standards	-.17	.426
Bargaining power of customers	.29	.256
Bargaining power of HR suppliers	-.03	.881
Bargaining power of technology suppliers	.07	.784
Competition	-.26	.270
Threat of substitutes	-.15	.450
Threat of new entrants	.09	.654
R^2	.161	
F	.646	.732

* : value is significant

As was theoretically expected, the regression analyses did not establish any relationship between external factors related to industry structure and the various performance indicators. However, it failed to establish a relationship between the global environment and Islamic bank performance.

Although this partly corroborates the hypotheses brought forward above in the analytical framework section, the missing correlation between the global environment variables – in particular (re)financing opportunities – and most of the performance indicators is at odds with the theoretical exposition, and needs to be explained. The global environment factors clearly depend on the geographical location of the bank concerned, as most of the banks operate in a single national market: (Re)financing opportunities mirror the macro-economic conditions of the country, while the regulatory framework and standards are set by government authorities. As was outlined in the theoretical exposition, both macro-economic conditions and the regulatory framework differ across the various GCC countries and Malaysia. At the same time, the performance of Islamic banks within a single national market will most likely differ, as conventional wisdom suggests. Therefore, banks within the same national market might report the same level of global environment factors, but differences in the performance indicators, leading to a missing correlation of the two groups of factors across banks of the same location. Moreover, bank performance is measured in this study in relative terms: respondents rated their performance in comparison with other Islamic banks, where these banks are most likely located in the same national market. Therefore, even if there are significant differences of the global environment factors leading to significant performance differences across the various geographical markets, respondents might not take this into account, as they do not assess their performance with banks in geographical locations other than their home base. Interestingly enough, the negative correlation between regulatory framework and customer loyalty can also not be attributed to the geographical location of the banks: the differences of customer loyalty performance across the various locations of Islamic banks present in the study are statistically not significant, as evidenced in Exhibit 65, nor are the differences of the regulatory framework and standards, as presented in Exhibit 66.

Exhibit 65: t-test for customer loyalty

	N	Average	t-test significance
GCC countries	25	.059	.515
Malaysia	11	-.135	

Exhibit 66: t-test for regulatory framework and standards

	N	Average	t-test significance
GCC countries	25	.042	.708
Malaysia	11	-.096	

But how can the negative correlation be explained, then, which implies that low performers are suffering from more unfavorable conditions of the regulatory framework than high performers. It can be argued that the observed relation between the regulatory framework and customer loyalty is due to the subjective measure of the factor "regulatory framework and standards". First, the discussion about the improvement potential of the regulatory environment is a hot topic in Islamic finance, regardless of location. Second, as has been evidenced in other empirical studies, low performers tend to attribute their lack of performance to external factors, while high performers attribute it to internal shortcomings.[291] Therefore, the observed correlation might be attributable to this imputation effect rather than a true relationship between the two factors.

3.2.2 Model 2: Impact of Internal Factors on Performance

In model 2, the analysis of the impact of internal factors on Islamic bank performance is in focus. Internal factors consist of market-access core competencies, functionality-related core competencies, and integrity-related core competencies – the areas of core competencies proposed in the literature –, as well as reputation as Islamic company, and Sharia board efficiency and effectiveness – two Islamic-finance specific assumed core competencies, which have been singled out for analytical purposes. In the empirical examination, the following two propositions have been tested: First, that variations in Islamic bank performance can be explained by differences in the resource and competency endowment of banks. Second, that bank performance depends on the adherence to strategic groups, which are largely defined by the socio-cultural background of the banks.

Exhibit 67 presents the results of the correlation analysis to the first proposition. Market-access core competencies, functionality-related core competencies, integrity-related core competencies, reputation as Islamic company, and Sharia board efficiency and effectiveness have been correlated with profitability, customer loyalty, and market share, respectively. As a first observation, it can be established that every internal factor is at least correlated with one performance indicator. Moreover, every performance indicator is correlated with at least one internal factor.

[291] Cf. Laudicina (2005), p. 4-5.

Exhibit 67: Correlation analysis to proposition 2

	Profitability (ROE)	Customer loyalty	Market share
Market-access core competencies	.09	.20	.45***
Functionality-related core competencies	-.01	.47***	.17
Integrity-related core competencies	.29**	.52***	.19
Reputation as Islamic company	-.04	.09	.23*
Sharia board efficiency and effectiveness	-.01	.41***	.00

***: 1% significance level (1-sided)
** : 5% significance level (1-sided)
* : 10% significance level (1-sided)

However, there are marked differences across the various internal factors as well as the performance indicators. On the one hand, integrity-related core competencies is the only factor that correlates with two performance indicators – profitability (ROE) and customer loyalty. On the other hand, while a relationship can be established for customer loyalty to three internal factors – functionality-related core competencies, integrity-related core competencies, and Sharia board efficiency and effectiveness –, this can be done to only two in the case of market share – market-access core competencies, and reputation as Islamic company –, and a single one in the case of profitability – integrity-related core competencies. In the first case, all three correlations are highly significant at the 1% level. In the second case, the correlation with market-access core competencies is highly significant (1% level), the correlation with reputation as Islamic company is significant at the 10% level only. In the last case, the correlation is significant at the 5% level.

At this point, the results suggest the following: the various internal factors have an uneven impact on the different performance indicators. In detail, profitability appears to be independent of market-access core competencies, functionality-related core competencies, reputation as Islamic company, and Sharia board efficiency and effectiveness. What is more, the relatively low correlation with integrity-related core competencies, although significant at the 5% level, suggests that there may be other factors influencing company performance. We would therefore expect to observe significant correlations between profitability and various company strategies presented in model 3. Customer loyalty seems to be independent of market-access core competencies, and reputation as Islamic company. Functionality-related core competencies, integrity-related core competencies, and Sharia board efficiency and effectiveness, however, have a high impact on customer loyalty. Finally, market share appears independent of functionality-related core competencies, integrity-related core competencies, and Sharia board efficiency and effectiveness. It is strongly impacted by market-access core competencies, and, to a lesser degree, by reputation as an Islamic company. Consequently, proposition 2 is only partly corroborated.

Exhibit 68: Correlation analysis to market-access core competencies

	Market share
Customer relations	.50***
Brand image	.35**
Distribution capabilities	.13

***: 1% significance level (1-sided)
** : 5% significance level (1-sided)
* : 10% significance level (1-sided)

In order to understand more about the driving forces of company performance, a correlation analysis of the individual items behind the strongly significant factors market-access core competencies, functionality-related core competencies, and integrity-related core competencies was undertaken. Exhibit 68 shows the results of the analysis of correlation between customer relations, brand image, and distribution capabilities – the individual items behind market-access core competencies – and market share. As is evidenced by the analysis, customer relations and brand image have a strong positive impact on market share, while the effect of distribution capabilities is not significant.

Exhibit 69 demonstrates the results of the correlation between customer loyalty and the individual items behind functionality-related core competencies – customer service, supporting processes, resource efficiency, technological capabilities and equipment, technological expertise, financial expertise, and financial processing capabilities. As can be seen, customer loyalty is impacted by all of them.

Exhibit 69: Correlation analysis to functionality-related core competencies

	Customer loyalty
Customer service	.51***
Supporting processes	.57***
Resource efficiency	.43***
Technological capabilities and equipment	.30**
Technological expertise	.29**
Financial expertise	.40***
Financial processing capabilities	.23*

***: 1% significance level (1-sided)
** : 5% significance level (1-sided)
* : 10% significance level (1-sided)

Exhibit 70: Correlation analysis to integrity-related core competencies

	Profitability (ROE)	Customer loyalty
Co-operation	.35**	.35**
Management quality	.21	.49***
Firm culture	.29*	.25*
Implementation capabilities	.24*	.51***
Financial standing	-.11	.20

***: 1% significance level (1-sided)
** : 5% significance level (1-sided)
* : 10% significance level (1-sided)

As is presented in Exhibit 70, the individual items behind integrity-related core competencies have an uneven impact on profitability (ROE), and customer loyalty, respectively. Co-operation, firm culture, and implementation capabilities correlate positively and significantly with profitability (ROE), while management quality and financial standing appear to have no impact. Customer loyalty, on the other hand, is positively and significantly correlated with all individual items except for financial standing.

Proposition 2 on the impact of internal factors on company performance was further examined by a linear regression analysis. The result of the regression analysis to the proposition for profitability (ROE) is documented in Exhibit 71. The regression explains approx. 21% of the variance of profitability (ROE). As was the case in the correlation analysis, integrity-related core competencies are the only factor that appears to be significant. However, with an F-value of 1.583 at a significance level of .195, the overall regression is not significant.

Exhibit 71: Regression analysis to proposition 2 for profitability (ROE)

	Std. Beta	Sig. level
Market-access core competencies	.27	.227
Functionality-related core competencies	-.47	.069
Integrity-related core competencies	.58*	.016
Reputation as Islamic company	-.03	.897
Sharia board efficiency and effectiveness	-.18	.439
R^2	.209	
F	1.583	.195

* : value is significant

Exhibit 72: Regression analysis to proposition 2 for customer loyalty

	Std. Beta	Sig. level
Market-access core competencies	-.21	.294
Functionality-related core competencies	.31	.180
Integrity-related core competencies	.19	.345
Reputation as Islamic company	-.17	.379
Sharia board efficiency and effectiveness	.42*	.047
R^2	.377	
F	3.625	.011

* : value is significant

Exhibit 73: Regression analysis to proposition 2 for market share

	Std. Beta	Sig. level
Market-access core competencies	.41	.054
Functionality-related core competencies	.21	.392
Integrity-related core competencies	.01	.957
Reputation as Islamic company	.19	.378
Sharia board efficiency and effectiveness	-.43	.052
R^2	.295	
F	2.505	.052

* : value is significant

Exhibit 72 documents the result of the regression analysis for customer loyalty. Here, only Sharia board efficiency and effectiveness has a positive, significant impact on customer loyalty, while the regression coefficients of functionality-related core competencies and integrity-related core competencies – both factors correlate significantly with customer loyalty – are not significant. The explained variance (approx. 38%) is relatively high. Moreover, the overall regression is also significant with an F-value of 3.625 at a significance level of .011.

The regression analysis results for market share are presented in Exhibit 73. Although the regression explains approx. 30% of the variance of market share, none of the regression coefficients is at a significant level, nor is the overall regression.

As was the case with the correlation analysis, the regression analysis only partially corroborates proposition 2. Moreover, it does so to a lesser degree than the correlation analysis. Integrity-related core competencies and Sharia board efficiency and effectiveness appear to be the only internal factors, which impact profitability (ROE) and customer loyalty, respectively.

This partial corroboration of proposition 2 calls for an explanation. Proposition 2 postulated that better endowment with resources and capabilities (core competencies) leads to better performance. As was argued in the conceptual model section, there is reason to believe that this statement holds true for every internal factor included in the study. However, as was also pointed out, core competencies that offer potential competitive advantages need to be distinguished from basic competencies, which are merely prerequisites for being active within an industry. Although the definition of core competencies gives some hints as to which competencies can be regarded core and which not, strategic management theory abuts on its limits in predicting core competencies. Rather, the distinction of core competencies and basic competencies is an empirical question. Hence, the results of the correlation and regression analyses can be interpreted as an identification of core and basic competencies. They suggest that integrity-related core competencies are the only core competencies for profitability (ROE), while market-access core competencies, functionality-related core competencies, reputation as Islamic company, and Sharia board efficiency and effectiveness are mere basic competencies here. For customer loyalty, functionality-related core competencies, integrity-related core competencies, and Sharia board efficiency and effectiveness offer competitive advantages as core competencies, while market-access core competencies and reputation as Islamic company are basic competencies. Finally, market-access core competencies and reputation as Islamic company appear to be core competencies for market share performance, while functionality-related core competencies, integrity-related core competencies, and Sharia board efficiency and effectiveness do not offer competitive advantage here.

Moreover, the relatively low correlation of profitability (ROE) with a single internal factor may be attributable to the fact that ROE is an accounting figure, the value of which is heavily influenced by accounting standards and practices. As was evidenced before in the theoretical framework section, there is a lack of standard accounting practices across the GCC countries and Malaysia, leading to considerable differences in reported profitability across banks in these regions. Variations in ROE might therefore be more a reflection of differing accounting practices than differences in the endowment of resources and capabilities.

Besides the impact of internal factors on Islamic bank performance, model 2 also developed the proposition that bank performance depends on strategic groups, namely Islamic subsidiaries of conventional banks whose corporate headquarters are located in the West, Islamic subsidiaries of conventional banks whose corporate headquarters are located in the GCC countries or Malaysia, and Islamic banks that are either stand-alone or belong to another Islamic bank.

Exhibit 74 documents the ANOVA to this proposition for all three performance indicators used in the study. As can be seen, the performance differences across the three proposed resource-based strategic groups are not significant. Therefore, it can be concluded that bank performance does not depend on the adherence of companies to these groups. On average, there are no performance differences between Islamic subsidiaries of conventional banks whose headquarters are located in the West, Islamic subsidiaries of conventional banks whose corporate headquarters are located in the GCC countries or Malaysia, and Islamic banks that are either stand-alone or belong to another Islamic bank.

Exhibit 74: ANOVA to proposition 3

	Significance
Profitability (ROE)	.242
Customer loyalty	.345
Market share	.777

3.2.3 Model 3: Impact of Company Strategies on Performance

Model 3 analyzes the impact of company strategies on Islamic bank performance. Company strategies include cost leadership, price leadership, product differentiation, marketing and sales differentiation, focus, emulation of conventional products, and reputation as Islamic company. The empirical analysis tested the following proposition: Company strategies have an uneven impact on Islamic bank performance. While no correlation is expected between cost leadership strategy, price leadership strategy, and emulation of conventional products on bank performance, a positive correlation is expected between product differentiation strategy, marketing and sales differentiation strategy, focus strategy, and reputation as Islamic company on Islamic bank performance.

Exhibit 75 presents the results of the correlation analysis to this proposition. The various strategies described above have been correlated with profitability (ROE), customer loyalty, and market share, respectively, as performance indicators. A first look at the table suggests the following: cost leadership, price leadership, and emulation of conventional products do not correlate with any of the performance indicators, which is line with what has been predicted theoretically. Moreover, the other company strategies – product differentiation, marketing and sales differentiation, focus, and reputation as Islamic company – correlate with at least one of the performance indicators. The customer loyalty performance indicator is even linked to all four company strategies predicted to impact it. Besides, the focus strategy does not correlate with market share. Again, all this complies with the theoretical expectations.

Exhibit 75: Correlation analysis to proposition 4

	Profitability (ROE)	Customer loyalty	Market share
Cost leadership	.18	.12	.06
Price leadership	.00	.09	.16
Product differentiation	.08	.42***	.08
Marketing and sales differentiation	-.01	.39***	.01
Focus	.18	.25*	.08
Emulation of conventional products	.06	-.16	.20
Reputation as Islamic company	.05	.24*	.44***

***: 1% significance level (1-sided)
** : 5% significance level (1-sided)
* : 10% significance level (1-sided)

However, there are two results, which are at odds with the hypotheses brought forward in the conceptual model section. First, no relationship could be established between profitability (ROE) and any of the company strategies, suggesting that company strategies have no impact on ROE. Second, market share is correlated with reputation as Islamic company only, suggesting that all other theoretically relevant company strategies do not influence market share performance. Consequently, company strategies have an even more uneven impact on Islamic bank performance than predicted and proposition 4 is only partly corroborated.

In order to get a more detailed view on the driving forces of company performance, a correlation analysis of the individual items behind the strongly significant factors product differentiation strategy and marketing and sales differentiation strategy was conducted. Exhibit 76 presents the results of this analysis for product quality and design, and product diversification – the two items behind the factor product differentiation strategy. As can be observed, both have a strongly significant positive impact on customer loyalty performance.

Exhibit 76: Correlation analysis to product differentiation strategy

	Customer loyalty
Product quality and design	.38**
Product diversification	.37**

***: 1% significance level (1-sided)
** : 5% significance level (1-sided)
* : 10% significance level (1-sided)

Exhibit 77 documents the results of the correlation between customer orientation strategy, distribution strategy, and brand and image strategy – the individual items behind the factor marketing and sales differentiation strategy – and customer loyalty. As is evidenced, all three have a positive impact on customer loyalty, although at varying significance levels.

Exhibit 77: Correlation analysis to marketing and sales differentiation strategy

	Customer loyalty
Customer orientation	.45***
Distribution	.23*
Brand and image	.38**

***: 1% significance level (1-sided)
** : 5% significance level (1-sided)
* : 10% significance level (1-sided)

Proposition 4 on the impact of company strategies on company performance was further examined using a linear regression analysis. The result of the regression analysis to the proposition for profitability (ROE) is presented in Exhibit 78. None of the single regression coefficients are significant. Moreover, with an R^2 of .036, an F-value of .151 at a significance level of .992, the overall regression is not significant. Just like the correlation analysis, the regression analysis does not establish any impact of company strategies on Islamic bank profitability (ROE).

Exhibit 78: Regression analysis to proposition 4 for profitability (ROE)

	Std. Beta	**Sig. level**
Cost leadership	.08	.751
Price leadership	.02	.934
Product differentiation	.13	.685
Marketing and sales differentiation	-.15	.646
Focus	.16	.404
Emulation of conventional products	-.09	.703
Reputation as Islamic company	-.02	.922
R^2	.036	
F	.151	.992

* : value is significant

Exhibit 79: Regression analysis to proposition 4 for customer loyalty

	Std. Beta	Sig. level
Cost leadership	-.09	.630
Price leadership	.02	.921
Product differentiation	.54*	.032
Marketing and sales differentiation	.20	.427
Focus	.18	.239
Emulation of conventional products	-.42*	.024
Reputation as Islamic company	-.15	.379
R^2	.439	
F	3.125	.014

* : value is significant

Exhibit 79 documents the regression results to proposition 4 for customer loyalty. The regression explains approx. 44% of the variance of the customer loyalty performance indicator. Moreover, the overall regression is significant with an F-value of 3.125 at a significance level of .014. However, the results are only partially in line with the findings of the correlation analysis and partially at odds with theoretical expectations: While product differentiation appears to have a positive impact on customer loyalty – as is theoretically predicted –, emulation of conventional products has a negative regression coefficient – theoretically, no impact was expected.

Exhibit 80: Regression analysis to proposition 4 for market share

	Std. Beta	Sig. level
Cost leadership	.16	.462
Price leadership	-.10	.594
Product differentiation	-.12	.651
Marketing and sales differentiation	-.13	.650
Focus	-.02	.922
Emulation of conventional products	.34	.096
Reputation as Islamic company	.54*	.007
R^2	.300	
F	1.718	.145

* : value is significant

The regression analysis results for the market share performance indicator are presented in Exhibit 80. In line with the outcome of the correlation analysis, reputation as Islamic company is the only strategy with a significant positive regression coefficient. Although the regression explains approx. 30% of the variance of the market share performance indicator, the overall regression is not significant with an F-value of 1.718 at a significance level of .145.

As in the case of the correlation analysis, the regression analysis only partially corroborates proposition 4. Moreover, it does so to a lesser degree than the correlation analysis, given the fact that two out of the three regressions are overall not significant, and that the significant regression is partially at odds with theoretical expectations. Product differentiation and emulation of conventional products appear to be the only factors, which impact customer loyalty, and reputation as Islamic company appears to be the only factor influencing market share.

This partial corroboration of proposition 4 as well as the findings of the regression analysis contradicting the theoretical expectations call for an explanation. The statements of proposition 4 that are not supported by the analysis are the following: First, profitability (ROE) is positively impacted by product differentiation strategy, marketing and sales differentiation strategy, focus strategy, and reputation as Islamic company. Second, emulation of conventional products has no impact on customer loyalty. Third, product differentiation strategy, and marketing and sales differentiation strategy have a positive impact on market share.

In the empirical analysis, the missing impact of the theoretically relevant strategies is particularly puzzling. One possible explanation for this may be that company strategies are the fundamental, long-term oriented behavior of firms in order to realize their long-term objectives. Looking at the three performance indicators used, customer loyalty maybe is the indicator, which is most long-term oriented, followed by market share – which may be influenced in the short term by tactical behavior – and finally profitability (ROE), which probably is a more short-term oriented indicator. The empirical observation that customer loyalty is influenced by all company strategies predicted to do so, market share is influenced by one, and profitability (ROE) by none is in line with this potential explanation. However, this explanatory attempt implies that there is some sort of tactical behavior – i.e. more short-term oriented – which needs to be taken into account to explain company performance differences. One such tactical behavior concerning ROE may be related to accounting standards and practices. As was argued before along similar lines for internal factors, variations in ROE might be more a reflection of differing accounting practices than differences in company strategies. However, there may be other causes for this empirical result, either related to the research design or leading to a refinement of strategic management theory.

The negative impact of the emulation of conventional products strategy on customer loyalty in the regression analysis is also surprising. On theoretical grounds, no impact was expected, as Islamic banks are in competition with conventional banks, and therefore all have reason to emulate the financial conditions of conventional products.

A possible explanation for the empirical observation may be that the more financial conditions of conventional products are emulated, the blurrier the distinction between the Islamic financial product offered and the conventional product becomes for the customer, which in turn impairs customer satisfaction. However, as before, there may be other reasons for this empirical result.

3.2.4 Summary of Empirical Results

The empirical analysis tested the theoretical propositions developed in the conceptual model section. The conceptual model is divided into three different areas: Model 1 looks at potential effects of external factors on Islamic bank performance. Model 2 develops hypotheses about the potential impact of internal factors on Islamic bank performance. Model 3, finally, considers company strategies as potential explanatory factors for Islamic bank performance. Overall, most of the research findings are in line with the theoretical propositions, as will be recapitulated in the following.

Model 1 predicted that external factors have an uneven impact on Islamic bank performance. While the industry structure was not expected to explain intra-industry performance differences in Islamic finance, a more favorable global environment was assumed to lead to better performance. Both the correlation analysis and the regression analysis could not establish a link between external factors and the various performance indicators, with one exception: the factor regulatory framework and standards correlated significantly with customer loyalty, and had a significant regression coefficient in the analysis for profitability (ROE), where the overall regression was not significant, though. Therefore, the proposition of model 1 related to industry structure could be supported, while the proposition related to global environment was only partly corroborated.

In model 2, two propositions were brought forward. First, it was predicted that better endowment with core competencies leads to better performance. Second, it was assumed that Islamic banks could be classified into three resource-based strategic groups, with a corresponding difference in performance. As for the first proposition, both the correlation analysis and the regression analysis could establish a link between various internal factors and various performance indicators. However, not all internal factors impacted all performance indicators. This observation can maybe attributed to the distinction between core competencies and basic competencies. Consequently, the proposition was largely supported, although, again, with a salt of grain. Concerning the second proposition, no significant performance differences across the three assumed resource-based strategic groups were found. Therefore, the proposition had to be rejected.

Model 3 predicted an uneven impact of company strategies on Islamic bank performance. While no correlation was expected between cost leadership strategy, price leadership strategy, and emulation of conventional products on bank performance, a positive correlation was expected between product differentiation strategy, marketing and sales differentiation strategy, focus strategy, and reputation as Islamic company on Islamic bank performance. Here, the empirical results are mixed.

The first part of the proposition – the non-existence of an impact of various strategies on performance – could be largely supported in both the correlation and the regression analyses, with the exception of a significant negative regression coefficient of the emulation of conventional products strategy on customer loyalty. The empirical test, however, is only somewhat supportive of the second part of the proposition. Significant correlations were found for all relevant strategies with customer loyalty, for one with market share, and for none with profitability (ROE). Therefore, the proposition is only partly corroborated.

4 Summary and Concluding Remarks

This chapter serves as a summary appraisal of the main arguments and major results of both the analytical framework and the empirical study. It is organized in three sections. It starts with an analytical and empirical summary. Next, implications of the study for Islamic financial institutions are described. Finally, research limitations and suggestions for future research are discussed.

4.1 Analytical and Empirical Summary

The present research developed a holistic conceptual framework for identifying and testing key success factors of Islamic financial institutions. The framework integrated insights into the current practices in Islamic finance, a variety of theories – namely the market-based view, the resource-based view, and, to some extent, New Institutional Economics approaches – as well as previous research from the fields of strategic management and economics. It was empirically examined using a questionnaire-based survey of 36 Islamic financial institutions with the major region of operations in the GCC area and in Malaysia. The intended purpose of this model and its subsequent empirical analysis was twofold: on the one hand, general theoretical propositions of the strategic management literature should be tested; on the other hand, the concrete Islamic finance-specific manifestations of the various influencing factors on company performance should be examined.

Accordingly, there are also two overall conclusions of this study. First, the general theoretical propositions of the strategic management literature were largely validated. In detail, three general propositions were put to the test:

- External factors have an uneven impact on performance. While the industry structure does not explain intra-industry performance differences in Islamic finance, a more favorable global environment leads to better performance.
- Better endowment with core competencies leads to better performance.
- Company strategies have an uneven impact on performance. Some will have a positive impact on performance, others will have none.

All were essentially supported by the empirical results, albeit with a salt of grain. Second, the Islamic-finance specific manifestations of key success factors – in terms of core competencies and company strategies – were identified. It was found that

- Integrity-related core competencies are the driving force behind profitability.
- Functionality-related core competencies, integrity-related core competencies, and Sharia board efficiency and effectiveness – as internal factors – as well as product differentiation and marketing and sales differentiation, focus, and reputation as Islamic company – as company strategies – are the main drivers for customer loyalty.

- Market-access core competencies, and reputation as Islamic company – as internal factors – as well as reputation as Islamic company – as company strategy – are the main drivers for market share.

However, for both external and internal factors as well as company strategies, not all theoretically relevant factors proved to have an impact on Islamic bank performance. In the case of external factors, the relative measurement of performance could potentially explain the missing correlations of global environment and performance. In the case of internal factors, it was suggested that the empirical analysis might have isolated basic and core competencies. In the case of company strategies, the differences of implied time horizon of the various performance indicators was seen as a potential explanation for the empirical results. In all three cases, accounting practices might blur the relationship between profitability and the various influencing factors. The implications of these observations for future research will be discussed below in the last section of the study.

Another important finding of the study concerned a proposed resource-based strategic grouping of Islamic financial institutions into Islamic subsidiaries of conventional banks whose headquarters are located in the West, Islamic subsidiaries of conventional banks whose corporate headquarters are located in the GCC countries or Malaysia, and Islamic banks that are either stand-alone or belong to another Islamic bank. Performance differences across the three proposed groups were found not to be significant.

The present study made key contributions both to theoretical and empirical research. From a theoretical point of view, identifying and adding Islamic-finance specific parameters further refined the external factors, internal factors, and company strategies proposed in the literature. In particular, factors like Sharia board efficiency and effectiveness, and reputation as Islamic company were singled out.

From an empirical point of view, three important contributions were made. First, this affects the operationalisation of theoretical constructs: Reliable and valid variables for strategic management research were developed or further refined drawing on previous empirical studies. This is of particular importance for core competencies, where empirical research still has not reached maturity, and thus measurement scales are scarcely available. As is called for in the literature, they were measured at a low level of aggregation.[292]

Second, the empirical study adds to the discussion of firm performance and its various influencing factors in the strategic management literature. Its findings are in accordance with both the market-based view and the resource-based view of strategic management, and therefore seems to support the notion that the two perspectives are supplementary in explaining firm performance. This also suggests that there is a need for a composite framework that will synthesize premises from both perspectives. The

[292] Cf. Mauri and Michaels (1998).

analysis is also in line with other studies that found no effect of company strategies on profitability.[293]

Third, the present research provides valuable empirical data about a particular industry. Moreover, it is the first examination of this kind for Islamic finance. This is all the more important as sources of persistent firm success might prove fundamentally context specific.[294]

4.2 Implications for Islamic Financial Institutions

The statistical analysis evidenced the importance of several internal factors as well as company strategies for various performance indicators, even though some of the (significant) correlation coefficients were ranging below .5. If one takes the interdependencies discovered at face value, some implications of the empirical results for the management of Islamic financial institutions can be discussed. This will be done along the lines of the individual internal factors and company strategies, respectively, starting with market-access core competencies.

Market-access core competencies proved to have a significant effect on market share. In a more detailed view, the factors customer relations and brand image correlated significantly with market share, while distribution capabilities did not. Therefore, Islamic banks do not seem to take competitive advantage of their well-built distribution networks composed of a branch and ATM network, or direct banking facilities, such as internet banking and call centers. As is proposed in the literature, distribution capabilities should rather be viewed as basic competencies.[295] Islamic banks should, however, build up favorable customer relations and a favorable brand image. The former relates to their ability to access capital, the competitive strength of their current customer base, and the general relations with their customers. The latter concerns their reputation as financial services provider and their general brand image. Islamic financial institutions should take appropriate measures to enhance their capabilities in this field.

One of the significant factors affecting customer loyalty was functionality-related core competencies. In particular, all individual items behind it – customer service, supporting processes, resource efficiency, technological equipment and capabilities, technological expertise, financial expertise, and financial processing capabilities – correlated significantly with customer loyalty, albeit to varying degrees. This suggests that Islamic banks should pay particular attention to the acquisition of such competencies. Regarding customer service, Islamic banks are advised to respond fast to customer requests, and constantly monitor and enhance the service quality in marketing and sales and transaction processing. Competencies in the supporting processes require a strong risk management, good research capabilities, a superior

---

293 Cf. Spanos and Lioukas (2001).

294 Cf. Collis (1994)

295 Börner (2000b), p. 231-232.

knowledge and data management, and outstanding HR processes and administration. Resource efficiency is another highly significant factor and relates to all principal services rendered by a bank. In a similar manner, banks require strong technological capabilities and equipment – the tangible hard- and software – as well as technological expertise – the know-how – in all major areas of banking services. The financial expertise seems to be another domain, which needs to be strengthened for effective competition. It encompasses inter alia competencies in product development innovation, know-how of both Islamic and financial market requirements, and market knowledge in general. Among the functionality-related core competencies, financial processing capabilities had the weakest correlation with customer loyalty. Obviously, strengths in this area have a tendency towards becoming basic competencies.

Integrity-related core competencies had a significant effect on both profitability (ROE) and customer loyalty. They are the only internal factor, which impacted two profitability indicators. In detail, the factors co-operation, firm culture, and implementation capabilities correlated significantly with profitability (ROE); the same factors along with management quality correlated significantly with customer loyalty. Among these four, management quality and implementation capabilities had the highest significance level. All these factors relate to the organization and the self-conception of the firms, and many are rather soft, behavioral factors. Co-operation, for example, includes strengths in vertical communication across the organization, cross-functional information exchange, and the degree to which the company works in a team-based approach. Firm culture regards the extent of transparency and openness across the company and hierarchies, the ability of the company to attract and retain high-quality people, the prevalence of a meritocracy culture, and reward of creativity and innovation, among other things. Management quality becomes a little bit more tangible as it includes managerial competencies, and knowledge and skills of employees. Implementation capabilities are even more tangible with strengths in controlling, the compensation and reward system, and the use of strategy-enforcing tools as exemplary components of this factor. The results suggest that Islamic financial institutions should set up an organizational framework, which supports the build-up of strengths and competencies in these areas. It also commends that Islamic banks should use state-of-the-art controlling, compensation, and strategy-enforcing tools in order to ensure effective implementation of their strategies. As an example, Islamic banks could use the balanced scorecard for strategy enforcement. Financial standing – a factor including asset quality, equity base, and financial rating, and the last component of integrity-related core competencies – had, by the way, no significant effect on any of the performance indicators. This may point to the fact that the financial standing is a basic competence rather than a core competence of Islamic banks.

Reputation as Islamic company was the second factor, which had a significant effect on market share, although at a relatively low significance level. Among the individual items behind this factor are the engagement of the firm in socially beneficial activities, and the reputation of the Sharia board. Just like the brand image in general, the "Islamic" image of the company must be cultivated. Islamic banks should therefore take special care in the selection of their Sharia board members. It may not be a coincidence that a small group of highly reputed Sharia scholars is shared by a number of firms. Moreover, some Sharia scholars specialize in Islamic finance issues and signal their competence in this domain by a high number of publications. A good means to show socially beneficial engagement might be charitable donations or some sort of sponsorship. By the way, this is also done by conventional banks, and is generally viewed as a good means to enhance their global image. Of course, the reputation as Islamic company may potentially also be strengthened through such means as corporate design, corporate language, or the provision of Islamic facilities, such as prayer rooms in the banks' branch offices.

Besides other factors mentioned above, customer loyalty was impacted by Sharia board efficiency and effectiveness, at a highly significant level. This factor is composed of the relative strength of the speed and efficiency of the Sharia-approval process (both in product development and marketing and sales), Sharia compliance, and the overall effectiveness and efficiency of the Sharia board. This means that Islamic financial institutions have to find the right balance between two seemingly contradictory requirements: On the one hand, the Sharia-approval process must be fast, which, by the way, corresponds with the above-mentioned observation that Islamic banks are advised to respond fast to customer requests. On the other hand, Sharia compliance may entail a thorough, rather time-consuming process. Obviously, further standardization of rules and regulations as well as products and services will alleviate the effects of this task.

Among the company strategies, product differentiation proved to have a significant effect on customer loyalty in the correlation analysis. In a more detailed view, both components of product differentiation – product quality and design, and product diversification – correlated significantly with customer loyalty. This result is unsurprising, as product innovation is one of the hot topics among Islamic finance practitioners. The empirical analysis suggests that Islamic financial institutions should follow a strategy, which emphasizes product and service quality control, product design, and product innovation, and builds product-related brands. Moreover, products should be introduced fast into the market. Besides, it is advised that Islamic banks refine their products to local needs and demands, provide variations within the product lines, and tailor-make products according to customer specification.

Another significant factor affecting customer loyalty was marketing and sales differentiation. As before, all individual items behind it – customer orientation, distribution, and brand and image – correlated significantly with customer loyalty, albeit to varying degrees. Customer orientation puts particular stress on innovation in marketing techniques and methods, immediate responses to customer requests, and quick decision-making processes. Brand and image relates, among other things, to the brand-identification of the company, and the reputation in the industry. These results are somewhat consistent with what has been observed in the area of market-access and functionality-related core competencies. There, too, marketing and sales service quality, fast responses to customer requests, brand image, and reputation were of particular importance. The concordant strategies can therefore be seen as a prerequisite to acquire the relevant competencies. Apart from that, the empirical results suggest that Islamic banks should follow a strategy of acquiring high-caliber workforce, providing extensive employee training, and building up efficient internal communication channels. Islamic financial institutions are also advised to gain control over strong distribution channels. Finally, promotion expenditures above industry-average seem to be helpful.

In the correlation analysis, focus strategy correlated significantly with customer loyalty, although at a low significance level. Focusing on a few main product lines, and focusing on a few customer segments are the two items behind that strategy. At a first glance, one of the suggestions of the product differentiation strategy – namely the provision of a broad variation within the product lines – could be in contradiction to the focus strategy. However, focusing on a few main product lines does not preclude a broad variation within these product lines.

Reputation as Islamic company is the last strategy that showed a significant association with company performance, more precisely with customer loyalty and market share. The importance of this strategy is consistent with the importance of reputation as Islamic company as a competence area. Therefore, this result suggests again that Islamic financial institutions should take appropriate steps to strengthen their "Islamic" image.

4.3 Limitations and Future Research Suggestions

Considering the limitations of the study will put the findings and implications of the research into perspective, and help identify suggestions for future research. The overall limitations of the study will be discussed first, followed by considerations for each of the three different models examined.

As was detailed in the research methodology section, self-reported data were used to test the theoretical propositions of the various models. This procedure entails the potential of survey biases, despite the application of stringent construct tests to confirm reliability, content validity, convergent validity, and discriminant validity of the observed variables. The questionnaire asked for the respondents' perceptions regarding the various issues of this study, which might not necessarily match objective reality. Although subjective measures are widely used in strategic management research, and can be justified by both practical and theoretical considerations[296], they might be prone to subjective biases. First, respondents might be inclined to rationalize their firms' competitive behavior based on conventional

[296] As a practical consideration, it was anticipated in this study that most participants would not be willing to share potentially confidential hard financial and competitive data (e.g. balance sheet, profit and loss sheet, market share), which was actually the case. As a theoretical consideration, one could follow the social constructionist view that reality as such is socially constructed and therefore there is no objective environment. In a more attenuated manner, one can still argue that managerial perceptions have considerable impact on the strategic behavior of companies (cf. Chattopadhyay et. al. (1999)).

wisdom about strategic management. Second, respondents have a subjective definition of industry boundaries, which might affect their relative positioning compared to competitors regarding their core competencies, strategies and performance. This is especially relevant for Islamic financial institutions, which might consider either the financial industry at large, or the Islamic finance segment, as their competitive realm.

Apart from potential biases resulting from the use of perceptual measures, further limitations arise from the time period considered, research design, and sample size. First, performance was looked at at a certain point in time, therefore precluding the possibility to account for any business cycle effects, or transient problems. Second, the research design was cross-sectional rather than longitudinal. In cross-sectional studies, different subjects are compared to each other at one point in time, while subjects are compared with themselves at different points in time in a longitudinal study. Therefore, cause effect relationships may not be definitely inferred from the results, as association is not causation. Last, the sample is with n=36 only slightly above what is normally considered a small sample in empirical research. Although the sample covered a large part of the GCC area and Malaysia markets, the statistical methods used are often viewed to be more powerful with a larger sample size. It is therefore suggested that future research adopts a longitudinal approach, possibly with a larger sample, to substantiate the results of this study.

Such an approach could also remedy another limitation of this study, which is the inherently static character of this research. However, in order to do this, further theoretical work is needed that explains the dynamic process how firms build up their competencies and employ certain strategies within a given industry. In contrast to such a dynamic approach, this study focused on effects within a static equilibrium context.

This study, although quite holistic in its general approach, nevertheless has limitations in the selection of individual factors included in the research. Admittedly, there is quite some leeway in the decision about which factors were considered. Therefore, some extensions of the model are suggested. Regarding external factors, one could for example include the prevailing interest rate, inflation, or GDP growth as additional macroeconomic factors. Internal factors, although quite comprehensive with regard to the resource-based view, could also be further refined. As an example, there could be differences across Islamic banks depending on whether they are state-owned or privately owned, as this might influence their respective company goals. Finally, the strategies included in the study, especially as regards the various differentiation strategies, could also be classified differently by other researchers.

Furthermore, as will be highlighted specifically for model 1 later, the possibility to draw general conclusions for the whole Islamic finance industry is limited by the fact that this research focused on Islamic finance in the GCC area and Malaysia. Therefore, a further roll-out to other geographic markets is suggested for future research.

Model 1, which examined the impact of external factors on Islamic banks performance, predicted that industry structure factors do not explain intra-industry performance differences in Islamic finance. However, there are mainly two reasons why this proposition was developed and found to hold true. First, a single industry was analyzed, therefore excluding the possibility to detect distinctive performance differences across industries. Second, the various geographic markets included were found to be quite homogeneous in terms of the industry structure factors considered. Therefore, the research results do not suggest that Islamic banks can ignore industry structure factors in general, but rather that they do not offer any sources for competitive advantages in the markets considered. According to the market-based view of strategic management, industry structure factors should play a role when more than one industry is looked at, or when differences in market conditions – e.g. across various geographic markets – are expected. In particular, one might find idiosyncratic performance differences between Islamic and conventional finance, as the two might be affected differently by such external factors as regulatory framework and standards. Another example might be idiosyncratic differences between Islamic banks operating in countries that have introduced interest-free banking systems as the rule – such as Sudan – and those in other countries operating alongside conventional banks – as is the case in the GCC countries and Malaysia. Consequently, it is suggested that future research enlarges the scope and includes more geographic markets and/or more industries. The comparison with conventional banks would be especially interesting, as it is often lamented by practitioners as well as theorists that Islamic banks are at a competitive disadvantage compared to their conventional counterparts.

A potential explanation for the empirical results of model 2 – the impact of internal factors on Islamic bank performance – was, that the analysis might have isolated basic and core competencies. From a theoretical perspective, it is hard to predict which is which, as the definition of core competence is rather general, and the theoretical expositions have so far concentrated on developing heuristics for the identification of core competencies rather than detailing industry-specific core competence areas at low aggregation levels. Interestingly enough, the heuristics often propose the use of working groups or expert panels for this matter, and leave ample room for subjective assessments. Accordingly, empirical research so far has mainly determined ex post which of the competencies considered are core and which not – as is the case in the present research. Therefore, future research should work on two areas. First, empirical results such as the ones from this study should be used to refine strategic management theory in order to better define the determinants of core competencies, and better explain the impact of core competencies on various performance indicators. Second, in order to support this task, further empirical studies could look at other, single industries.

In the same vein, strategic management theories could be further refined in the explanation of the use of various strategies and their influence on different performance indicators. As was evidenced in the empirical results of model 3 – the impact of company strategies on Islamic bank performance – not all performance indicators were affected by all theoretically relevant company strategies. This is in line with other empirical research, as was demonstrated above, but still calls for an explanation. It was suggested that there might be some sort of tactical behavior, potentially related to accounting practices, which influences company performance, in particular with regard to short-term performance. Future theoretical research should take this observation into consideration. Besides this enhancement of strategic management theory, future research should also focus on the conditions of the use of cost and price leadership strategies. In this study, it was predicted that these two strategies do not correlate with Islamic bank performance. However, the main reason for this was a statistical one, as a single or only very few companies should follow these strategies – provided that companies act rationally. Consequently, a statistical correlation cannot be established in a cross-sectional study, although one or a few companies might successfully apply such a strategy. Therefore, the empirical results of this study do not suggest that such strategies are futile in an Islamic finance setting. This research area could be further studied in case studies concentrating on Islamic banks, which apply cost or price leadership strategies.

References

Abdullah, Nazatul Izma (2004): "Malaysia's vision for Islamic finance", *asiamoney*, March 2004, pp. 20-22.

Abdul-Rahman, Yahia (1999): "Islamic Instruments for Managing Liquidity", *International Journal of Islamic Financial Services*, Vol. 1, No. 1.

Achenbach, Wieland, Steffens, Udo and Strohhecker, Jürgen (2003): „Strategisches Management", in: Bankakademie (Ed.): *Kompendium Management in Banking & Finance*, 2nd ed., Frankfurt a.M.

Adil, Ahmed (2004): *Risky business – Building investor confidence through* risk management and governance, www.megaevents.net/wibc/presentations/ 2004/ conference/268,1,Risky Business Building Investor Confidence Through Risk Management & Governance Ahmed Adil Partner, Ernst & Young Bahrain

Aggarwal, Rajesh K. and Yousef, Tarik (2000): "Islamic Banks and Investment Financing", *Journal of Money, Credit and Banking*, Vol. 32, No. 1 (February), pp. 93-120.

Al-Amine, Muhammad and Al-Bashir Muhammad (2001): "Istisna' and its application in Islamic banking", *Arab Law Quarterly*, Vol. 16, No. 1, pp. 22-48.

Al-Deehani, Talla, Abdel Karim, Rifaat Ahmed and Murinde, Victor (1999): „The Capital Structure of Islamic Banks under the Contractual Obligation of Profit Sharing", *International Journal of Theoretical and Applied Finance*, Vol. 2, No. 3, pp. 243-283.

Al-Harran, Saad (1999): "Introduction: Cases in Islamic Finance", *Arab Law Quarterly*, Vol. 14, No. 3, pp. 193-202.

Al-Laham, Andreas (1997) : *Strategieprozesse in deutschen Unternehmungen. Verlauf, Struktur und Effizienz*, Wiesbaden.

Altundag, Paolo and Haldi, Nadia (2003): *Handbuch Islamic Banking*, Pfäffikon.

Amit, Raphael and Schoemaker, Paul J.H. (1993): "Strategic Assets and Organizational Rent", *Strategic Management Journal*, Vol. 14, pp. 33-46.

Antes, Peter (1991): *Der Islam als politischer Faktor*, 2nd ed., Bonn.

Archer, Simon and Abdel Karim, Rifaat (2003): *Islamic Finance – Innovation and Growth*, London.

Arrow, Kenneth J. (1985): "The economics of agency", in: Pratt, John W. and Zeckhauser, Richard J. (Eds.): *Principals and agents: The structure of business,* Boston, pp. 37-51.

At-Tabari (Reprint 1954): *Jami'al-bayan 'an tawil aya al-qur'an, Cairo.*

Bacha, Obiyathullah Ismath (1999): "Derivative instruments and Islamic finance: Some thoughts for a reconsideration", *International Journal of Islamic Financial Services*, Vol. 1, No. 1.

Backhaus, Klaus, Erichson, Bernd, Plinke, Wulff and Weiber, Rolf (2003): *Multivariate Analysemethoden*, 10th ed., Berlin et.al.

Bahrain Monetary Agency (2002): *Islamic Banking and Finance in the Kingdom of Bahrain*, Manama.

Bahrain Monetary Agency (2003): *Islamic Banking Hub*, October 2003.

Bahrain Monetary Agency (2004): *Islamic Banking Hub*, January 2004.

Bain, Joe S. (1968): *Industrial Organization*, 2nd ed., New York.

Bälz, Kilian (2002): "Islamische Bankgeschäfte vor europäischen Gerichten", *Zeitschrift für vergleichende Rechtswissenschaft*, Vol. 101, pp. 379-383.

Bankakademie e.V. (Ed.) (2003): *Kompendium Management in Banking & Finance*, 2nd ed., Frankfurt a.M..

Barney, Jay (1991): "Firm Resources and Sustained Competitive Advantage", *Journal of Management*, Vol. 17, No. 1, pp. 99-120.

Barney, Jay B. (2001): "Is the Resource-Based 'View' a Useful Perspective for Strategic Management Research? Yes", *Strategic Management Journal*, Vol. 26, No. 1, pp. 41-56.

Bashir, Abdel-Hameed M. (2000): "Determinants of Profitability and Rate of Return Margins in Islamic Banks: Some Evidence from the Middle East", The ERF 7th Annual Conference, www.erf.org.eg/html/finance4.pdf

Basle Committee on Banking Supervision (1997): *Core Principles for Effective Banking Supervision*, Basle.

Bea, Franz Xaver and Göbel, Elisabeth (1999): *Organisation*, Stuttgart.

Bea, Franz Xaver and Haas, Jürgen (2001): *Strategisches Management*, 3rd ed., Stuttgart.

Bellalah, Mondher and Ellouz, Siwar (2004): „Islamic Finance, Interest Rates and Islamic Banking: A Survey of the Literature", *Finance India*, Vol. XVIII, pp. 533-546.

Bharadwaj, Sundar G., Varadarajan, P. Rajan and Fahy, John (1993): "Sustainable Competitive Advantage in Service Industries: A Conceptual Model and Research Propositions", *Journal of Marketing*, Vol. 57 (October), pp. 83-99.

Börner, Christoph J. (1999): "Verbundeffekte bei Unternehmenszusammenschlüssen aus Sicht des ‚Resource-based View' – dargestellt am Beispiel der Finanzdienstleistungswirtschaft", *Mitteilungen und Berichte der Abteilung Bankwirtschaft des Instituts für Bankwirtschaft und Bankrecht an der Universität zu Köln*, Vol. 30, No. 82, pp. 7-36.

Börner, Christoph J. (2000a): "Allfinanz, neue Bankvertriebswege und Resource-based View", *Mitteilungen und Berichte der Abteilung Bankwirtschaft des Instituts für Bankwirtschaft und Bankrecht an der Universität zu Köln*, Vol. 31, No. 83, pp. 49-73.

Börner, Christoph J. (2000b): *Strategisches Bankmanagement*, Munich et. al.

Börner, Christoph J. and Zmuda, Piotr (2001): "Kernkompetenzmanagement bei Sparkassen", *Mitteilungen und Berichte der Abteilung Bankwirtschaft des Instituts für Bankwirtschaft und Bankrecht an der Universität zu Köln*, Vol. 32, No. 84, pp. 39-68.

Bowman, Edward H. and Helfat, Constance E. (2001): "Does Corporate Strategy Matter?", *Strategic Management Journal*, Vol. 22, pp. 1-23.

Bronner, Rolf, Appel, Wolfgang and Wiemann, Volker (1999): *Empirische Personal- und Organisationsforschung*, Munich and Vienna.

Brown, Kym (2003): "Islamic Banking Comparative Analysis", *The Arab Bank Review*, Vol. 5, No. 2 (October), pp. 43-50.

Brush, Thomas H., Bromiley, Philip and Hendrickx, Margaretha (1999): "The Relative Influence of Industry and Corporation on Business Segment Performance: An Alternative Estimate", *Strategic Management Journal*, Vol. 20, No. 6, pp. 519-547.

Büschgen, Hans E. (1999): *Grundlagen des Bankmanagements*, Frankfurt a.M..

Buzzell, Robert D. and Bradley, T. Gale (1989): *Das PIMS-Programm*, Wiesbaden.

Buzzell, Robert D. and Gale, Bradley T. (1987): *The PIMS Principles – Linking Strategy to Performance,* New York.

Central Intelligence Agency (2004): *World Factbook*, Washington.

Cezanne, Wolfgang and Mayer, Annette (1998): "Neue Institutionenökonomik – Ein Überblick", *WISU*, 11/98, pp. 1345-1353.

Chahin, Hassan (2000): *Chancen und Risiken im islamischen Bankwesen*, Freiburg.

Chattopadhyay, Prithviraj, Glick, William H., Miller, C. Chet And Huber, George P. (1999): „Determinants of executive beliefs: comparing functional conditioning and social influence", *Strategic Management Journal*, Vol. 20, pp. 763-789.

Choi, Sun (1997): *Strategien von Banken im globalen Wettbewerb*, Wiesbaden.

CIBEDO (Ed.) (1980): *Universal Islamic Declaration – Politisch-religiöse islamische Grundsatzerklärung*, CIBEDO-Texte 4, Cologne.

Citicorp (no date): *Instruments of Islamic Finance*, www.citibank.com/ciib/download/instruif.pdf

Coase, Ronald H. (1937): "The nature of the firm", *Economica*, Vol. 4, pp. 386-405.

Collis, David (1994): "How valuable are organizational capabilities?", *Strategic Management Journal*, Vol. 15, pp. 143-152.

Conner, Kathleen R. and Prahalad, C.K. (1996): „A Resource-based Theory of the Firm: Knowledge Versus Opportunism“, *Organization Science*, Vol. 7, No. 5, pp. 477-501.

Cornelius, Peter and Schwab, Klaus (2003): *The Arab World Competitiveness Report 2002-2003*, Oxford.

Cummings, John Thomas, Askari, Hossein and Mustafa, Ahmad (1980): "Islam and Modern Economic Change", in: Esposito, John L. (Ed.): *Islam and Development*, New York, pp. 25-47.

Dadhaboy, Ismail (2004): *Strategic Innovation in Islamic Finance*, www.megaevents .net/ wibc/presentations/2004/conference/dadabhoy.ppt

Dar, Humayon A. and Presley, John R. (2000): "Lack of Profit Loss Sharing in Islamic Banking: Management and Control Imbalances", *Economic Research Paper No. 00/24*, Loughborough University.

Dar, Humayon A., Hall, Maximilian J.B. and Muljawan, Dadang (2001): "A Strategic Design of Islamic Banking Regulations", *Middle East Business and Economic Review*, Vol. 13, Iss. 2 (December), pp. 28-38.

Deans, Graeme K. and Kroeger, Fritz (2003): *Stretch! How Great Companies Grow In Good Times and Bad*, New York et. al.

Delley, Thierry (2001): *Management von Kernkompetenzen in Banken*, Zürich.

Deutsch, Karl J., Diedrichs, Eva P., Raster, Max and Westphal, Jörg (Eds.) (1997): *Gewinnen mit Kernkompetenzen*, Munich et. al.

Dichtl, Erwin and Issing, Otmar (Eds.) (1993): *Vahlens Großes Wirtschaftslexikon*, 2nd ed., Munich.

Dierickx, Ingemar and Cool, Karel (1989): "Asset stock accumulation and sustainability of competitive advantage", *Management Science,* Vol. 35, pp. 1504-1511.

Dudley, Nigel (2004): „Islamic finance needs solid foundations“, *euromoney*, January 2004, pp. 38-43.

Economic Research Forum (2003): *Economic Trends in the MENA Region 2002*, Cairo.

Edwardes, Warren (2003): "Islamic Liquidity Management", *http://dc3.co.uk/ IslamicLiquidity031008.pdf.*

El-Gamal, Mahmoud A. (1997): "Can Islamic Banking Survive? A Micro-evolutionary Perspective", *http://www.ssc.wisc.edu/econ/archive/wp9705.pdf.*

El-Gamal, Mahmoud A. (2000): "A Basic Guide to Contemporary Islamic Banking and Finance", *http://www.ruf.rice.edu/~elgamal/files/primer.pdf.*

Ende, Werner and Steinbach, Udo (Eds.) (1996): *Der Islam in der Gegenwart*, 4th ed., Munich.

Errico, Luca and Farahbaksh, Mitra (1998): "Islamic Banking: Issues in Prudential Regulations and Supervision", *IMF Working Paper 98/30.*

Eschenbach, Rolf (Ed.) (1993): *Strategische Konzepte*, Stuttgart.

Fiegenbaum, Avi and Thomas, Howard (1995): "Strategic Groups as Reference Groups: Theory, Modeling and Empirical Examination of Industry and Competitive Strategy", *Strategic Management Journal*, Vol. 16, pp. 461-476.

FTSE International Limited (2001): *Ground Rules fort he Management of the FTSE Global Islamic Index Series*, www.ftse.com/indices_marketdata/ground_rules/ global-islamic-ground-rules.pdf.

Furubotn, Eirik G. and Richter, Rudolf (1996): *Neue Institutionenökonomik: Eine Einführung und kritische Würdigung*, Tübingen.

Furubotn, Eirik G. and Richter, Rudolf (Eds.) (1991): *The New Institutional Economics: A Collection of Articles from the Journal of Institutional and Theoretical Economics*, Tübingen.

Gerbach, Stephan (2002): *Wettbewerbsstrategien von Auslandsniederlassungen: Empirische Studie zur Bestimmung von Erfolgsfaktoren deutscher und amerikanischer Niederlassungen in Singapur*, Doctoral dissertation, Heidelberg.

Gerbing, David W. and Anderson, James C. (1988): "An Updated Paradigm for Scale Development Incorporating Unidimensionality and its Assessment", *Journal of Marketing Research*, Vol. 25, pp. 186-192.

Ghaussy, A. Ghanie (1994): *Islamic Countries and Europe*, Bern et.al.

Grant, Robert M. (1996): "Toward a knowledge-based theory of the firm", *Strategic Management Journal*, Vol. 17, pp. 109-122.

Grossman, Sanford and Hart, Oliver (1983): "An analysis of the principal-agent problem", *Econometrica*, Vol. 51, pp. 7-46.

Hahn, Dietger and Taylor, Bernard (Eds.) (1999): *Strategische Unternehmensführung*, 8th ed., Heidelberg.

Hair, Joseph F., Anderson, Rolph E., Tatham, Ronald L. and Black, William C. (1998): *Multivariate Data Analysis*, 5th ed., Upper Saddle River.

Hakim, Sam and Neaime, Simon (2001): "Performance & Credit Risk in Banking: A Comparative Study for Egypt and Lebanon", *ERF Working Paper Series 200137.*

Hamel, Gary (1994): "The Concept of Core Competence", in: Hamel, Gary and Heene, Aimé (Eds.): *Competence-based Competition*, Chichester et.al.

Hamel, Gary and Prahalad, Coimbatore K. (1994): *Competing for the future*, Boston.

Hamel, Gary and Prahalad, Coimbatore K. (1995): *Wettlauf um die Zukunft*, Vienna.

Hammann, Peter and Erichson, Bernd (2000): *Marktforschung*, Stuttgart.

Hammer, Richard M. (1988): *Unternehmensplanung*, 3rd ed., Munich.

Haron, Sudin (1996): "Competition and other external determinants of the profitability of Islamic banks", *Islamic Economic Studies*, Vol. 4, No. 1, pp. 49-63.

Haron, Sudin and Ahmad, Norafifah (2000): "The effects of conventional interest rates and rate of profit on funds deposited with Islamic banking system in Malaysia", *International Journal of Islamic Financial Services*, Vol. 1, No. 4.

Hartmann, Richard (1992): *Die Religion des Islam*, 2nd ed., Darmstadt.

Hasan, Zubair (2002): „Mudarabah as a Mode of Finance in Islamic Banking: Theory, Practice and Problems", *Middle East Business and Economic Review*, Vol. 14, Iss. 2 (December), pp. 41-53.

Hassan, Kabir M., Farhat, Joseph and Al-Zu'bi, Bashir (2002): "Dividend Signaling Hypothesis and Short-term Asset Concentration of Islamic Interest-Free Banking", The ERF 9th Annual Conference, www.erf.org.eg/9th%20annual%20conf/9th%20PDF%20Background/Finance/FB%20Kabir%20&%20Farhat.pdf

Hassan, M. Kabir and Bashir, Abdel-Hameed M. (2003): "Determinants of Islamic Banking Profitability", The ERF 10th Annual Conference, www.erf.org.eg/tenthconf/Financial_Markets_Presented/Kabir_Bashir.pdf

Hassoune, Anouar (2002): "Islamic Banks' Profitability in an Interest Rate Cycle", *The Arab Bank Review*, Vol. 4, No. 2 (October), pp. 54-58.

Hatten, Kenneth J. and Hatten, M. Louise (1988): *Effective Strategic Management*, Englewood Cliffs.

Hawawini, Gabriel, Subramanian, Venkat and Verdin, Paul (2003): "Is Performance Driven by Industry- or Firm-Specific Factors? A New Look at the Evidence", *Strategic Management Journal*, Vol. 24, No. 1, pp. 1-16.

Hax, Arnoldo C. and Majluf, Nicolas S. (1991): *The Strategic Concept and Process*, Englewood Cliffs.

Heimer, Thomas and Rossbach, Peter (Eds) (2001): *Management der Ressource Wissen in Banken*, Frankfurt a.M..

Henry, Clement M. and Wilson, Rodney (Eds.) (2004): *The Politics of Islamic Finance*, Edinburgh.

Heritage Foundation (2005): *2005 Index of Economic Freedom*, www.heritage.org/research/features/index/downloads.cfm.

Herrmann, Andreas and Homburg, Christian (Eds.) (2000): *Marktforschung*, Wiesbaden.

Herrmann, Andreas, Jasny, Ralf and Vetter, Ingrid (1999): *Kundenorientierung von Banken*, Frankfurt a. M.

Hinterhuber, Hans H. (1992): *Strategische Unternehmensführung*, 5th ed., Berlin et. al.

Hinterhuber, Hans H., Al-Ani, Ayad and Handlbauer, Gernot (Eds.) (1996): *Das Neue Strategische Management*, Wiesbaden.

Hinterhuber, Hans H., Handlbauer, Gernot and Matzler, Kurt (1997): *Kundenzufriedenheit durch Kernkompetenzen*, Munich et. al.

Homburg, Christian (2000): *Kundennähe von Industriegüterunternehmen – Konzeptualisierung, organisationale Determinanten und Erfolgsauswirkungen*, Wiesbaden.

Homburg, Christian and Giering, Annette (1996): "Konzeptionalisierung und Operationalisierung komplexer Konstrukte", *Marketing ZFP*, No. 1, pp. 5-24.

Hüttemann, Hans-Hermann (1993): *Anreizsysteme in schrumpfenden Unternehmnungen*, Wiesbaden.

Ibrahim, Badr-El-Din A. and Vijaykumar, K.C. (1998): " 'Islamic *Musharaka*' versus 'limited conventional' partnership modes of finance – Is *Musharaka* really different from limited conventional partnership?", The ERF 10th Annual Conference, www.erf.org.eg/tenthconf/Financial_Markets_background/Ibrahim.pdf

International Monetary Fund (1999): "Malaysia: Selected Issues", *IMF Staff Country Report 99/86.*

International Monetary Fund (2000): *IMF Survey*, Vol. 29, No. 17.

International Monetary Fund (2001): "Malaysia: Statistical Appendix", *IMF Country Report 01/187.*

Iqbal, Munawar (Ed.) (2001): *Islamic Banking and Finance: Current Developments in Theory and Practice*, Markfield.

Iqbal, Munawar and Llewellyn, David T. (Eds.) (2002): *Islamic Banking and Finance*, Cheltenham and Northampton.

Iqbal, Zubair (1997): "Islamic Financial Systems", *Finance & Development*, June.

Iqbal, Zubair (Ed.) (2001): *Macroeconomic Issues and Policies in the Middle East and North Africa*, Washington.

Islam, Mazhar M. (2003a): "Development and Performance of Domestic and Foreign Banks in GCC Countries", *Managerial Finance*, Vol. 29, No. 2/3, pp. 42-72.

Islam, Mazhar M. (2003b): "Regulations and Supervision of Financial Institutions in GCC Countries", *Managerial Finance*, Vol. 29, No. 7, pp. 17-42.

Ismail, Mohamed (2001): "Islamic Banking: How Developed is it in Malaysia today?", *Malayan Law Journal*, www.mlj.com.my/free/articles/mohdismail.htm

Jacoby, Jacob H. (1978): „Consumer Research – A State of the Art Review", *Journal of Marketing*, Vol. 42(4), pp. 87-96.

Jendruschewitz, Boris (2003): *Value at Risk – Ein Ansatz zum Management von Marktrisiken in Banken*, 3rd ed., Frankfurt a.M.

Jensen, Michael C. and Meckling, William H. (1976): "Theory of the firm: Managerial behavior, agency costs and ownership structure", *Journal of Financial Economics*, Vol. 3, pp. 305-360.

Juncker, Klaus and Priewasser, Erich (Eds.) (2002): *Handbuch Firmenkundengeschäft*, 2nd ed., Frankfurt a.M.

Kahf, Monzer (2002): "Strategic Trends in the Islamic Banking and Finance Movement",*http://monzer.kahf.com/papers/english/strategic%20trends%20in%20islamic%20banking%20and%20finance.pdf*.

Kaleem, Ahmad and Isa, Mansor Md (2003): "Causal relationship between Islamic and conventional banking instruments in Malaysia", *International Journal of Islamic Financial Services*, Vol. 4, No. 4.

Kaplan, Robert S. and Norton, David P. (1996): *The balanced scorecard*, Boston.

Kaplan, Robert S. and Norton, David P. (2001): *Die strategiefokussierte Organisation*, Stuttgart.

Keuper, Frank (2001): *Strategisches Management*, Munich et. al.

Kieser, Alfred (Ed.) (1999): *Organisationstheorien*, 3rd ed., Stuttgart.

Kirsch, Werner (1996): *Wegweiser zur Konstruktion einer evolutionären Theorie der strategischen Führung*, Herrsching.

Knaese, Birgit (1996): *Kernkompetenzen im strategischen Management von Banken*, Wiesbaden.

Knyphausen-Aufseß, Dodo zu (1995): *Theorie der strategischen Unternehmensführung – State of the Art und neue Perspektiven*, Wiesbaden.

Kornmesser, Christian and Schreiber, Jürgen (1998): „Die Messbarkeit der Kundenzufriedenheit", *controller magazin*, 5/98, pp. 359-362.

Kreikebaum, Hartmut (1989): *Strategische Unternehmensplanung*, 3rd ed., Stuttgart et.al.

Kumar, Nirmalya, Scheer Lisa K., Steenkamp, Jan-Benedict (1993): "Powerful Suppliers, Vulnerable Resellers, and the Effects of Supplier Fairness: A Cross-National Study", *Working Paper*, Institute for the Study of Business Markets, Pennsylvania State University, State College.

Kuran, Timur (1986): „The economic system in contemporary Islamic thought: interpretation and assessment", *International Journal of Middle Eastern Studies*, Vol. 18, pp. 135-164.

Kuran, Timur (1995): "Interest", *The Oxford Encyclopedia of the Modern Islamic World*, New York and Oxford, pp. 205-207.

Kwan, Simon (2001): „Financial Modernization and Banking Theories", *FRBSF Economic Letter*, No. 2001-37.

Laudicina, Paul A. (2005): *World Out of Balance*, New York.

Lehmann, Donald R., Gupta, Sunil and Steckel, Joel H. (1998): *Marketing Research*, Reading et. al.

Lehmann, Marcus (1999): „Strategieformulierung im Bankgeschäft“, *Die Bank*, 5/99, pp. 305-309.

Levitas, Edward and Chi, Tailan (2002): "Rethinking Rouse and Daellenbach's Rethinking: Isolating Vs. Testing for Sources of Sustainable Competitive Advantage", *Strategic Management Journal*, Vol. 23, No. 10, pp. 957-962.

Lewis, Mervyn K. and Algaoud, Latifa (2001): *Islamic banking*, Cheltenham.

Limam, Imed (2001): „A Comparative Study of GCC Banks Technical Efficiency“, *ERF Working Paper Series 200119*.

Litfin, Thorsten, Teichmann, Maik-Henrik and Clement, Michel (2000): "Beurteilung der Güte von explorativen Faktorenanalysen im Marketing", *Wirtschaftswissenschaftliches Studium*, Vol. 29, No. 5, pp. 283-286.

Lumma, Katrin (2003): *Markenstrategien für Finanzdienstleister*, Frankfurt a.M.

Malhotra, Naresh K. (1999): *Marketing Research: An Applied Orientation*, 3rd ed., Upper Saddle River.

Marighetti, Luca P., Jasny, Ralf, Herrmann, Andreas and Huber, Frank (Eds.) (2001): *Management der Wertschöpfungsketten in Banken*, Wiesbaden.

Mason, Edward S. (1939): "Price and Production Policies of Large-Scale Enterprise", *American Economic Review*, Vol. 29, pp. 61-74.

Maßmann, Jens and Schmidt, Reinhard H. (1998): „Recht, internationale Unternehmensstrategien und Standortwettbewerb“, *Johann Wolfgang Goethe-Universität Frankfurt am Main Working Paper Series: Finance & Accounting*, No. 25 (December).

Mauri, Alfredo J. and Michaels, Max P. (1998): "Firm and Industry Effects Within Strategic Management: An Empirical Examination", *Strategic Management Journal*, Vol. 19, pp. 211-219.

McAllister, Daniel J. (1995): "Affect- and cognition-based trust as foundations for interpersonal cooperation in organizations", *Academy of Management Journal*, Vol. 38, pp. 24-59.

McGahan, Anita M. and Porter, Michael E. (1997): "How Much Does Industry Matter, Really?", *Strategic Management Journal*, Vol. 18, pp. 15-30.

McGee, John and Thomas, Howard (1986): "Strategic groups: Theory, research and taxonomy", *Strategic Management Journal*, Vol. 7, pp. 141-160.

Meesook, Kanitta, Lee, Il Houng, Liu, Olin, Khatri, Yougesh, Tamirisa, Natalia, Moore, Michael and Krysl, Mark H. (2001): *Malaysia: from crisis to recovery*, Washington, D .C.

Mehra, Ajay (1996): "Resource and Market Based Determinants of Performance in the U.S. Banking Industry", *Strategic Management Journal*, Vol. 17, pp. 307-322.

Meschi, Pierre-Xavier (1997): "Longevity and Cultural Differences of International Joint Ventures: Toward Time-Based Cultural Management", *Human Relations*, Vol. 50, No. 2, pp. 211-228.

Metawa, Saad A. and Almossawi, Mohammed (1997): "Banking Behavior of Islamic Bank customers: Perspectives and Implications", *International Journal of Bank Marketing*, Vol. 16, No. 1, pp. 299-313.

Meyer, Klaus E. and Estrin, Saul (2001): „Brownfield Entry in Emerging Markets", *Journal of International Business Studies*, Vol. 32, No. 3, pp. 575-584.

Milgrom, Paul and Roberts, John (1992): *Economics, Organization and Management*, Englewood Cliffs.

Mills, Paul S. and Presley, John R. (1999): *Islamic Finance: Theory and Practice*, Houndmills et. al.

Möller, Martin (2000): *Strategische Konzepte von Universalbanken*, Frankfurt a.M.

Montagu-Pollock, Matthew (2002): "One for the history books", *asiamoney*, July 2002, pp. 17-18.

Montagu-Pollock, Matthew and Wright, Chris (2002): "The many faces of Islamic finance", *asiamoney*, August 2002, pp. 31-37.

Moormann, Jürgen and Rossbach, Peter (Eds.) (2001): *Customer Relationship Management in Banken*, Frankfurt a.M.

Müller, Joachim (1996): *Islamischer Weg und islamistische Sackgasse*, Münster.

Nienhaus, Volker (1982): *Islam und moderne Wirtschaft*, Graz et.al.

Nienhaus, Volker (1983): "Profitability of Islamic PLS Banks Competing with Interest Banks: Problems and Prospects", *Journal of Research in Islamic Economics*, Vol. 1, No. 1, pp. 37-47.

Nienhaus, Volker (1988): "The performance of Islamic banks: Trends and cases", in: Mallat, Chibli (Ed.): *Islamic Law and Finance*, London, pp. 129-160.

Nienhaus, Volker (1991): "Islamische Wirtschaft. Einführung und Würdigung des zinslosen Bankwesens aus institutionsökonomischer Sicht", in *Jahrbuch für neue politische Ökonomie*, Vol. 10, pp. 247-273.

Nienhaus, Volker (1994): „Conceptual and Economic Foundations of Islamic Banking", in Piccinelli, Gian Maria (Ed.): *Banche Islamiche in Contesto Non Islamico*, Rome.

Nienhaus, Volker (1995): „Developments in Regulatory and Supervisory Issues Relating to Islamic Banking", Paper prepared for the conference *Accessing Islamic Finance-Market and Investment Opportunities,* London.

Nienhaus, Volker (1999): „Islam", in Korff, Wilhelm et. al. (Ed.): *Handbuch der Wirtschaftsethik,* Gütersloh.

Nienhaus, Volker (2004): "The 'Westernization' of Islamic Finance: Towards More Efficiency and Less Distinctiveness", 2nd International Islamic Banking and Finance Conference, Malaysia.

No Author (2002): "How Malaysia approaches Islamic finance", *asiamoney*, August 2002, pp. 43-47.

No Author (2003): "Top 100 Arab Banks", *Al-Iktissad Wal-Amal*, September 2003, pp. 128-164.

Noman, Abdullah M (2002): "Imperatives of financial innovation for Islamic banks", *International Journal of Islamic Financial Services*, Vol. 4, No. 3.

Nonaka, Ikujiro and Takeuchi, Hirotaka (1995): *The Knowledge-Creating Company*, Oxford.

OICV-IOSCO (2004): *Islamic Capital Market Fact Finding Report*, www.sc.com.my/eng/html/icm/ICM-IOSCOFact%20finding%20Report.pdf

Paret, Rudi (1991): *Mohammed und der Koran*, 7th ed., Stuttgart et.al.

Penrose, Edith (1959): *The theory of the growth of the firm*, New York.

Peter, J. Paul (1981): "Construct Validity: A Review of Basic Issues and Marketing Practices", *Journal of Marketing Research*, Vol. 18, pp. 133-145.

Picot, Arnold, Dietl, Helmut M. and Franck, Egon (1997): *Organisation. Die ökonomische Perspektive*, Stuttgart.

Pitelis, Christos N. and Sugden, Roger (Eds.) (2000): *The Nature of the Transnational Firm*, 2nd ed., New York.

Platzek, Heinz-Jörg (1998): "Private Banking als strategisches Geschäftsfeld deutscher Banken", *Mitteilungen und Berichte der Abteilung Bankwirtschaft des Instituts für Bankwirtschaft und Bankrecht an der Universität zu Köln*, Vol. 29, No. 80, pp. 1-11.

Porter, Michael E. (1980): *Competitive strategy*, New York.

Porter, Michael E. (1981): "The contributions of industrial organization to strategic management", *Academy of Management Review*, Vol. 6, pp. 609-620.

Porter, Michael E. (1983): *Wettbewerbsstrategie*, Frankfurt a.M. et. al.

Porter, Michael E. (1985): *Competitive Advantage*, New York and London.

Porter, Michael E. (1996): *Wettbewerbsvorteile*, 4th ed., Frankfurt a.M. et. al.

Porter, Michael E. (Ed.) (1986): *Competition in Global Industries*, Boston.

Post, James E., Frederick, William C., Lawrence, Anne T. and Weber, James (1996): *Business and Society*, 8th ed., New York et.al.

Pratt, John W. and Zeckhauser, Richard J. (Eds.) (1985): *Principals and agents: The structure of business,* Boston.

Priem, Richard L. and Butler, John E. (2001): "Is the Resource-Based 'View' a Useful Perspective for Strategic Management Research?", *Strategic Management Journal*, Vol. 26, No. 1, pp. 22-40.

Priem, Richard L. and Butler, John E. (2001): "Tautology in the Resource-Based View and the Implications of Externally Determined Resource Value: Further Comments", *Strategic Management Journal*, Vol. 26, No. 1, pp. 57-66.

Rasche, Christoph (1994): *Wettbewerbsvorteile durch Kernkompetenzen – Ein ressourcenorientierter Ansatz*, Wiesbaden.

Rindfleisch, Ari and Heide, Jan B. (1997): "Transaction Cost Analysis: Past, Present, and Future Applications", *Journal of Marketing*, Vol. 61 (October 1997), pp. 30-54.

Rodinson, Maxime (1971): *Islam und Kapitalismus*, Frankfurt a. M.

Rosly, Saiful Azhar and Sanusi, Mahmood M. (1999): "The application of bay' al-'inah and bay' al-dayn in Malaysian Islamic bonds: An Islamic analysis", *International Journal of Islamic Financial Services*, Vol. 1, No. 2.

Rouse, Michael J. and Daellenbach, Urs S. (2002): "More Thinking on Research Methods for the Resource-Based Perspective", *Strategic Management Journal*, Vol. 23, No. 10, pp. 963-967.

Ruefli, Timothy W. and Wiggins, Robert R. (2003): "Industry, Corporate and Segment Effects and Business Performance: A Non-Parametric Approach", *Strategic Management Journal*, Vol. 24, pp. 861-879.

Rumelt, Richard P. (1984): "Toward a Strategic Theory of the Firm", in: Lamb, R. (Ed.): *Competitive Strategic Management*, Englewood Cliffs.

Rumelt, Richard P. (1991): "How Much Does Industry Matter?", *Strategic Management Journal*, Vol. 12, pp. 167-185.

Saeed, Abdullah (1996): *Islamic Banking and Interest*, Leiden.

Saif, Abdulla H. (2003): "A magnet for Islamic finance", *Arab Banker*, www.arab-banker.com/dir/1703/1703-IslamicBanking.asp.

Sala-I-Martin, Xavier and Artadi, Elsa V. (2003): "Economic Growth and Investment in the Arab World", in Cornelius, Peter and Schwab, Klaus (Eds.): *The Arab World Competitiveness Report 2002-2003*, Oxford.

Salehabadi, Ali and Aram, Mohammad (2002): "Islamic justification of derivative instruments", *International Journal of Islamic Financial Services*, Vol. 4, No. 3.

Saunder, Anthony (2000): *Financial Institutions Management*, 3rd ed., Boston et. al.

Schacht, Joseph (1964): *An Introduction to Islamic Law*, Oxford.

Schierenbeck, Henner (1997): *Ertragsorientiertes Bankmanagement*, 5th ed., Wiesbaden.

Schmalensee, Richard (1985): "Do markets differ much?", *American Economic Review*, Vol. 75 (3), pp. 341-351.

Schmidt, Reinhard H., Hackethal, Andreas and Tyrell, Marcel (1998): „Disintermediation and the Role of Banks in Europe: An International Comparison", *Johann Wolfgang Goethe-Universität Frankfurt am Main Working Paper Series: Finance & Accounting*, No. 10 (January).

Schnell, Rainer, Hill, Paul B. and Esser, Elke (1999): *Methoden der empirischen Sozialforschung*, Munich.

Schumeckers, Gerd and Krause, Jürgen (2000): „Spezialbanken – ein Konzept mit Zukunft", *bank und markt*, 3 (March 2000), pp. 20-24.

Schutjens, Veronique A.J.M. and Wever, Egbert (2000): "Determinants of New Firm Success", *Papers in Regional Science*, Vol. 79, pp. 135-159.

Scott, W. Richard (1995): *Institutions and Organizations*, London

Shaver, J. Myles (1998): "Accounting for Endogeneity When Assessing Strategy Performance: Does Entry Mode Choice Affect FDI Survival?", *Management Science*, Vol. 44, No. 4, pp. 571-585.

Spanos, Yiannis E. and Lioukas, Spyros (2001): "An Examination into the Causal Logic of Rent Generation: Contrasting Porter's Competitive Strategy Framework and the Resource-based Perspective", *Strategic Management Journal*, Vol. 22, pp. 907-934.

Spanos, Yiannis E., Zaralis, George and Lioukas, Spyros (2004): "Strategy and Industry Effects on Profitability: Evidence from Greece", *Strategic Management Journal*, Vol. 25, pp. 139-165.

Steffens, Udo and Achenbach, Wieland (Eds.) (2002): *Strategisches Management in Banken*, Frankfurt a. M.

Stewart, David P. (1981): "The Application and Misapplication of Factor Analysis in Marketing Research", *Journal of Marketing Research*, Vol. 18, pp. 51-62.

Süchting, Joachim and Paul, Stephan (1998): *Bankmanagement*, 4th ed., Stuttgart.

Sundararajan, V. and Errico, Luca (2002): "Islamic Financial Institutions and Products in the Global Financial System: Key Issues in Risk Management and Challenges Ahead", *IMF Working Paper 02/192.*

Sundararajan, V., Marston, David and Shabsigh, Ghiath (1998): "Monetary Operations and Government Debt Management Under Islamic Banking", *IMF Working Paper 98/144.*

Svoboda, Michael (1997): "Führen durch Zielvereinbarung", *Die Bank*, 9/97, pp. 522-526.

Thompson, Arthur A. Jr. and Strickland III, A.J. (1998): *Strategic Management: Concepts & Cases*, Boston and New York.

Timberg, Thomas A. (2003): "Islamic Banking and Its Potential Impact", *http://www.basis.wisc.edu/live/rfc/cs_06b.pdf.*

Tirole, Jean (1995): *The Theory of Industrial Organization*, 8th ed., Cambridge and London.

Ul Haque, Nadeem and Mirakhor, Abbas (1998): "The Design of Instruments for Government Finance in an Islamic Economy", *IMF Working Paper 98/54.*

Usmani, Muhammad Taqi (2002): *An introduction to Islamic finance*, The Hague.

van Schaik, Diederik (2001): "Islamic Banking", *The Arab Bank Review*, Vol. 3, No. 1 (April), pp. 45-52.

Visser, Hans (2004): *Islamic Finance*, Amsterdam.

Vogel, Frank E. and Hayes, Samuel L. (1998): *Islamic Law and Finance*, The Hague et. al.

Warde, Ibrahim (2000): *Islamic Finance in the Global Economy*, Edinburgh.

Welge, Martin K. and Al-Laham, Andreas (1999): *Strategisches Management*, 2nd ed., Wiesbaden.

Wernerfelt, Birger (1984): "A Resource-based View of the Firm", *Strategic Management Journal*, Vol. 5, pp. 171-180.

Wernerfelt, Birger and Montgomery, Cynthia A. (1988): "Tobin's q and the Importance of Focus in Firm Performance", *The American Economic Review*, Vol. 78, No. 1, pp. 246-250.

Wild, Jürgen (1974): *Grundlagen der Unternehmensplanung*, Reinbek bei Hamburg.

Williamson, Oliver E. (1975): *Markets and Hierarchies: Analysis and Antitrust Implications*, New York.

Williamson, Oliver E. (1979): "Transaction-Cost Economics: The Governance of Contractual Relations", *The Journal of Law and Economics*, Vol. 22, No. 2, pp. 233-261.

Williamson, Oliver E. (2000): "The New Institutional Economics: Taking Stock, Looking Ahead", *Journal of Economic Literature*, Vol. 38 (September 2000), pp. 595-613.

Wilson, Rodney (2002): "Arab Government Responses to Islamic Finance: The Cases of Egypt and Saudi Arabia", *Mediterranean* Politics, Vol. 7, pp. 143-163.

Yeoh, Poh-Lin and Roth, Kendall (1999): "An Empirical Analysis of Sustained Advantage in the U.S. Pharmaceutical Industry: Impact of Firm Resources and Capabilities", *Strategic Management Journal*, Vol. 20, No. 7, pp. 637-653.

Zaheer, Srilata and Mosakowski, Elaine (1997): "The Dynamics of the Liability of Foreignness: A Global Study of Survival in Financial Services", *Strategic Management Journal*, Vol. 18, No. 6, pp. 439-464.

Zaher, Tarek S. and Hassan, M. Kabir (2001): "A Comparative Literature Survey of Islamic Finance and Banking", *Financial Markets, Institutions and Instruments*, Vol. 10, No. 4 (November), pp. 155-199.

Zaman, M.R. and Movassaghi, H. (2001): "Islamic banking: A performance analysis", *Journal of Global Business*, Vol. 12, No. 22, pp. 31-38.

Zerr, Konrad, Gaiser, Brigitte and Decker, Dominik (2003): *Die Rolle des Marketing bei der Entwicklung und Vermarktung von Dienstleistungen*, Frankfurt a.M.

Zopounidid, Constantin (Ed.) (2002): *New Trends in Banking Management*, Heidelberg.

Appendix

Questionnaire

Questionnaire

- Strategic Management in Islamic Finance -

Bochum, February 2004

Research study conducted by

Alexander von Pock

Faculty of Economics and Business Administration

RUHR-UNIVERSITÄT BOCHUM

Germany

CONFIDENTIALITY DECLARATION

All answers given in the questionnaire will be treated in the strictest confidence and will not be disclosed by the receiving party to any third party. The data will be used exclusively for academic research purposes. Findings will be published in the form of anonymous statistical analyses only.

Introduction

Background

In the last decades, the Islamic finance sector has consistently grown with 2-digit growth rates. Although still a niche market, the segment is experiencing ever increasing competition and, especially in recent years, has become a highly dynamic and quickly developing business area. While academic research has extensively covered the basics and a selection of special issues regarding Islamic finance and Islamic economics, the determinants of strategic management in Islamic finance have not drawn the same degree of attention in the literature. The present study intends to fill that research gap.

Completion of the Questionnaire

It will take 30-40 min. to complete the questionnaire. It should be filled in by (a) the managing director in case of a full-fledged Islamic bank; (b) the head of Islamic finance in case of an Islamic "window" of a conventional bank.

Please answer all questions (starting on page 3) to the best of your knowledge. *If not noted otherwise, your answers should refer to your Islamic finance activities!* If you are missing exact figures, your answers should be based on traceable estimations – please make a note on the side of estimated figures.

If a tick-marking question allows for a *single answer only*, input boxes are in the form of O or ①. If it allows for *multiple answers*, input boxes look like this: ☐ (in addition, "multiple answers possible" will be explicitly stated!).

Shaded fields should not be filled in. All text should be written in block letters.

If not noted otherwise, all data should refer to the year 2003. We suggest that you double-check all your answers before returning the questionnaire.

Return of the Questionnaire

Please return the filled-in questionnaire until 3 March 2004 via fax (+49 69 7474 6999).

Please send additional background information (organigram, latest annual report, company or product brochures) to:

Alexander von Pock
c/o Chair of Economic Policy II (Prof. Dr. Volker Nienhaus)
Ruhr-Universität Bochum: Faculty of Economics and Business Administration

D-44780 Bochum, Germany

If you have any questions concerning this study or the completion of the questionnaire please contact Mr. von Pock (+49 175 2659 545 or alexander.vonpock@rub.de)

As a participant, you may receive a benchmark report summarizing the results of this study (tick-mark on next page).

Respondent Contact Information

Please fill in the blanks:

Name of company: ____

Business Unit: ____

Address: ____

____

____

____

Name of Respondent: ____

Function: ____

Tel.: ____

Fax: ____

Email: ____

I would like to receive the benchmark report.

O Yes O No

Industry and Market Environment

For your subsequent assessment of the industry and market environment, please indicate the geographical focus of your company
(please refer your answers in this section to that focus):

O Bahrain	O Kuwait	O Qatar
O Saudi Arabia	O United Arab Emirates	O GCC area
O Malaysia	O South-east Asia	O Global

O Other (please explain): ____________________

Please indicate how you view the importance of the following factors affecting the Islamic finance industry:
(① = Not important ... ⑦ = Very important)

	Not important ...... Very important
▪ Disintermediation	① ② ③ ④ ⑤ ⑥ ⑦
▪ Sophistication of banking information technology	① ② ③ ④ ⑤ ⑥ ⑦
▪ Decrease of long-term customer-relationships	① ② ③ ④ ⑤ ⑥ ⑦
▪ Increased competition and cost pressure	① ② ③ ④ ⑤ ⑥ ⑦
▪ Deregulation	① ② ③ ④ ⑤ ⑥ ⑦
▪ Innovation	① ② ③ ④ ⑤ ⑥ ⑦
▪ Other: ____________________	① ② ③ ④ ⑤ ⑥ ⑦

Please indicate the attractiveness of the following market segments for Islamic finance:
(① = Not attractive ... ⑦ = Highly attractive)

	Not attractive ..... Highly attractive
▪ Trade financing	① ② ③ ④ ⑤ ⑥ ⑦
▪ Medium- to long-term corporate financing	① ② ③ ④ ⑤ ⑥ ⑦
▪ Venture capital	① ② ③ ④ ⑤ ⑥ ⑦
▪ Personal advances for consumption purposes	① ② ③ ④ ⑤ ⑥ ⑦
▪ Personal advances for consumer durables (e.g. cars)	① ② ③ ④ ⑤ ⑥ ⑦
▪ Home financing	① ② ③ ④ ⑤ ⑥ ⑦
▪ Asset management	① ② ③ ④ ⑤ ⑥ ⑦
▪ Public sector financing	① ② ③ ④ ⑤ ⑥ ⑦
▪ Investment banking	① ② ③ ④ ⑤ ⑥ ⑦
▪ Other: ____________________	① ② ③ ④ ⑤ ⑥ ⑦

For those market segments that you rated highest in the previous question, indicate the major factors contributing to their attractiveness (multiple answers possible):

☐ Low risk ☐ Asset-deposit maturity matching
☐ Low funding costs ☐ Low operational costs
☐ High margins ☐ High demand
☐ High growth potential ☐ Other: ____________________

In most countries, Islamic banks (IBs) are in competition with conventional banks. Please indicate to what extent you disagree or agree.
(① = Strongly disagree … ⑦ = Strongly agree)

Compared to conventional banks or financial products…	*Strongly disagree……Strongly agree*
▪ …IBs benefit from higher market growth rates	① ② ③ ④ ⑤ ⑥ ⑦
▪ …Islamic products can be priced more expensively	① ② ③ ④ ⑤ ⑥ ⑦
▪ …IBs have easier access to shareholder's equity	① ② ③ ④ ⑤ ⑥ ⑦
▪ …IBs have easier access to capital (deposits or funding)	① ② ③ ④ ⑤ ⑥ ⑦
▪ …IBs are exposed to lower risk (e.g. borrower default risk)	① ② ③ ④ ⑤ ⑥ ⑦
▪ …IBs incur lower funding costs	① ② ③ ④ ⑤ ⑥ ⑦
▪ …IBs incur lower operation costs	① ② ③ ④ ⑤ ⑥ ⑦
▪ …IBs gain higher profit margins	① ② ③ ④ ⑤ ⑥ ⑦
▪ …IBs benefit from a larger market size (cater to both conventional and Islamic investors)	① ② ③ ④ ⑤ ⑥ ⑦

When evaluating the various forces shaping the Islamic finance industry, please indicate for each of the following statements to what extent you disagree or agree. Please refer to your own geographic focus!
(① = Strongly disagree … ⑦ = Strongly agree)

	Strongly disagree……Strongly agree
▪ Competition in the industry is very high	① ② ③ ④ ⑤ ⑥ ⑦
▪ The clients have a strong bargaining position	① ② ③ ④ ⑤ ⑥ ⑦
▪ Clients prefer short-term deposits & investments	① ② ③ ④ ⑤ ⑥ ⑦
▪ Most clients regard conventional banks as substitutes for Islamic banks	① ② ③ ④ ⑤ ⑥ ⑦
▪ The industry's liquidity market is too restricted	① ② ③ ④ ⑤ ⑥ ⑦
▪ The industry's regulatory & legal framework could improve	① ② ③ ④ ⑤ ⑥ ⑦
▪ There is a lack of standardization of Sharia opinions	① ② ③ ④ ⑤ ⑥ ⑦
▪ The industry's capital market is underdeveloped	① ② ③ ④ ⑤ ⑥ ⑦
▪ There is not enough attractive profit-and-loss-sharing investment opportunities	① ② ③ ④ ⑤ ⑥ ⑦

▪ The threat of substitutes is high (conventional banks)	① ② ③ ④ ⑤ ⑥ ⑦
▪ There is low barriers to enter the Islamic finance market	① ② ③ ④ ⑤ ⑥ ⑦
▪ Overall, attractive investment opportunities are hard to find	① ② ③ ④ ⑤ ⑥ ⑦
▪ Access to capital is limited	① ② ③ ④ ⑤ ⑥ ⑦
▪ There is a lack of skilled human resources	① ② ③ ④ ⑤ ⑥ ⑦
▪ Suppliers of state-of-the-art technology have high bargaining power (e.g. IT vendors)	① ② ③ ④ ⑤ ⑥ ⑦
▪ There is a lack of standardization of products (incl. documentation)	① ② ③ ④ ⑤ ⑥ ⑦
▪ There is a lack of customer education regarding the characteristics of Islamic finance	① ② ③ ④ ⑤ ⑥ ⑦

In order to compete effectively with conventional banks and to provide products that meet all financial requirements, how do you view the following statements?
(① = Strongly disagree … ⑦ = Strongly agree)

	Strongly disagree.....Strongly agree
▪ Islamic banks should actively approach non-Muslim clients	① ② ③ ④ ⑤ ⑥ ⑦
▪ Islamic banks must charge late-payment fees	① ② ③ ④ ⑤ ⑥ ⑦
▪ Islamic banks should offer Islamic hedge funds	① ② ③ ④ ⑤ ⑥ ⑦
▪ There is a need for consolidation in the Islamic finance industry (e.g. through mergers)	① ② ③ ④ ⑤ ⑥ ⑦
▪ Financial conditions of Islamic financial instruments must match conditions of conventional alternatives	① ② ③ ④ ⑤ ⑥ ⑦
▪ Islamic banks should offer Islamic derivative instruments (options, futures)	① ② ③ ④ ⑤ ⑥ ⑦
▪ In general, Islamic banks should offer products that closely emulate the features of conventional financial products	① ② ③ ④ ⑤ ⑥ ⑦

Company Key Characteristics

Please indicate your form of activity:

O Full-fledged Islamic bank
O Islamic "window" of conventional bank

Please indicate the scope of your Islamic banking activities (multiple answers possible):

☐ Corporate & government financing
☐ Venture capital
☐ Corporate & institutional asset management
☐ Corporate advisory (e.g. sukuk issues)
☐ Personal financing (incl. home financing)
☐ Personal wealth management
☐ Personal banking (checking, cards,....)
☐ Other: ______________________

Please indicate your ownership structure:

O Fully owned by parent firm (100%)
O State-owned (>50% of capital)
O Joint venture
O Privately owned (>50% of capital)

If parent company, please name parent: ____________________________________

If joint venture, please list partners: ____________________________________

If your company is not privately owned, please indicate the following:
(① = Fully dependant on directives... ⑦ = Fully autonomous)

Fully dependant.. Fully autonomous

- Degree of autonomy in decision-making ① ② ③ ④ ⑤ ⑥ ⑦

Please indicate the following figures:

Figure	*2000*	*2003*	*Target 2004*
Total assets, in €m	€m	€m	€m
Current accounts, in €m	€m	€m	€m
Unrestricted investment accounts, in €m	€m	€m	€m
Restricted investment accounts, in €m	€m	€m	€m
Mutual funds under management, in €m	€m	€m	€m
Earnings before tax (EBT), in €m	€m	€m	€m
Number of employees			

Which management / steering tools do you use? (multiple answers possible)

☐ Balanced scorecard
☐ Performance-related compensation
☐ Business plan
☐ Milestone planning
☐ Management by objectives
☐ Measurement of customer satisfaction
☐ Key performance indicators
☐ Other: ________________________

What principal goals does your company pursue? (multiple answers possible)

☐ Providing highest-standard banking services
☐ Maximizing the shareholder value
☐ Developing the economy
☐ Promoting social welfare
☐ Maximizing profits
☐ Encouraging people to save & invest
☐ Promoting the precepts of Islam
☐ Other: ____________________

Which of the following customer segments do you focus on? (multiple answers possible)

☐ Small- and medium-sized companies
☐ Large companies
☐ Small- and medium-sized financial institutions
☐ Large financial institutions
☐ Mass and affluent private clients
☐ High net worth individuals

Please indicate the following figures regarding your customer segments for 2003:

Customer segment	*Assets on your balance sheet*	*Liabilities on your balance sheet*	*Off-balance sheet funds under management*
Corporate clients	%	%	%
Institutional clients	%	%	%
Private clients	%	%	%
Total	100%	100%	100%

Please select your three most important areas of investment of customer funds and indicate their share of total customer fund investments (multiple answers possible):

☐ Trade financing: ____________%
☐ Corporate CapEx: ____________%
☐ Company shares: ____________%
☐ Commercial property: ____________%
☐ Home financing: ____________%
☐ Consumer durables: ____________%
☐ Public infrastructure: ____________%
☐ Government/ corporate bonds: ______%
☐ Other: ____________ ______%

Please indicate the number of people on your Sharia board:

○ 1 ○ 2 ○ 3 ○ 4 ○ 5 ○ >5

Please indicate the scope of your Sharia board's functions (multiple answers possible):

☐ Ex ante approval general rules & guidelines
☐ Ex ante approval new products
☐ Ex ante approval non-standard transactions
☐ Ex ante approval standard transactions
☐ Ex post review non-standard transactions
☐ Ex post review standard transactions
☐ Issuance of Sharia compliance report
☐ Other: ____________________

Do you share your Sharia board or members of it with other companies?

O Yes O No

Please indicate the following figures regarding your balance sheet for 2003:

Assets	*% of total*
Cash and cash equivalent	%
Advances to other financial institutions	%
Murabaha	%
Ina	%
Salam/ Istisna	%
Ijara/ Ijara muntahia bittamleek	%
Mudaraba/ Muqarada	%
Musharaka	%
Investment in securities	%
Other, specify:	%
Total	100 %
Liabilities, investment accounts & shareholder's equity	*% of total*
Deposits from other financial institutions	%
Current accounts	%
Investment accounts	%
Shareholder's equity	%
Other, specify:	%
Total	100 %

Please indicate the following figures regarding your sources of income for 2003:

Source	*% of total income*
Bank's income as mudarib	%
Bank's income from self-financed investments (i.e. shareholders funds)	%
Revenue from financial advisory services	%
Revenue from letters of credit/ guarantees	%
Other fees and charges	%
Total	100 %

Please indicate for each of the following your firm's *strength* relative to competition:
(① = Much weaker than competitors ... ⑦ = Much stronger than competitors)

Organization Structure & Communication	*Much weaker .... Much stronger*
▪ Clearly structured roles and responsibilities	① ② ③ ④ ⑤ ⑥ ⑦
▪ Vertical communication	① ② ③ ④ ⑤ ⑥ ⑦
▪ Cross-functional information exchange	① ② ③ ④ ⑤ ⑥ ⑦
▪ Cross-functional co-operation	① ② ③ ④ ⑤ ⑥ ⑦
▪ Team-based approach	① ② ③ ④ ⑤ ⑥ ⑦
▪ Market-oriented organization	① ② ③ ④ ⑤ ⑥ ⑦
Management Quality	
▪ Managerial competencies	① ② ③ ④ ⑤ ⑥ ⑦
▪ Quality of leadership	① ② ③ ④ ⑤ ⑥ ⑦
▪ Clear strategic vision	① ② ③ ④ ⑤ ⑥ ⑦
▪ Strategy-implementation	① ② ③ ④ ⑤ ⑥ ⑦
▪ Effective resource management	① ② ③ ④ ⑤ ⑥ ⑦
▪ Knowledge and skills of employees	① ② ③ ④ ⑤ ⑥ ⑦
Firm Culture	
▪ Transparency and openness across company/ hierarchies	① ② ③ ④ ⑤ ⑥ ⑦
▪ Ability to attract and retain high-quality people	① ② ③ ④ ⑤ ⑥ ⑦
▪ Prevalence of a meritocracy culture	① ② ③ ④ ⑤ ⑥ ⑦
▪ Highly motivating environment	① ② ③ ④ ⑤ ⑥ ⑦
▪ Reward of creativity and innovation	① ② ③ ④ ⑤ ⑥ ⑦
▪ Coordination	① ② ③ ④ ⑤ ⑥ ⑦
Product Development	
▪ Innovation	① ② ③ ④ ⑤ ⑥ ⑦
▪ Technological expertise	① ② ③ ④ ⑤ ⑥ ⑦
▪ Technological capabilities and equipment	① ② ③ ④ ⑤ ⑥ ⑦
▪ Resource efficiency	① ② ③ ④ ⑤ ⑥ ⑦
▪ Know-how of both Islamic & financial market requirements	① ② ③ ④ ⑤ ⑥ ⑦
▪ Quick & efficient Sharia-approval process (if applicable)	① ② ③ ④ ⑤ ⑥ ⑦
Marketing and Sales	
▪ Reputation as financial services provider	① ② ③ ④ ⑤ ⑥ ⑦
▪ Brand image	① ② ③ ④ ⑤ ⑥ ⑦
▪ Placing power	① ② ③ ④ ⑤ ⑥ ⑦
▪ Market knowledge	① ② ③ ④ ⑤ ⑥ ⑦
▪ Reputation as Islamic company	① ② ③ ④ ⑤ ⑥ ⑦
▪ Information processing capabilities	① ② ③ ④ ⑤ ⑥ ⑦
▪ Control of and access to distribution channels	① ② ③ ④ ⑤ ⑥ ⑦
▪ Advantageous relationships with customers	① ② ③ ④ ⑤ ⑥ ⑦
▪ Engagement in socially beneficial activities	① ② ③ ④ ⑤ ⑥ ⑦

▪ Current customer base	① ② ③ ④ ⑤ ⑥ ⑦
▪ Branch network	① ② ③ ④ ⑤ ⑥ ⑦
▪ ATM network	① ② ③ ④ ⑤ ⑥ ⑦
▪ Internet banking	① ② ③ ④ ⑤ ⑥ ⑦
▪ Call center	① ② ③ ④ ⑤ ⑥ ⑦
▪ Deal and customer assessment	① ② ③ ④ ⑤ ⑥ ⑦
▪ Customer counseling	① ② ③ ④ ⑤ ⑥ ⑦
▪ Private equity/ venture capital expertise	① ② ③ ④ ⑤ ⑥ ⑦
▪ Response time to customer requests	① ② ③ ④ ⑤ ⑥ ⑦
▪ Financial expertise	① ② ③ ④ ⑤ ⑥ ⑦
▪ Sharia board reputation	① ② ③ ④ ⑤ ⑥ ⑦
▪ Service quality	① ② ③ ④ ⑤ ⑥ ⑦
▪ Technological expertise	① ② ③ ④ ⑤ ⑥ ⑦
▪ Technological capabilities and equipment	① ② ③ ④ ⑤ ⑥ ⑦
▪ Resource efficiency	① ② ③ ④ ⑤ ⑥ ⑦
▪ Quick & efficient Sharia-approval process (if applicable)	① ② ③ ④ ⑤ ⑥ ⑦
Transaction Processing	
▪ Service quality	① ② ③ ④ ⑤ ⑥ ⑦
▪ Securitization of investment products	① ② ③ ④ ⑤ ⑥ ⑦
▪ Technological expertise	① ② ③ ④ ⑤ ⑥ ⑦
▪ Technological capabilities and equipment	① ② ③ ④ ⑤ ⑥ ⑦
▪ Resource efficiency	① ② ③ ④ ⑤ ⑥ ⑦
▪ Trading & treasury	① ② ③ ④ ⑤ ⑥ ⑦
Steering and Supporting Functions	
▪ Sharia compliance	① ② ③ ④ ⑤ ⑥ ⑦
▪ Effectiveness and efficiency of Sharia board	① ② ③ ④ ⑤ ⑥ ⑦
▪ Strategic planning	① ② ③ ④ ⑤ ⑥ ⑦
▪ Controlling	① ② ③ ④ ⑤ ⑥ ⑦
▪ Risk management	① ② ③ ④ ⑤ ⑥ ⑦
▪ Research capabilities	① ② ③ ④ ⑤ ⑥ ⑦
▪ Asset quality	① ② ③ ④ ⑤ ⑥ ⑦
▪ Equity base	① ② ③ ④ ⑤ ⑥ ⑦
▪ Knowledge and data management	① ② ③ ④ ⑤ ⑥ ⑦
▪ Compensation and reward system	① ② ③ ④ ⑤ ⑥ ⑦
▪ HR processes and administration	① ② ③ ④ ⑤ ⑥ ⑦
▪ Use of strategy-enforcing tools (e.g. balanced scorecard)	① ② ③ ④ ⑤ ⑥ ⑦
▪ Access to short-term capital	① ② ③ ④ ⑤ ⑥ ⑦
▪ Access to mid- and long-term capital	① ② ③ ④ ⑤ ⑥ ⑦
▪ Financial rating (e.g. Moody's)	① ② ③ ④ ⑤ ⑥ ⑦

Strategy

Which is your preferred strategy for growth?

O Internal / organic growth

O Co-operation with competitors (e.g. joint-venture, strategic alliance)

O Acquisition of competitors

O None, please explain: ______________________________

Does your company operate fully independently, using only its own resources?

O Yes O No

If no, which external resources does it use and in which areas (multiple answers possible)?

	Support by parent company/ other subsidiaries of parent	*Co-operation with competitors (e.g. joint-venture, strategic alliance)*	*Contracting companies*
Product development	☐	☐	☐
Marketing	☐	☐	☐
Sales/ Distribution	☐	☐	☐
Transaction processing	☐	☐	☐
Steering & supporting functions	☐	☐	☐

Which strategies does your company pursue to effectively compete in the market place? (① = Not considered ... ⑦ = Major emphasis)

Not considered ...... Major emphasis

- Pricing below competitors ① ② ③ ④ ⑤ ⑥ ⑦
- Providing extensive customer service ① ② ③ ④ ⑤ ⑥ ⑦
- Strict product & service quality control ① ② ③ ④ ⑤ ⑥ ⑦
- Achieving the lowest cost position in the industry ① ② ③ ④ ⑤ ⑥ ⑦
- Focusing on a few main product lines ① ② ③ ④ ⑤ ⑥ ⑦
- Providing a broad variation within the product lines ① ② ③ ④ ⑤ ⑥ ⑦
- Building brand identification of company ① ② ③ ④ ⑤ ⑥ ⑦
- Refining existing products to local needs and demands ① ② ③ ④ ⑤ ⑥ ⑦
- Control over distribution channels ① ② ③ ④ ⑤ ⑥ ⑦
- Promotion/ advertising expenditures above industry average ① ② ③ ④ ⑤ ⑥ ⑦

- Tailor-make products according to customer specification ① ② ③ ④ ⑤ ⑥ ⑦
- Developing the existing market ① ② ③ ④ ⑤ ⑥ ⑦
- Concerted effort to build/ maintain reputation in the industry ① ② ③ ④ ⑤ ⑥ ⑦
- Offering the main products in lower priced market segments ① ② ③ ④ ⑤ ⑥ ⑦
- Innovation in marketing techniques and methods ① ② ③ ④ ⑤ ⑥ ⑦
- Emphasis on quick market penetration/ product introduction ① ② ③ ④ ⑤ ⑥ ⑦
- Closely emulating the financial conditions of conventional banking products ① ② ③ ④ ⑤ ⑥ ⑦
- Immediate response to customer requests ① ② ③ ④ ⑤ ⑥ ⑦
- Acquiring high caliber work-force ① ② ③ ④ ⑤ ⑥ ⑦
- Emphasis on building reputation as an Islamic company ① ② ③ ④ ⑤ ⑥ ⑦
- Providing discounts to customers ① ② ③ ④ ⑤ ⑥ ⑦
- Extensive marketing research ① ② ③ ④ ⑤ ⑥ ⑦
- Extensive employee training ① ② ③ ④ ⑤ ⑥ ⑦
- Entering into and developing new market segments ① ② ③ ④ ⑤ ⑥ ⑦
- Emphasis on design and quality of products ① ② ③ ④ ⑤ ⑥ ⑦
- Efficient internal communication channels ① ② ③ ④ ⑤ ⑥ ⑦
- Unobstructed and quick decision making process ① ② ③ ④ ⑤ ⑥ ⑦
- Emphasis on product innovation ① ② ③ ④ ⑤ ⑥ ⑦
- Efforts to achieve economies of scale ① ② ③ ④ ⑤ ⑥ ⑦
- High capacity utilization ① ② ③ ④ ⑤ ⑥ ⑦
- Emphasis on strong distribution channels ① ② ③ ④ ⑤ ⑥ ⑦
- Highly automized transaction and administrative processes ① ② ③ ④ ⑤ ⑥ ⑦
- Differentiated pricing for various distribution channels ① ② ③ ④ ⑤ ⑥ ⑦
- Standardization & modularization of products / services ① ② ③ ④ ⑤ ⑥ ⑦
- Focusing on a few customer segments ① ② ③ ④ ⑤ ⑥ ⑦
- Emphasis on gaining a high or dominant market share ① ② ③ ④ ⑤ ⑥ ⑦
- Building product-related brands ① ② ③ ④ ⑤ ⑥ ⑦
- Entering into and developing new geographic markets ① ② ③ ④ ⑤ ⑥ ⑦

Performance Data

What was your absolute market share over the past 3 years and what is your target for 2004?

By assets: 2000: __________% 2003: __________% Target 2004: __________%

By profit: 2000: __________% 2003: __________% Target 2004: __________%

Which Economic Value did your company create?

Economic Value Created (EVC)	*2000*	*2003*	*Target 2004*
Net Operating Profit After Tax, in €m	€m	€m	€m
Equity (book value), in €m	€m	€m	€m
Cost of Equity (dividend paid), in %	%	%	%

Please indicate the following figures:

Figure	*2000*	*2003*	*Target 2004*
Net profit after tax as % of total assets	%	%	%
Net profit after tax as % of shareholders' equity and reserves	%	%	%

Please indicate for each item to what extent you disagree or agree.
(① = Strongly disagree … ⑦ = Strongly agree)

Compared to other Islamic banks…	*Strongly disagree……Strongly agree*
▪ …the market share of our products & services is very high	① ② ③ ④ ⑤ ⑥ ⑦
▪ …the market share of our products & services grows rapidly	① ② ③ ④ ⑤ ⑥ ⑦
▪ …we gain above-average profit margins	① ② ③ ④ ⑤ ⑥ ⑦
▪ …we gain above-average return on equity (ROE)	① ② ③ ④ ⑤ ⑥ ⑦
▪ …we have a high degree of customer retention	① ② ③ ④ ⑤ ⑥ ⑦
▪ …our customers are highly satisfied with our products and services	① ② ③ ④ ⑤ ⑥ ⑦

Answers

fallnum	geo	disint	it_soph	cust_rel	comp	dereg
1	Malaysia	5	5	5	6	6
2	GCC	3	5	4	6	6
3	GCC	6	7	7	7	6
4	GCC	5	3	4	7	6
5	Global	5	7		7	5
6	GCC	5	6	5	6	5
7	GCC	6	6	3	6	5
8	GCC	6	6	6	6	5
9	Malaysia	5	7	6	6	
10	Malaysia	3	7	6	7	6
11	Global	2	4	6	7	7
12	GCC	4	7	7	6	2
13	Malaysia	7	7	6	7	7
14	Malaysia	4	5	7	7	6
15	GCC	7	5	3	4	3
16	GCC	5	7	6	5	6
17	GCC	4	2	2	5	6
18	Global	4	7	7	5	5
19	GCC	6	6	5	6	5
20	GCC	4	6	4	7	4
21	Malaysia	5	7	6	7	7
22	GCC	5	6	5	7	3
23	GCC		7			
24	Malaysia	5	7	2	6	3
25	GCC	4	6	4	6	3
26	GCC		6	5	6	6
27	GCC		6	4	4	3
28	GCC	5	6	6	6	7
29	Malaysia	3	5	5	6	5
30	GCC	3	5	4	6	6
31	GCC	5	7	6	6	5
32	GCC	5	7	6	5	6
33	Malaysia		6	6	4	4
34	Malaysia	6	7	6	7	6
35	Global	2	4	1	5	2
36	Malaysia	3	4	4	4	5

innov	trade	corp_fin	venture	pers_con	pers_dur	home_fin
7	6	4	3	6	6	7
6	5	6	2	7	7	7
7	7	6	5	5	5	6
3	5	5	3	7	7	7
7	7	5	3	5	7	7
7	6	6	5	6	6	6
7	7	6	5	6	7	7
7	7	5	3	5	6	5
7	7	6	7	6	4	7
7	7	5	7	6	6	6
7	3	4	6	7	7	7
7	7	7	3	3	4	4
7	6	6	3	4	4	6
7	5	7	6	7	7	7
6	7	7	7	7	7	7
7	6	6	6	5	4	7
5	7	6	3	3	6	6
4	6	5	3	5	6	6
5	7	3	2	6	5	6
7	5	5	4	6	7	7
7	6	5	5	5	6	6
7	6	5	5	1	6	7
	7	4	4	6	7	7
7	6	6	1	7	6	6
7	6	7	7	5	6	5
7	7	3	1	4	6	5
6	6	6	6	6	6	6
7	5	5	4	4	5	6
7	6		4	6	7	6
7	6	7	4	6	6	7
6	5	6	6	5	7	7
6	6	6	4	5	6	6
6	4	6	3	6	6	5
7	7	6	7	7	7	7
6	7	5	7	2	4	5
5	6	6		4	6	6

asset_mg	public_f	inv_bank	risk	maturity	funding	operatio
5	5	5	1	0	0	0
5	2	4	1	0	0	0
7	7	7	0	1	1	0
2	6	6	1	0	0	0
7	5	5	1	1	0	0
6	6	6	1	1	0	1
5	6	7	1	0	0	0
5	6	6	1	1	0	0
7	6	7	1	0	0	0
7	6	7	0	0	0	0
6	4	5	0	0	0	0
7	6	6	1	0	0	0
5	4	4	0	0	0	0
5	5	5	0	0	0	0
7	7	7	0	0	0	0
7	7	7	0	1	0	1
7	4	7	1	1	1	1
6	6	6	0	0	0	0
4	4	4	1	0	1	1
5	6	5	1	1	0	0
5	5	5	1	0	0	0
6	5	7	0	1	0	1
5	7	6	1	0	0	0
6	5	7	1	0	1	0
6	6	7	0	1	0	0
7	6	6	1	0	0	0
5	5	6	1	0	0	0
6	4	6	0	0	1	0
6	5	6	0	0	0	0
5	7	6	1	0	1	1
6	5	6	0	0	1	0
6	6	6	0	1	0	0
4	4	6	0	0	1	0
6	7	7	1	0	0	0
7	6	6	0	0	0	0
5	5	5	0	1	1	0

margins	demand	growth	ib_grow	ib_price	ib_equit	ib_capit
1	1	1	7	3	3	2
1	0	1	4	1	1	1
1	1	1	7	4	5	5
1	0	1	6	6	4	3
1	1	0	7	2	2	5
1	1	1	5	2	2	3
1	1	1	6	4	4	6
1	0	0	7	2	4	1
1	1	0	6	3	5	5
1	0	1	5	5	3	4
1	1	1	6	5	5	4
0	0	1	6	4	1	1
0	1	1	6	1	4	5
1	1	1	7	4	4	5
0	1	0	6	4	4	5
0	0	1	5	3	6	3
1	1	1	4	6	4	6
1	1	1	6	2	2	2
1	1	0	6	5	2	4
1	1	0	4	2	5	5
0	1	1	6	3	3	3
1	0	1	6	3	4	4
0	0	1	6	1	1	3
1	0	1	7	1	3	6
1	1	1	6	3	4	6
1	1	1	6	3	4	4
0	0	0	4	5	5	5
1	1	1	5	4	4	5
1	1	0	5	4	3	6
1	1	1	7	3	6	6
1	0	0	6	5	4	4
1	0	0	6	6	5	5
0	1	1	4	4	3	3
1	1	1	7	1	4	4
0	0	1	6	2	4	5
0	1	1	5	2	4	

ib_risk	ib_fund	ib_opera	ib_margi	ib_marke	competit	clients
3	5	5	5	6	4	4
3	5	2	2	1	4	2
4	4	4	4	4	6	4
1	3	1	3	3	4	3
3	3	3	5	4	3	4
2	4	2	4	4	4	4
2	3	2	5	6	6	3
5	5	4	2	5	5	6
7	5	5	6	6	7	6
5	5	5	6	6	7	7
1	2	1	5	5	5	6
1	1	1	1	4	6	2
4	5	3	4	2	5	6
4	5	4	5	7	5	5
2	3	2	5	6	4	3
4	5	4	6	5	5	4
6	5	5	5	4	6	6
2	3	1	4	7	7	4
5	4	4	5	6	5	4
5	4	4	3	6	4	5
3	2	3	2	7	7	6
4	5	4	3	5	6	5
3	1	1	1	6	6	7
1	5	1	1	6	6	6
3	3	3	5	3	5	5
1	4	2	3	4	5	4
2	3	3	3	6	6	3
3	6	4	6	6	6	6
5	6	5	5	5	6	6
4	4	4	3	5	6	5
5	4	2	3	5	6	5
5	2	2	4	3	5	5
4	5	5	6	6	4	4
1	1	2	2	7	6	6
1	1	1	1	1	3	3
4	5	5	5	5	4	5

deposits	substit	liquidit	regulat	shar_st	capital	pls
6	7	5	5	2	2	5
6	4	4	6	6	6	6
4	2	2	6	6	5	5
7	4	5	6	3	5	4
6	2	6	5	5	6	6
6	4	6	6	7	7	6
6	1	6	7	5	7	2
6	4	6	5	6	7	4
6	7	5	6	6	5	5
4	5	5	6	7	5	6
6	5	7	5	1	7	6
4	4	7	7	7	6	2
7	2	2	6	5	6	6
6	6	6	6	6	6	5
6	3	6	6	6	7	7
6	5	5	7	6	7	6
6	1	4	5	1	4	4
5	7	4	6	6	7	6
6	3	3	6	4	5	2
6	5	4	6	6	6	1
7	4	6	6	3	6	6
3	3	5	6	6	7	6
7	4	3	5	5	5	6
6	6	2	7	7	7	2
6	1	6	6	7	6	6
6	2	7	5	5	4	4
4	5	5	7	6	7	5
6	4	4	5	6	7	4
7	7	3	7	6	5	6
2	2	2	6	1	5	2
6	4	3	7	7	5	5
5	5	6	7	7	6	5
5	4	2	6	1	1	1
7	2	2	7	7	7	7
6	1	6	7	6	6	6
6	4	3	6	5	3	4

substit2	barriers	investm	capital2	hr	it_suppl	prod_st
7	5	6	5	5	2	5
3	5	4	4	5	4	6
4	6	3	4	3	5	5
2	2	2	2	5	2	2
4	5	6	5	6	5	6
4	4	5	4	6	5	6
1	3	3	3	6	3	6
5	6	5	6	3	4	6
7	6	5	5	4	6	5
5	5	5	6	6	6	6
2	5	6	4	5	6	4
4	2	4	4	1	5	7
7	4	6	3	6	3	7
6	4	5	3	6	4	3
4	2	5	2	6	3	4
5	4	5	3	7	6	6
6	5	6	4	4	4	4
2	2	4	3	5	6	7
3	4	2	4	5	4	5
2	6	2	2	5	4	5
6	7	6	6	6	7	6
4	5	5	5	5	5	6
2	1	2	2	2	6	3
6	6	3	3	7	6	6
3	6	6	5	7	4	6
3	5	5	2	5	3	6
4	5	4	5	6	4	5
5	3	6	5	6	7	7
6	6	6	5	4	4	6
2	6	2	5	6	5	5
7	4	3	2	1	7	7
5	6	5	2	3	4	5
6	1	1	2	5	5	2
2	2	1	1	7	7	2
2	6	2	2	6	3	6
6	6	4		5	5	4

educ	non_musl	late_fee	hedge_fu	consolid	fin_cond	deriv
6	6	6	6	4	7	6
6	2	4	6	4	7	6
4	5	4	1	6	4	6
4	2	2	2	4	7	2
5	7	7	6	6	7	7
6	4	4	5	3	6	5
5	7	7	5	7	2	1
6	7	6	4	5	6	4
6	6	5	5	6	7	7
7	7	7	7	7	7	7
3	6	5	5	4	6	5
5	2	1	4	7	2	1
6	7	5	6	4	6	4
5	7	6	5	5	5	6
5	4	2	2	6	6	2
7	7	6	7	7	6	7
4	4	4	2	4	4	2
6	7	4	6	4	6	4
3	4	1	4	3	2	1
6	6	4	7	6	4	4
3	6	4	5	4	4	4
5	7	4	7	7	4	7
6	7	6	6	6	7	5
6	6	6	6	6	6	6
6	5	3	6	6	4	6
6	5	5	4	7	6	6
4	5	5	4	2	6	5
5	4	6	1	5	2	1
6	6	6	7	5	5	6
5	2	5	5	1	1	1
7	6	6	5	4	4	7
7	7	7	6	2	4	4
6	5	4	5	5	5	3
3	7	4	4	6	7	6
6	5	2	2	5	2	6
5	7	7	7	7	7	7

emulate	act_form	corp_gov	pers_fin	vent_cap	pers_wea	corp_as
5	0	1	1	0	1	0
7	0	1	1	1	1	1
6	1	1	1	1	0	0
2	1	1	0	1	0	0
7	1	1	0	0	0	0
4	1	1	1	0	0	0
1	0	1	1	0	0	0
4	0	1	0	0	0	0
6	0	1	1	0	0	0
6	0	1	1	1	0	1
2	1	0	0	1	0	1
1	0	1	0	0	0	1
5	0	1	1	0	0	0
5	0	1	1	0	0	0
5	1	1	1	0	0	1
5	1	1	0	0	1	1
2	1	1	1	1	1	1
2	1	1	0	0	1	1
2	1	1	1	0	0	0
4	1	0	0	1	1	1
	0	1	1	0	1	0
4	1	1	1	0	0	1
6	1	1	1	0	0	0
6	1	1	1	0	0	0
5	1	1	1	0	0	1
6	1	1	0	0	0	1
5	1	1	1	1	1	1
1	0	0	1	0	1	1
4	0	1	1	0	0	1
3	1	1	1	1	1	1
6	1	1	1	1	1	1
7	1	1	1	0	0	1
2	0	1	1	0	1	0
2	1	1	1	1	0	0
3	0	1	1	1	1	1
7	0	1	1	0	0	1

pers_ban	corp_ad	own_str	autonomy	asset00	asset03
1	1	Fully owned by parent firm	5		
1	1	Joint venture	6		
0	0	Privately owned			
0	1	Privately owned			
0	1	Fully owned by parent firm			
1	1	Privately owned		1126	1954
1	0	Joint venture	6		
0	0	State-owned	6		
1	0	Fully owned by parent firm			
1	1	Fully owned by parent firm	5		
0	0	Privately owned		500	800
0	0	Fully owned by parent firm	2		
1	0	Fully owned by parent firm	5		
1	0	Fully owned by parent firm		299	635
0	1	Fully owned by parent firm	3		
1	1	Privately owned			
1	1	Joint venture	4		
0	1	Fully owned by parent firm			
1	0	Privately owned			
0	1	Joint venture	4		232
1	0	Fully owned by parent firm	4		
1	1	Fully owned by parent firm	5	1079	976
1	1	Privately owned			
0	1	Privately owned			
1	1	State-owned	6	942	1991
0	1	Fully owned by parent firm		195	245
1	1	Fully owned by parent firm			225
1	0	Privately owned			2000
1	0	Fully owned by parent firm	2		
1	0	Privately owned		1021	1072
1	1	Privately owned		7155	8188
1	0	State-owned	7		578
1	0	Fully owned by parent firm			
1	1	Fully owned by parent firm	7	2121	3430
1	1	Privately owned			
1	0	Fully owned by parent firm	2		

asset04	curr_00	curr_03	curr_04	u_inv_00	u_inv_03	u_inv_04
2015	97	350	416	0	0	0
	0	0		76	162	
975	14	50	74	249	399	485
332						
1105	53	43	47	559	505	399
2231	81	222	262	541	1100	1409
317				137	213	282
400		25	33		19	73
		800				
1080	170	179	181	482	506	510
				5463	6193	
634		124	139		278	311
3879	308	672	687	1595	1983	1821

r_inv_00	r_inv_03	r_inv_04	funds00	funds03	funds04	ebt00
0	0	0	51	39	42	11
0	0		0	0		36
0	0	0	0	0	0	-1
1344	1059	1453				8
16	0	0	47	44		13
231	180	180				4
				2000		
20	21	25	0	0	0	16
						171
	0	0		0	0	
2275	2275	2275				11

ebt03	ebt04	empl00	empl03	empl04	bal_sc	mbo
					0	1
					1	1
					0	1
					0	1
					1	0
20	30	321	507	804	1	1
					0	1
					0	0
					1	0
					1	0
44		90	114		0	0
					0	0
					0	1
11	5	40	59	84	0	0
					1	0
					0	1
					1	1
					0	1
					0	1
22	32		25	30	0	1
		21	28	32	1	0
21	25	157	186	218	1	0
					0	1
					0	0
22	27	241	483	677	1	0
9	3	20	19	21	1	1
7			86	120	0	0
			12		1	0
					0	0
22	46	400	410		0	0
161		1328	1452		0	1
13	15		275	325	0	1
					1	1
33	37	1622	2022		0	0
					1	0
		27	27		1	0

perf_com	cust_sat	bus_plan	kpi	mil_plan	high_st	share_va
1	0	1	1	0	1	1
1	1	1	0	0	1	1
1	1	1	1	0	1	1
1	0	0	1	0	0	1
0	0	0	0	0	1	1
1	1	1	1	0	1	1
1	0	1	1	0	1	1
1	1	1	0	0	1	1
0	0	0	0	0	1	1
0	0	1	1	1	1	1
1	0	1	0	0	1	1
0	0	1	0	0	1	1
1	0	1	1	0	1	1
1	1	1	1	1	1	1
1	0	1	1	1	1	1
1	1	1	1	0	1	1
1	1	1	1	1	1	1
1	0	1	1	0	1	1
1	1	1	0	0	1	1
0	1	1	0	1	1	1
0	0	1	1	0	1	1
0	1	1	1	0	1	1
0	1	1	1	0	1	1
1	0	0	1	0	1	1
1	1	1	1	0	1	1
1	0	1	0	0	1	1
1	0	0	1	0	1	1
0	1	1	1	0	0	1
1	0	1	0	0	1	1
0	1	1	0	0	1	1
1	1	1	1	0	1	1
1	1	1	1	0	1	1
1	1	1	1	1	1	1
0	0	1	1	0	1	1
1	0	0	0	0	1	1
1	1	1	1	0	1	1

dev_econ	soc_welf	max_prof	enc_peop	prec_isl	sme	smfi
0	0	1	0	0	1	1
0	0	1	0	1	1	1
1	1	1	1	1	1	1
1	0	0	0	0	0	0
0	0	0	0	0	0	0
0	0	0	0	0	1	0
1	0	1	1	0	1	1
1	0	1	0	0	0	1
1	0	1	1	0	1	0
0	0	1	0	1	1	1
0	0	1	0	0	0	0
0	0	0	0	0	1	1
0	0	0	1	1	1	0
0	1	1	1	1	1	0
0	0	1	0	0	0	1
1	0	1	0	0	0	1
1	1	1	1	1	1	1
0	0	1	0	0	0	1
0	0	1	0	1	1	0
1	0	1	1	1	1	1
0	0	0	1	0	1	0
1	0	0	0	1	1	1
1	0	1	0	0	1	0
0	0	1	0	0	0	1
1	1	1	1	1	0	1
0	0	1	0	0	0	0
1	1	1	1	1	1	1
0	0	1	1	0	1	0
0	0	1	0	0	1	0
0	0	1	1	1	0	0
1	0	0	1	0	0	0
0	1	1	0	0	1	0
0	0	1	1	0	1	0
0	0	0	1	1	1	0
0	0	0	0	1	1	1
0	0	1	1	1	1	1

mapc	large_co	large_fi	hnwi	cc_asset	ic_asset	pc_asset
1	1	1	0	20	40	40
1	1	1	1			
1	1	1	1	50	15	35
0	1	1	1			
0	1	1	1			
1	0	0	1	26	45	29
1	1	1	1			
0	1	1	0			
1	1	0	1			
1	1	0	0	30	10	60
0	0	0	1			
0	1	1	0			
1	0	0	0	15	5	80
1	1	0	0	6	14	80
0	1	1	1			
0	0	1	1			
1	1	1	1	29	51	20
0	1	1	1			
1	1	1	0			
0	0	0	1	88	11	1
1	0	0	0	48	14	38
1	0	0	1	37	42	21
0	0	0	1	24	28	48
0	1	0	1			
0	1	0	1	52	14	34
0	1	1	1	33	67	0
1	1	1	1	25	50	25
0	1	0	1	25	10	65
0	0	0	1	2	0	98
1	1	1	1	48	29	23
1	1	1	1			
0	1	0	1	50	39	11
1	0	0	1			
1	1	0	0	51	2	47
1	1	1	1			
1	1	1	1	40		60

cc_liab	ic_liab	pc_liab	cc_funds	ic_funds	pc_funds	ia_trade
20	0	80	0	0	0	0
45	10	45	0	0	0	1
						0
						1
33	42	25	0	0	100	0
						1
60	10	30	70	20	10	1
			20	0	80	
33	15	52	0	0	0	1
80	15	5	0	100	0	0
						1
10	76	14	26	3	71	
11	89	0	35	0	65	1
83	0	17	0	0	0	1
23	41	36	20	30	50	0
35	5	60				1
39	20	41	78	0	22	
1	94	5	10	85	5	1
10	75	15	70	0	30	
15	15	70	20	10	70	1
40	0	60	0	0	0	0
			30	60	10	1
51	2	47	0	0	0	1
						1
31	55	14				1
45		55				1

ia_share	ia_home	ia_publi	ia_capex	ia_compr	ia_durab	ia_bonds
0	1	0	0	0	0	1
1	0	0	0	0	0	1
0	0	0	0	0	0	0
0	0	1	0	0	0	1
1	0	0	1	0	0	1
1	0	0	0	0	1	0
0	1	0	1	1	0	1
1	1	1	0	1	1	0
0	1	0	0	1	1	0
0	1	0	1	1	0	0
1	0	0	0	1	0	0
0	1	0	0	0	0	0
0	1	0	0	0	0	1
0	0	1	0	0	1	1
0	0	0	0	0	0	1
0	1	0	0	0	1	0
0	1	1	0	1	0	0
0	0	0	0	1	1	0
0	1	1	1	1	1	0
0	1	0	0	1	0	0
0	1	0	0	0	0	0
0	1	0	1	0	0	0

ia_other	ia_p_tra	ia_p_sha	ia_p_hom	ia_p_pub	ia_p_cap	ia_p_com
1	0	0	60	0	0	0
0	55	15	0	0	0	0
1						
0						
1	0	5	0	0	55	0
0						
1	10	0	5	0	5	20
0	5	5	62	2	0	25
0	0	0	26	0	0	20
0	20	0	5	0	35	40
1	5	52	0	0	0	29
1	15	0	47	0	0	0
1	0	0	9	0	0	0
0	28	0	0	39	9	9
1	51	0	0	0	0	0
0	50	0	10	0	0	0
0	0	0	50	30	0	20
0	20	0	0	0	0	50
0						
1	1	0	10	0	0	29
1	21	0	27	0	0	0
0	20	0	50	0	25	0

ia_p_dur	ia_p_bon	ia_p_ot1	shb_num	appr_gg	appr_np	appr_nst
0	30	10	2	1	1	0
			5	1	1	1
0	20	0	4	1	1	1
			5	1	1	1
			3	0	1	1
0	12	28	5	1	1	1
			1	1	1	1
			0			
			4	1	1	0
0	10	50	3	1	1	1
			4	1	1	1
			0			
1	0	0	3	1	1	1
54	0	0	3	1	1	1
0	0	0		1	1	1
			3	1	1	1
			5	1	1	1
			3	1	1	0
			6	1	1	1
0	0	15	3	1	1	1
0	0	37	6	1	1	1
0	63	20	4	1	1	1
30	7	0	4	1	1	0
			6			
			4	1	1	1
0	8	13	4	1	1	1
			6	1	1	1
40	0	0	3	1	1	0
0	0	0	3	1	1	0
20	0	0	6	0	1	1
			6	0	1	0
			3	1	1	1
0	0	60	3	1	1	0
0	0	11		1	1	1
			4	1	1	1
0	0	0	3	1	1	0

appr_st	rev_nst	rev_st	compl_re	share_sh	bs_cash	bs_advan
0	0	0	0	1	4	49
1	0	0	0	1		
1	1	1	1	1	5	42
1	1	1	1	1	2	0
0	1	0	1	1		
1	1	1	1		7	20
1	1	1	1	1		
0	0	0	1	0		
1	0	1	0	1	7	0
1	1	1	1	1	2	36
0	0	1	0	1		
1	0	0	1	1	4	1
1	0	0	0	1		
0	0	0	1	1		
1	1	1	1	1	22	0
1	0	1	1	1		
1	1	1	1	1		
0	1	0	1	0	11	0
0	0	0	1	1	0	8
0	1	1	1	1	27	0
1	1	0	1	1	5	28
				0		
0	0	0	1	1	5	22
1	1	1	1	1	1	0
1	1	1	1	1	6	0
0	1	1	0	1		
0	0	0	0	1		
0	0	1	1	1	13	0
0	0	0	0	1		
0	1	0	1		7	30
0	0	1	1	1		
0	0	0	1	1	4	13
0	0	1	1	1		
1	0	0	1	1		

bs_murab	bs_ina	bs_salam	bs_ijara	bs_mudar	bs_musha	bs_inv_s
9	0	0	0	0	0	37
19	0	0	2	4	1	20
2	0	0	0	0	0	5
39	0	0	2	0	0	16
1	31	1	42	1	2	12
31	0	0	0	0	0	32
1	2	1	37	0	0	18
62	0	0	5	1	0	5
2	0	0	3	0	0	52
1	0	0	6	0	0	24
20	4	3	3	26	4	6
50	0	3	7	1	0	3
36	0	1	28	1	0	7
52	0	0	13	0	0	34
41	0	0	6	9	0	0
48	0	9	1	3	0	0
10	0	0	45	0	0	2
44	1	0	1	1	2	27

bs_ass_o	bs_depos	bs_curac	bs_invac	bs_equit	bs_lia_o	is_mudar
1	0	14	61	15	10	60
6	16	13	53	17	2	20
89	10	0	0	97	-9	46
16	4	18	66	10	1	
3	60	15	10	15	0	60
1	39	0	20	25	16	0
36	14	6	63	8	9	81
5	7	5	71	15	2	49
33	40	0	0	53	8	39
62	0	20	57	7	16	82
7	16	4	53	24	4	27
5	5	23	62	8	3	65
1	17	11	55	15	1	79
1	81	6	0	12	1	6
38	41	11	9	38	1	0
25	1	17	47	8	2	84
6	1	22	48	25	4	2
8	1	20	70	8	2	87

is_self	is_advis	is_loc	is_fees	org_role	org_vert	org_info
10	0	0	30	4	5	4
				6	4	4
73	0	3	4	6	6	5
48	0	0	6	3	4	7
				4	5	7
				4	4	5
				5	5	5
				5	5	6
				7	5	5
10	10	15	5	6	6	7
100	0	0	0	5	6	6
				4	4	5
				5	6	5
10	0	9	1	6	6	6
				5	6	5
				5	6	6
30	0	13	8	6	6	6
				6	5	6
				5	4	3
44	17	0	0	4	4	5
17	0	0	1	6	6	5
47	23	2	1	5	5	4
8	0	2	25	5	5	5
				5	5	4
5	12	2	3	5	4	3
70	0	4	20	6	6	5
88	10	0	2	4	4	5
				5	5	4
				5	6	5
2	0	5	1	7	5	6
				6	5	5
68	0	5	25	5	6	6
				6	5	5
8	0	0	5	4	5	4
				6	7	5
				6	6	5

org_coop	org_team	org_mark	mgmt_com	mgmt_qua	mgmt_vis	mgmt_str
5	6	6	5	5	4	4
4	6	5	6	6	6	6
7	6	6	7	7	6	6
7	7	7	5	5	6	5
6	6	6	6	6	5	5
4	5	4	5	5	4	4
5	6	6	6	6	6	5
6	5	5	6	6	5	4
5	7	5	7	7	7	7
6	7	7	6	6	6	6
6	7	6	7	6	6	6
5	6	6	6	6	5	5
6	6	7	7	7	6	6
7	6	6	5	6	6	5
6	7	7	6	7	7	6
6	6	6	6	6	6	6
6	6	6	6	6	6	6
6	6	4	6	6	5	6
3	3	4	4	4	3	4
5	6	6	4	5	5	5
6	5	6	6	6	6	5
4	4	5	6	5	6	6
5	6	5	5	6	6	6
5	5	5	5	4	6	6
3	4	5	5	6	5	5
5	7	6	6	6	5	5
4	4	6	6	7	5	5
4	4	5	5	5	6	5
6	5	5	5	5	5	6
6	6	7	7	7	6	6
5	4	6	6	7	6	5
6	6	5	4	6	6	6
6	6	5	5	4	6	5
3	4	2	5	5	4	4
6	6		7	7	7	6
5	5	6	6	6	6	6

mgtm_res	mgmt_kno	cul_tran	cul_peop	cul_meri	cul_moti	cul_rewa
4	4	4	4	4	4	5
6	6	6	6	5	5	5
7	6	7	7	6	6	7
5	6	7	6		5	6
5	7	7	7	7	6	6
4	5	5	4	5	4	5
5	6	6	5	5	5	5
5	5	5	6	5	5	6
5	7	3	7	4	4	4
5	5	6	6	7	6	6
5	6	6	6	6	6	7
5	6	6	5	4	4	4
5	5	6	7	6	5	6
6	6	6	6	5	6	6
5	6	7	5	6	6	6
6	6	5	6	6	6	6
6	6	6	6	6	6	6
5	6	4	5	5	6	6
6	4	4	2	4	3	3
5	5	5	5	4	6	6
5	6	6	6	6	5	6
5	5	4	5	4	3	4
5	5	7	5	4	5	4
4	4	6	4	2	4	4
4	5	4	3	4	4	4
6	7	7	4	5	2	4
4	5	6	7	6	7	6
5	5	5	4	4	5	5
4	6	5	4	4	4	5
6	6	6	6	5	6	6
5	5	5	5	6	5	6
6	6	6	4	6	6	6
4	4	6	5	3	4	5
1	6	4	2	2	4	3
6	6	6	7	7	7	7
6	5	5	6	6	5	5

cul_coor	prd_inno	prd_expe	prd_capa	prd_effi	prd_know	prd_appr
4	6	4	4	5	5	5
5	6	6	5	5	6	6
6	6	6	6	6	7	6
5	6	6	5	4	6	5
6	6	6	7	6	7	7
5	6	5	5	5	6	5
5	5	6	5	5	5	6
6	5	5	5	5	5	
4	7	6	5	5	7	6
6	5	5	5	5	6	6
6	7	6	5	5	5	5
3	2	3	3	3	5	
5	5	5	4	4	5	4
6	5	5	5	5	5	6
5	6	5	4	5	7	6
6	6	6	6	6	6	6
6	6	6	6	6	6	6
6	7	6	6	5	6	6
4	2	4	5	5	4	3
6	5	5	5	5	6	6
6	6	6	5	5	6	5
4	7	6	6	4	6	5
5	4	5	5	5	6	6
4	4	5	4	4	5	6
3	5	5	4	5	5	4
6	6	6	6	7	7	5
4	6	5	5	5	5	5
4	5	6	6	5	5	6
5	5	5	6	5	5	4
7	5	6	6	6	7	7
6	7	5	5	5	7	7
6	5	6	6	5	6	5
5	5	3	3	4	5	5
4	7	7	7	4	7	4
6	6	6	6	6	6	6
5	5	6	6	5	5	5

ms_repfi	ms_brand	ms_placi	ms_marke	ms_repui	ms_ipcap	ms_distr
6	7	5	6	2	5	5
7	7	5	6	3	4	4
7	6	6	7	7	6	7
6	6	6	6	5	3	1
7	7	7	7	6	6	7
3	4	3	5	5	5	5
6	6	5	6	1	5	5
6	6	6	6	4	5	6
7	6	5	6	6	5	5
6	7	6	5	6	5	5
6	6	6	6	6	6	6
4	4	2	5	4	2	2
7	7	5	5	4	5	6
5	5	5	5	5	5	5
5	6	4	5	5	5	4
6	7	7	6	6	6	6
6	6	6	6	6	6	6
7	7	6	6	7	6	5
6	6	6	5	6	4	6
6	5	5	5	6	5	6
6	6	5	5	5	5	6
5	5	5	6	6	6	7
6	5	5	6	6	5	6
5	5	3	5	6	6	5
5	5	6	5	5	6	5
7	7	7	7	7	6	6
6	6	6	6	7	6	5
6	6	6	6	4	6	6
5	6	5	5	3	4	4
7	6	6	7	7	6	7
7	6	5	6	7	6	6
6	4	4	4	4	5	5
5	3	3	4	2	4	4
5	7	5	5	7	4	4
7	7	6	6	6	6	5
6	6	6	6	5	6	6

ms_relcu	ms_socbe	ms_curcu	ms_branc	ms_atm	ms_inter	ms_callc
2	4	2	3	3	2	6
4	3	6	5	5	7	7
7	6	6	6	6	4	5
3	2	3	1	1	1	1
6	5	5	2	2	1	1
3	3	2	2	2	3	1
5	4	5	5	4	6	7
5	4	5	2			
5	5	6	6	7	6	6
5	5	6	7	6	5	5
6	5	5				
6	5	4	2	2	1	1
4	4	5	5	4	4	4
5	5	5	5	4	1	2
3	2	3	2	1	1	1
7	7	6				5
6	6	6	6	5	4	4
6	3	5	1	1	1	1
6	3	6	6	6	7	6
6	6	5	4		4	
5	5	4	6	6	5	5
5	5	4	4	5	6	5
6	5	6	4	6	2	4
6	6	3	2	2	1	2
5	5	4	5	4	3	4
6	6	5	2	1	1	1
5	4	5	4	3	1	2
6	5	5	5	5	5	4
4	3		3	3	4	5
6	7	5	6	7	5	6
5	7	7	7	7	6	5
4	6	5	4	5	1	1
4	4	4	5	3	6	6
5	6	6	6	6	5	1
5	4	2	2	2	5	5
6	4	7	7	7	7	6

ms_deala	ms_custo	ms_pe	ms_respo	ms_finex	ms_shari	ms_servi
6	4	1	5	5	6	4
6	5	4	5	5	7	6
5	6	5	6	6	7	6
6	6	7	6	7	4	6
6	6	1	6	6	7	7
4	2	1	5	3	5	5
6	4	2	6	6	7	7
6	6		6	6		6
5	5	5	5	5	6	6
6	5	5	5	6	5	5
6	5	7	6	5	6	6
1	1	1	2	4		2
4	4	4	6	5	6	7
4	4	1	6	5	5	5
5	1	3	5	6	6	5
6	5	6	6	6	6	6
6	6	6	6	6	6	6
1	1	4	5	6	7	6
4	4	1	4	4	6	5
5	5	5	5	5	6	5
5	4	4	5	6	6	5
6	5	6	5	6	6	5
6	6	2	5	6	6	6
5	5	2	6	6	6	6
5	4	3	4	5	6	5
5	5	1	4	6	7	6
3	3	6	4	6	6	5
5	5	5	4	5	6	5
5	3	2	5	4	3	5
6	6	6	6	7	7	6
5	5	6	5	5	7	4
4	2	2	3	4	7	4
6	2	3	5	5	5	5
4	1	7	2	5	7	4
5	5		5	5	6	5

ms_teche	ms_techc	ms_resef	ms_shapp	tp_servi	tp_secur	tp_teche
4	4	4	5	5	1	5
6	6	5	6	5	4	5
6	6	6	6	6	6	6
6	4	6	6	3	7	7
7	7	7	6	6	6	6
5	5	5	4	5	5	5
6	5	5	6	6	5	6
5	5			6		6
6	6	6	6	6	6	7
5	5	5	6	4	5	6
6	6	5	6	6		6
	3	3		4	1	2
5	5	4	5	7	5	5
4	4	4	7	5	4	4
5	4	5	4	5	6	4
6	6	6	6	6	6	6
6	6	6	6	6	6	6
6	6	6	6	7	5	6
5	5	6	3	4	2	5
6	5	5	6	5	6	5
5	5	5	5	5	4	5
6	6	4	5	4	6	6
5	6	6	6	6	2	5
6	6	6	6	6	6	6
5	5	4	5	5	5	5
6	6	6	5	6	7	7
4	5	4	5	5	3	3
6	6	5	6	6	3	5
5	6	5		6	5	5
6	6	6	6	6	6	6
5	5	5	7	5	4	5
5	4	4	6	4	4	4
3	3		5	5	3	4
4	4	4	7	3	1	4
6		5	5	5	5	6

tp_techc	tp_resef	tp_tradi	sup_shar	sup_boar	sup_stra	sup_cont
4	4	5	5	5	5	6
5	5	6	6	6	5	5
6	6	6	7	7	6	6
5	4	4	4	4	6	4
7	7	5	6	6	5	6
6	5	4	5	5	4	4
5	5	6	7	7	5	6
6	5	6			5	6
7	7	6	6	7	7	5
6	5	5	5	7	6	5
5	5	5	6	6	5	6
3	3	4	4		4	4
5	4	4	5	5	5	5
4	4	5	7	6	5	5
4	5	6	5	5	6	6
6	6	6	6	6	6	6
6	6	6	6	6	6	6
6	6	6	7	7	6	6
5	6	5	6	4	4	4
5	5	6	6	6	5	5
4	5	5	7	6	5	5
6	5	6	6	6	6	5
6	6	6	7	7	5	5
6	6	4	6	6	6	6
5	5	4	5	5	5	5
7	6	6	7	7	6	6
3	4	5	7	5	5	5
5	5	5	5	6	6	5
6	6	6	7	5	5	5
7	7	6	7	7	6	6
4	5	5	7	7	5	5
4	4	5	5	5	5	6
4	4	4	5	5	6	5
4	3	4	7	7	4	4
			7	7	6	
5	5	5	6	5	5	5

sup_risk	sup_rese	sup_asse	sup_equi	sup_data	sup_comp	sup_hr
6	3	6	4	4	5	4
7	5	6	6	6	5	3
6	6	6	6	7	6	6
4	4	4	2	5	6	4
6	7	6	5	5	6	7
4	2	3	3	4	3	3
7	3	6	6	6	5	5
6	5	6	6	5	5	
6	7	6	6	4	4	4
6	5	5	6	6	6	5
5	6	5	6	5	7	5
4	4	1	5	4	4	4
5	4	7	7	5	6	5
3	3	5	5	4	5	5
6	6	5	5	4	6	6
6	6	6	6	6	6	6
6	6	6	6	6	6	6
6	7	7	3	6	6	6
3	5	6	6	4	4	4
5	5	5	6	5	5	5
6	4	5	5	5	5	5
6	4	5	6	5	4	5
6	4	6	6	5	5	4
4	6	5	6	6	6	6
6	5	6	6	5	4	4
7	6	7	6	6	4	5
5	4	5	4	5	5	3
5	4	6	6	5	4	4
7	5	7	6	5	5	4
5	6	6	6	7	7	6
5	5	6	6	5	6	5
4	2	5	5	5	5	5
6	6	5	2	6	6	4
4	4	2	4	4	2	2
6	6	6	6	5	5	5
5	5	6	6	5	5	5

sup_tool	sup_shor	sup_long	sup_rati	grow_int	grow_coo	grow_acq
5	4	4	6	1	1	0
5	5	5	5	1	0	1
6	6	6	6	1	1	1
5	2	6	2	1	0	1
7	7	7	7	1	7	7
3	4	4	3	0	1	0
7	5	5	6	1	0	0
4	6	6		1	0	0
5	4	4	5	0	0	1
6	6	6	5	0	1	0
	6	6		1	0	0
3	3	3	5	0	1	0
4	4	4	4	1	0	0
4	4	5	1	1	0	0
7	6	3	7	1	1	1
6	6	6	5	0	1	1
6	6	6	6	1	0	0
4	3	2	7	1	0	1
	6	5		1	0	0
5	5	5		0	1	0
6	5	5	6	1	0	0
5	5	5	4	1	0	0
4	5	4	5	0	1	0
6	6	6	6	0	1	0
6	5	4	6	1	0	0
6	6	6	1	1	0	0
4	5	5	5	1	0	0
6	6	5	6	1	0	0
6	6	6	6	1	0	0
4	6	6	7	1	0	0
4	4	4	5	1	0	0
6	5	5	5	0	1	0
4	7	7	5	1	0	0
7	5	5	7	1	0	0
5	6	6	5	1	0	0

grow_non	ops_ind	ops_pd_p	ops_pd_c	ops_pd_o	ops_m_p	ops_m_c
0	0	0	0	0	0	0
0	1	0	0	0	0	0
0	1	0	0	0	0	0
0	1	0	0	0	0	0
7	0	1	0	0	1	0
0	0	0	1	0	0	0
0	1	0	0	0	0	0
0	0	1	0	0	1	0
0	1	0	0	0	0	0
0	1	0	0	0	0	0
0	1	0	0	0	0	0
0	0	1	0	0	1	0
0	1	0	0	0	0	0
0	0	1	0	0	1	0
0	0	1	1	0	1	1
0	0	0	1	0	1	0
0	0	1	1	1	1	1
0	0	1	1	0	1	0
0	1	0	0	0	0	0
0	0	1	0	0	1	0
0	0	0	0	0	1	0
0	0	1	0	0	0	0
0	1	0	0	0	0	0
0	1	0	0	0	0	0
0	1	0	0	0	0	0
0	0	1	1	0	0	1
	1	0	0	0	0	0
0	1	0	0	0	0	0
0	1	0	0	0	0	0
0	1	0	0	0	0	0
0	0	1	0	0	1	0
0	1	0	0	0	0	0
0	1	0	0	0	0	0
0	1	0	0	0	0	0
0	0	1	0	0	1	0
0	0	1	0	0	1	0

ops_m_o	ops_s_p	ops_s_c	ops_s_o	ops_t_p	ops_t_c	ops_t_o
0	0	1	1	0	1	1
0	0	0	0	0	0	0
0	0	0	0	0	0	0
0	0	0	0	0	0	0
0	1	0	0	1	0	0
1	0	0	0	0	0	0
0	0	0	0	0	0	0
0	1	0	0	1	0	0
0	0	0	0	0	0	0
0	0	0	0	0	0	0
0	0	0	0	0	0	0
1	1	0	1	1	0	0
0	0	0	0	0	0	0
0	1	0	0	1	0	0
1	1	1	0	1	0	1
0	0	1	0	1	0	0
1	1	1	1	1	1	1
0	1	1	0	1	0	0
0	0	0	0	0	0	0
0	1	0	0	1	0	0
0	1	0	0	1	0	0
0	1	0	0	0	0	1
0	0	0	0	0	0	0
0	0	0	0	0	0	0
0	0	0	0	0	0	0
0	0	1	0	1	0	0
0	0	0	0	0	0	0
0	0	0	0	0	0	0
0	0	0	0	0	0	0
0	0	0	0	0	0	0
0	1	0	0	1	0	0
0	0	0	0	0	0	0
0	0	0	0	0	0	0
0	0	0	0	0	0	0
0	1	0	0	1	0	0
0	1	0	0	1	0	0

ops_su_p	ops_su_c	ops_su_o	st_prici	st_custs	st_qualc	st_lowco
0	0	0	2	6	6	4
0	0	0	1	5	5	2
0	0	0	2	7	7	7
0	0	0		0		
1	0	0	2	7	7	3
0	0	1	4	5	5	3
0	0	0	4	7	6	6
1	0	0	5	6	7	3
0	0	0	5	5	7	6
0	0	0	5	5	6	4
0	0	0	1	5	6	1
1	0	0	6	4	4	3
0	0	0	5	6	5	5
1	0	0	5	5	6	4
1	0	0	3	3	6	3
1	0	0	2	6	6	3
1	1	1	4	6	6	5
1	0	0	4	5	6	4
0	0	0	2	3	4	6
1	0	0	1	5	6	4
1	0	0	4	6	6	6
1	0	0	5	4	4	5
0	0	0	2	6	5	4
0	0	0	5	7	7	7
0	0	0	4	5	5	3
1	0	0	1	7	7	3
0	0	0	4	5	5	4
0	0	0	4	5	5	3
0	0	0	2	5	6	7
0	0	0	4	7	7	6
1	0	0	5	4	4	4
0	0	0	2	6	6	6
0	0	0	2	6	5	6
0	0	0	4	7	4	4
1	0	0	4	6	6	4
1	0	0	5	5	5	7

st_focus	st_varia	st_brand	st_local	st_distr	st_promo	st_tailo
5	5	5	3	3	3	5
2	5	6	6	5	4	4
6	6	7	7	7	7	6
6						7
6	6	7	6	6	2	7
5	4	5	5	3	3	6
2	7	7	6	6	5	5
6	5		5		3	6
7	6	7	6	5	6	6
6	5	5	5	6	6	5
5	5	6	6	7	6	5
6	3	4	5	3	6	6
5	4	5	5	5	4	5
5	6	6	5	6	3	6
5	3	6	6	3	5	7
6	6	7	6	7	7	6
4	6	4	6	6	4	5
6	6	7	6	7	4	6
6	3	3	5	5	4	3
5	5	5	5	5	5	5
6	5	5	6	4	3	5
3	6	6	6	5	5	6
5	3	4	5	6	4	4
5	7	6	6	4	5	5
4	5	5	4	5	4	5
3	4	7	6	5	4	7
4	5	6	6	5	6	5
5	6	6	5	6	5	2
6	4	3	4	3	3	5
2	6	6	6	6	5	5
6	6	6	6	5	5	6
5	7	7	7	7	6	5
6	5	4	6	5	2	5
1	7	7	7	7	2	7
3	4	5	6	6	3	6
5	5	5	5	2	4	5

st_devel	st_conc	st_lowpr	st_innov	st_marpe	st_emula	st_immed
4	4	2	5	3	6	5
6	6	4	6	6	5	4
6	7	6	6	6	6	7
4	5	2	4	5	6	6
6	6	3	6	6	7	6
5	5	2	4	4	4	4
5	7	4	6	6	6	7
6	7	1	4	5	5	7
7	6	5	7	6	5	7
5	5	4	5	6	5	5
5	6	1	6	6	3	5
6	6	4	2	2	2	5
5	6	3	6	5	6	6
6	5	4	4	4	5	6
6	6	3	5	4	5	5
6	6	4	6	5	6	6
5	5	4	5	4	4	6
6	6	4	5	6	4	5
3	4	4	4	3	5	3
5	5	4	5	5	4	5
5	5	4	5	5	5	5
5	6	3	5	5	5	5
6	6	3	5	5	4	5
5	5	5	5	5	5	5
5	5	4	4	5	5	5
6	7	4	7	5	5	7
6	6	6	6	5	4	4
5	6	2	4	4	4	3
4	5	4	4	3	5	4
5	7	6	6	6	2	7
7	7	4	5	5	5	5
5	5	4	6	6	6	6
6		2	6	5	4	5
6	7	1	1	4	5	2
6	6	2	4	3	4	6
5	6	6	6	5	6	6

st_workf	st_islre	st_disco	st_markr	st_emplo	st_newma	st_desig
4	1	2	5	4	3	6
4	4	1	4	5	5	5
7	7	5	5	6	7	7
7	4	1	3	5	6	5
7	7	3	3	5	6	7
4	5	3	3	3	5	5
6	1	5	6	6	5	6
7	6	2	5	6	6	6
6	6	6	7	7	6	7
5	5	4	6	4	6	6
6	6	1	2	5	5	6
5	6	2	2	5	5	5
5	4	4	4	4	4	4
7	5	4	4	7	5	6
6	6	3	6	5	5	6
6	6	3	6	6	6	6
6	6	4	6	6	5	5
6	7	2	6	3	6	6
3	6	3	4	4	4	4
5	6	4	5	5	5	5
6	5	2	3	5	4	5
6	6	3	4	5	5	6
5	6	4	4	5	4	5
6	6	3	5	5	5	5
5	6	4	5	4	5	5
5	7	1	5	6	6	6
6	6	4	4	5	6	6
4	2	2	5	5	5	5
3	4	3	4	5	4	6
6	7	5	5	7	6	6
5	7	5	5	6	6	4
6	6	5	5	6	6	6
5	3	1	5	5	5	5
2	7	6	2	4	6	4
6	6	2	6	5	6	6
5	6	6	4	5	6	6

st_intco	st_decis	st_prodi	st_eos	st_capau	st_distc	st_trans
5	2	7	6	5	5	6
4	5	6	4	4	5	5
6	6	6	6	6	6	6
3	6	7	7	7	3	4
6	6	6	6	6	6	6
4	5	6	4	4	2	4
6	6	7	4	5	5	5
7	6	5	6	6	5	6
6	5	7	5	6	5	5
5	4	6	6	5	6	6
6	6	6	5	5	6	6
5	4	2	3	5	2	2
5	5	5	5	4	4	5
5	6	7	5	6	5	5
6	5	5	3	3	3	3
6	6	6	6	6	6	6
6	6	5	5	5	6	5
5	3	7	5	5	6	6
4	3	3	5	5	6	5
5	5	5	5	5	5	5
5	5	6	6	4	6	5
5	5	7	5	6	6	5
5	5	4	6	5	6	5
5	6	6	6	6	6	6
4	4	5	4	4	4	5
4	4	6	6	7	7	6
5	5	5	4	5	4	5
4	5	3	5	4	6	4
5	5	5	5	5	5	6
6	6	7	6	5	5	6
5	3	4	4	5	5	4
6	6	6	7	6	6	6
5	4	5	5	5	6	3
4	1	6	1	6	1	1
5	5	6	6	5	6	6
5	5	6	6	6	6	6

st_diffp	st_stand	st_focse	st_marks	st_probr	st_newge	msh_a_00
3	5	5	6	3	3	1
4	4	4	5	6	6	
6	7	7	6	6	7	18
3	2	7	7	7	7	
4	5	5	6	6	6	
4	3	6	5	3	3	
6	6	2	6	6	6	
	6	6	6		2	
5	5	5	5	6	6	
6	7	6	5	6	5	7
1	4	6	6	6	5	
2	2	6	3	2	6	
5	4	5	5	5	4	3
2	5	5	5	5	5	3
6	4	5	3	6	5	
5	6	6	7	6	6	
6	4	6	6	5	6	
3	5	6	6	6	6	
3	4	2	6	4	4	
5	5	5	5	5	5	
4	5	5	5	5	4	1
6	5	4	5	6	6	1
5	5	4	5	4	3	
6	6	5	6	6	6	
5	4	5	5	5	5	
5	5	4	6	6	6	
5	4	5	4	5	5	
4	5	4	6	5	3	5
4	5	5	4	4	5	
5	6	5	6	6	5	8
6	5	5	6	6	7	16
6	6	6	6	5	5	
2	6	5	3	3	3	
2	4	3	6	7	3	1
4	6	2	6	4	6	
6	6	3	7	6	5	

msh_a_03	msh_a_04	msh_p_00	msh_p_03	msh_p_04	nopat_00	nopat_03
1	5	2	2	5		
25	30	11	13	20		
19	30	5	7	10		
4	4	3	6	6		
4	4	-1	5	3	-1	10
					2	2
3	4		4	4		24
1	2	1	1	2		
1	2				5	18
3	3				13	22
					4	0
7	10					
10	11		10	11		
7	10				9	
16		19	16		48	28
						19
2	2				5	20

nopat_04	equi_00	equi_03	equi_04	coe_00	coe_03	coe_04
4	5	69	73	0	0	0
2	74	76	77			
27		123	140		10	12
				11	11	11
24	191	231	238	0	8	
27	255	302	324		5	
3	50	84	26	0	20	0
40	74	114	222	10	14	14
	217	285		48	56	
19		146	152		10	10
25	245	278	308	2	7	7

npat_00	npat_03	npat_04	npat2_00	npat2_03	npat2_04	perf_msh
2	1	2	16	10	10	3
						2
1	1	2	7	6	10	6
						6
						6
						4
						2
						5
						3
1	1	1	15	9	14	4
	7			26		6
						1
1	1	2	23	7	8	6
0	2	0	-13	14	6	4
						4
						4
1	0	0	2	2	3	4
						4
						6
	9	11		18	20	4
1	1	1	6	15	15	3
3	8	2	3	8	11	2
2	2	2	20	21	21	4
						2
1	1	1	5	7	8	4
2	0	1	7	1	9	5
	5	10		9	25	5
						3
	0	0		13	13	4
1	3	4	13	28	29	5
2	2		22	20		6
	2	2		10	11	2
						2
0	1	1	2	7	8	6
						3
1	1		29	12		7

perf_msg	perf_pma	perf_roe	perf_cre	perf_csa
4	6	6	5	4
6	6	5	6	5
6	6	4	7	6
5	5	6	5	5
6	5	6	5	5
5	4	3	6	6
7	5	4	6	6
3	2	2	7	6
6	6	6	6	6
5	6	5	5	5
6	6	6	6	6
2	5	5	5	5
5	4	4	5	4
6	5	5	5	5
5	5	6	7	5
5	5	6	5	7
5	4	4	6	6
5	6	6	6	7
5	6	6	4	3
4	4	4	4	4
5	4	6	5	5
3	3	2	4	5
5	4	6	5	5
2	2	2	5	6
5	4	4	4	5
4	2	2	5	5
6	5	5	5	4
4	3	3	4	5
5	4	4	5	5
6	6	7	7	7
4	6		6	5
5	5	6	4	4
5	6	6	6	6
6	2	4	6	4
5	5		5	6
4	7	7	5	6

Variable Name Description

Variable name	Description
fallnum	Case number
geo	Geographical focus
disint	Factor: Disintermediation
it_soph	Factor: Bank IT sophistication
cust_rel	Factor: Decrease customer relationships
comp	Factor: Increased competition
dereg	Factor: Deregulation
innov	Factor: Innovation
trade	Attractive segments: trade finance
corp_fin	Attractive segments: corporate finance
venture	Attractive segments: venture capital
pers_con	Attractive segments: personal advances for consumption
pers_dur	Attractive segments: personal advances for durables
home_fin	Attractive segments: home finance
asset_mg	Attractive segments: asset management
public_f	Attractive segments: public sector financing
inv_bank	Attractive segments: investment banking
risk	Attractiveness: low risk
maturity	Attractiveness: asset-deposit maturity matching
funding	Attractiveness: low funding costs
operatio	Attractiveness: low operational costs
margins	Attractiveness: high margins
demand	Attractiveness: high demand
growth	Attractiveness: high growth potential
ib_grow	IBs enjoy higher growth rates
ib_price	Islamic products can be priced more expensively
ib_equit	IBs have easier access to equity
ib_capit	IBs have easier access to capital
ib_risk	IBs are exposed to lower risk
ib_fund	IBs incur lower funding costs
ib_opera	IBs incur lower operation costs
ib_margi	IBs gain higher profit margins
ib_marke	IBs benefit from larger market size
competit	Five forces: Competition in the industry is very high
clients	Five forces: Clients have a strong bargaining position
deposits	Five forces: Clients prefer short-term deposits & investments
substit	Five forces: Conventional banks are regarded as substitutes
liquidit	Five forces: Industry's liquidity market is too restricted
regulat	Five forces: Industry's regulatory & legal framework could improve
shar_st	Five forces: Lack of Sharia standardization

Variable name	Description
capital	Five forces: Industry's capital market is underdeveloped
pls	Five forces: Lack of attractive PLS investment opportunities
substit2	Five forces: High threat of substitutes
barriers	Five forces: There are low barriers to entry
investm	Five forces: Lack of overall attractive investment opportunities
capital2	Five forces: Limited access to capital
hr	Five forces: Lack of skilled human resources
it_suppl	Five forces: Technology suppliers have high bargaining power
prod_st	Five forces: Lack of product standardization
educ	Five forces: Lack of customer education
non_musl	Effective competition: IBs should approach non-Muslim clients
late_fee	Effective competition: IBs should charge late-payment fees
hedge_fu	Effective competition: IBs should offer hedge funds
consolid	Effective competition: there is a need for consolidation
fin_cond	Effective competition: Islamic products must match conventional conditions
deriv	Effective competition: IBs should offer Islamic derivative instruments
emulate	Effective competition: IBs should offer products that closely emulate conventional features
act_form	Form of activity
corp_gov	Scope: corporate & government financing
pers_fin	Scope: personal financing
vent_cap	Scope: venture capital
pers_wea	Scope: personal wealth management
corp_as	Scope: corporate & institutional asset management
pers_ban	Scope: personal banking
corp_ad	Scope: corporate advisory
own_str	Ownership structure
autonomy	Degree of autonomy in decision making
asset00	Total assets 2000
asset03	Total assets 2003
asset04	Total assets 2004
curr_00	Current accounts 2000
curr_03	Current accounts 2003
curr_04	Current accounts 2004
u_inv_00	Unrestricted investment accounts 2000
u_inv_03	Unrestricted investment accounts 2003
u_inv_04	Unrestricted investment accounts 2004
r_inv_00	Restricted investment accounts 2000
r_inv_03	Restricted investment accounts 2003
r_inv_04	Restricted investment accounts 2004
funds00	Funds under management 2000

Variable name	Description
funds03	Funds under management 2003
funds04	Funds under management 2004
ebt00	EBT 2000
ebt03	EBT 2003
ebt04	EBT 2004
empl00	Employees 2000
empl03	Employees 2003
empl04	Employees 2004
bal_sc	Mgmt tools: balanced scorecard
mbo	Mgmt tools: management by objectives
perf_com	Mgmt tools: performance-related compensation
cust_sat	Mgmt tools: measurement of customer satisfaction
bus_plan	Mgmt tools: business plan
kpi	Mgmt tools: key performance indicators
mil_plan	Mgmt tools: milestone planning
high_st	Goals: providing highest-standard banking services
share_va	Goals: maximizing shareholder value
dev_econ	Goals: developing the economy
soc_welf	Goals: promoting social welfare
max_prof	Goals: maximizing profits
enc_peop	Goals: encouraging people to save & invest
prec_isl	Goals: promoting the precepts of Islam
sme	Customer segments: small- and medium-sized companies
smfi	Customer segments: small- and medium-sized financial institutions
mapc	Customer segments: mass and affluent private clients
large_co	Customer segments: large companies
large_fi	Customer segments: large financial institutions
hnwi	Customer segments: high net worth individuals
cc_asset	Assets: corporate clients
ic_asset	Assets: institutional clients
pc_asset	Assets: private clients
cc_liab	Liabilities: corporate clients
ic_liab	Liabilities: institutional clients
pc_liab	Liabilities: private clients
cc_funds	Off-balance-sheet funds: corporate clients
ic_funds	Off-balance-sheet funds: institutional clients
pc_funds	Off-balance-sheet funds: private clients
ia_trade	Investment area: trade financing
ia_share	Investment area: company shares
ia_home	Investment area: home financing
ia_publi	Investment area: public infrastructure
ia_capex	Investment area: corporate CapEx
ia_compr	Investment area: commercial property
ia_durab	Investment area: consumer durables
ia_bonds	Investment area: government/corporate bonds
ia_other	Investment area: other
ia_p_tra	Investment area (%): trade financing

Variable name	Description
ia_p_sha	Investment area (%): company shares
ia_p_hom	Investment area (%): home financing
ia_p_pub	Investment area (%): public infrastructure
ia_p_cap	Investment area (%): corporate CapEx
ia_p_com	Investment area (%): commercial property
ia_p_dur	Investment area (%): consumer durables
ia_p_bon	Investment area (%): government/corporate bonds
ia_p_ot1	Investment area (%): other
shb_num	Sharia board: Number of people
appr_gg	Sharia board function: ex ante approval general rules
appr_np	Sharia board function: ex ante approval new products
appr_nst	Sharia board function: ex ante approval non-standard transactions
appr_st	Sharia board function: ex ante approval standard transactions
rev_nst	Sharia board function: ex post review non-standard transactions
rev_st	Sharia board function: ex post review standard transactions
compl_re	Sharia board function: issuance of compliance report
share_sh	Sharia board: Shared with other companies?
bs_cash	Balance sheet: Cash and cash equivalents
bs_advan	Balance sheet: Advances to other financial institutions
bs_murab	Balance sheet: Murabaha
bs_ina	Balance sheet: Ina
bs_salam	Balance sheet: Salam/Istisna
bs_ijara	Balance sheet: Ijara/Ijara muntahia bittamleek
bs_mudar	Balance sheet: Mudaraba/Muqarada
bs_musha	Balance sheet: Musharaka
bs_inv_s	Balance sheet: Investment in securities
bs_ass_o	Balance sheet: Other
bs_depos	Balance sheet: Deposits from other financial institutions
bs_curac	Balance sheet: Current accounts
bs_invac	Balance sheet: Investment accounts
bs_equit	Balance sheet: Shareholders' equity
bs_lia_o	Balance sheet: Other
is_mudar	Income statement: bank's income as mudarib
is_self	Income statement: bank's income from self-financed investments
is_advis	Income statement: revenue from financial advisory services
is_loc	Income statement: revenue from LOCs/guarantees
is_fees	Income statement: Other fees and charges
org_role	Competencies - Organization: Clearly structured roles and responsibilities

Variable name	Description
org_vert	Competencies - Organization: Vertical communication
org_info	Competencies - Organization: Cross-functional information exchange
org_coop	Competencies - Organization: Cross-functional co-operation
org_team	Competencies - Organization: Team-based approach
org_mark	Competencies - Organization: Market-oriented organization
mgmt_com	Competencies - Management quality: Managerial competencies
mgmt_qua	Competencies - Management quality: Quality of leadership
mgmt_vis	Competencies - Management quality: Clear strategic vision
mgmt_str	Competencies - Management quality: Strategy-implementation
mgtm_res	Competencies - Management quality: Effective resource management
mgmt_kno	Competencies - Management quality: Knowledge and skills of employees
cul_tran	Competencies - Firm culture: Transparency across company
cul_peop	Competencies - Firm culture: Ability to attract and retain high-quality people
cul_meri	Competencies - Firm culture: Prevalence of a meritocracy culture
cul_moti	Competencies - Firm culture: Highly motivating environment
cul_rewa	Competencies - Firm culture: Reward of creativity and innovation
cul_coor	Competencies - Firm culture: Coordination
prd_inno	Competencies - Product development: Innovation
prd_expe	Competencies - Product development: Technological expertise
prd_capa	Competencies - Product development: Technological capabilities and equipment
prd_effi	Competencies - Product development: Resource efficiency
prd_know	Competencies - Product development: Know-how of both Islamic and financial market requirements
prd_appr	Competencies - Product development: Quick and efficient Sharia-approval process
ms_repfi	Competencies - Marketing & sales: Reputation as financial services provider
ms_brand	Competencies - Marketing & sales: Brand image
ms_placi	Competencies - Marketing & sales: Placing power
ms_marke	Competencies - Marketing & sales: Market knowledge

Variable name	Description
ms_repui	Competencies - Marketing & sales: Reputation as Islamic company
ms_ipcap	Competencies - Marketing & sales: Information processing capabilities
ms_distr	Competencies - Marketing & sales: Control of and acces to distribution channels
ms_relcu	Competencies - Marketing & sales: Advantageous relationships with customers
ms_socbe	Competencies - Marketing & sales: Engagement in socially benefitial activities
ms_curcu	Competencies - Marketing & sales: Current customer base
ms_branc	Competencies - Marketing & sales: Branch network
ms_atm	Competencies - Marketing & sales: ATM network
ms_inter	Competencies - Marketing & sales: Internet banking
ms_callc	Competencies - Marketing & sales: Call center
ms_deala	Competencies - Marketing & sales: Deal and customer assessment
ms_custo	Competencies - Marketing & sales: Customer counseling
ms_pe	Competencies - Marketing & sales: Private equity/venture capital expertise
ms_respo	Competencies - Marketing & sales: Response time to customer requests
ms_finex	Competencies - Marketing & sales: Financial expertise
ms_shari	Competencies - Marketing & sales: Sharia board reputation
ms_servi	Competencies - Marketing & sales: Service quality
ms_teche	Competencies - Marketing & sales: Technological expertise
ms_techc	Competencies - Marketing & sales: Technological capabilities and equipment
ms_resef	Competencies - Marketing & sales: Resource efficiency
ms_shapp	Competencies - Marketing & sales: Quick & efficient Sharia-approval process
tp_servi	Competencies - Transaction processing: Service quality
tp_secur	Competencies - Transaction processing: Securitization of investment products
tp_teche	Competencies - Transaction processing: Technological expertise
tp_techc	Competencies - Transaction processing: Technological capabilities and equipment
tp_resef	Competencies - Transaction processing: Resource efficiency
tp_tradi	Competencies - Transaction processing: Trading & treasury

Variable name	Description
sup_shar	Competencies - Steering/Supporting functions: Sharia compliance
sup_boar	Competencies - Steering/Supporting functions: Effectiveness and efficiency of Sharia board
sup_stra	Competencies - Steering/Supporting functions: Strategic planning
sup_cont	Competencies - Steering/Supporting functions: Controlling
sup_risk	Competencies - Steering/Supporting functions: Risk management
sup_rese	Competencies - Steering/Supporting functions: Research capabilities
sup_asse	Competencies - Steering/Supporting functions: Asset quality
sup_equi	Competencies - Steering/Supporting functions: Equity base
sup_data	Competencies - Steering/Supporting functions: Knowledge and data management
sup_comp	Competencies - Steering/Supporting functions: Compensation and reward system
sup_hr	Competencies - Steering/Supporting functions: HR processes and administration
sup_tool	Competencies - Steering/Supporting functions: Use of strategy-enforcing tools
sup_shor	Competencies - Steering/Supporting functions: Access to short-term capital
sup_long	Competencies - Steering/Supporting functions: Access to mid- and long-term capital
sup_rati	Competencies - Steering/Supporting functions: Financial rating
grow_int	Growth strategy: Internal growth
grow_coo	Growth strategy: Co-operation with competitors
grow_acq	Growth strategy: Acquisition of competitors
grow_non	Growth strategy: None
ops_ind	Operations: Independent?
ops_pd_p	Operations - Product development: Parent support
ops_pd_c	Operations - Product development: Competitor support
ops_pd_o	Operations - Product development: Contracting company support
ops_m_p	Operations - Marketing: Parent support
ops_m_c	Operations - Marketing: Competitor support
ops_m_o	Operations - Marketing: Contracting company support
ops_s_p	Operations - Sales & distribution: Parent support
ops_s_c	Operations - Sales & distribution: Competitor support
ops_s_o	Operations - Sales & distribution: Contracting company support
ops_t_p	Operations - Transaction processing: Parent support

Variable name	Description
ops_t_c	Operations - Transaction processing: Competitor support
ops_t_o	Operations - Transaction processing: Contracting company support
ops_su_p	Operations - Steering & supporting functions: Parent support
ops_su_c	Operations - Steering & supporting functions: Competitor support
ops_su_o	Operations - Steering & supporting functions: Contracting company support
st_prici	Competitive strategy: Pricing below competitors
st_custs	Competitive strategy: Providing extensive customer service
st_qualc	Competitive strategy: Strict product & service quality control
st_lowco	Competitive strategy: Achieving the lowest cost position in the industry
st_focus	Competitive strategy: Focusing on a few main product lines
st_varia	Competitive strategy: Providing a broad variation within the product lines
st_brand	Competitive strategy: Building brand identification of company
st_local	Competitive strategy: Refining existing products to local needs and demands
st_distr	Competitive strategy: Control over distribution channels
st_promo	Competitive strategy: Promotion/advertising expenditures above industry average
st_tailo	Competitive strategy: Tailor-make products according to customer specification
st_devel	Competitive strategy: Develop the existing market
st_conc	Competitive strategy: Concerted effort to build/maintain reputation in the industry
st_lowpr	Competitive strategy: Offering the main products in lower priced market segments
st_innov	Competitive strategy: Innovation in marketing techniques and methods
st_marpe	Competitive strategy: Emphasis on quick market penetration/product introduction
st_emula	Competitive strategy: Closely emulating the financial conditions of conventional banking products
st_immed	Competitive strategy: Immediate response to customer requests
st_workf	Competitive strategy: Acquiring high-caliber work-force
st_islre	Competitive strategy: Emphasis on building reputation as an Islamic company
st_disco	Competitive strategy: Providing discounts to customers

Variable name	Description
st_markr	Competitive strategy: Extensive marketing research
st_emplo	Competitive strategy: Extensive employee training
st_newma	Competitive strategy: Entering into and developing new market segments
st_desig	Competitive strategy: Emphasis on design and quality of products
st_intco	Competitive strategy: Efficient internal communication channels
st_decis	Competitive strategy: Unobstructed and quick decision making process
st_prodi	Competitive strategy: Emphasis on product innovation
st_eos	Competitive strategy: Efforts to achieve economies of scale
st_capau	Competitive strategy: High capacity utilization
st_distc	Competitive strategy: Emphasis on strong distribution channels
st_trans	Competitive strategy: Highly automized transaction and administrative processes
st_diffp	Competitive strategy: Differentiated pricing for various distribution channels
st_stand	Competitive strategy: Standardization & modularization of products / services
st_focse	Competitive strategy: Focusing on a few customer segments
st_marks	Competitive strategy: Emphasis on gaining a high or dominant market share
st_probr	Competitive strategy: Building product-related brands
st_newge	Competitive strategy: Entering into and developing new geographic markets
msh_a_00	Market share - by assets 2000
msh_a_03	Market share - by assets 2003
msh_a_04	Market share - by assets 2004 (target)
msh_p_00	Market share - by profit 2000
msh_p_03	Market share - by profit 2003
msh_p_04	Market share - by profit 2004 (target)
nopat_00	Net operating profit after tax 2000
nopat_03	Net operating profit after tax 2003
nopat_04	Net operating profit after tax 2004 (target)
equi_00	Equity 2000
equi_03	Equity 2003
equi_04	Equity 2004 (target)
coe_00	Cost of equity 2000
coe_03	Cost of equity 2003
coe_04	Cost of equity 2004 (target)
npat_00	Net profit after tax as % of total assets 2000
npat_03	Net profit after tax as % of total assets 2003
npat_04	Net profit after tax as % of total assets 2004 (target)

Variable name	Description
npat2_00	Net profit after tax as % of shareholders' equity and reserves 2000
npat2_03	Net profit after tax as % of shareholders' equity and reserves 2003
npat2_04	Net profit after tax as % of shareholders' equity and reserves 2004 (target)
perf_msh	Performance: Market share of products & services is very high
perf_msg	Performance: Market share of products & services grows rapidly
perf_pma	Performance: Above-average profit margins
perf_roe	Performance: Above-average return on equity
perf_cre	Performance: High degree of customer retention
perf_csa	Performance: Customers are highly satisfied with products & services